TABLE OF CONTENTS

INTRODUCTION

HOW TO USE THIS BOOK

AURICULAR TREATMENT (EAR ACUPUNCTURE) 3

THE TREATMENT OF SPECIFIC DISORDERS 4

HOW TO USE THE INDEX 4

THE TREATMENT OF PAIN 5

THE TREATMENT OF BACK PAIN 6

UNITS OF MEASUREMENT 7

LOCATING KEY POINTS 8

HOW TO TREAT EYES 11

THE HISTORY AND THEORY OF TRADITIONAL ACUPUNCTURE 15

HOW DOES ACUPUNCTURE WORK? 17

GENERAL HEALTH PLAN 0.1

ANTI AGEING & GOOD HEALTH 0.2

1. PAINFUL DISORDERS 1.1

2   E.N.T. PROBLEMS 2.1

3. HEART AND CIRCULATORY DISORDERS 3.1

4. ABDOMINAL PROBLEMS 4.1

5. SKIN DISORDERS 5.1

6. CHEST DISEASES 6.1

7. GENITO-URINARY PROBLEMS 7.1

8. MISCELLANEOUS DISORDERS 8.1

9. SPORTS AND INDUSTRIAL INJURIES 9.1

EAR TREATMENT POINTS 10.1

INDEX 10.3

THE AUTHOR

Robert Redfern

Robert's interest in health started when he and his wife Anne decided to take charge of their family's health in the late 80's. Up until 1986, Robert did not take much notice of his health - in spite of Anne's loving persuasion. It took the premature death of his parents, Alfred and Marjorie, who died in their 60's, to shock Robert into evaluating his priorities.

They looked at the whole field of health, available treatments and the causes of health problems. They found, from doctors researching the causes of disease, that lifestyle and diet were the most important contributions to Health.

They researched the benefits of acupuncture and together developed the HealthPoint, the world's foremost electronic acupressure device. This was based upon the electronic waveform research of Dr. Julian Kenyon MD. This has become the Gold Standard Electro-Acupressure device and is now successfully used by tens of thousands of users throughout the world and in many UK hospitals by Physiotherapists.

Robert and Anne changed their lifestyle and diet and, together with the use of HealthPoint, the improvement to their health became remarkable. As well as good health, they feel and look younger and more energetic than all those years ago - before they started their plan. Robert is now over 60 and, together with Anne, is still planning to look younger with continuing care.

Enzymes have been a major part of their life for nearly ten years, after reading a book by Dr Edward Howell, 'Enzyme Nutrition, The Food Enzyme Concept'
This filled in some of the gaps as to why just taking nutrition did not give the full benefit for everyone.

Over the past 10 years, tens of thousands of people have followed the plans and the majority that stayed with the program have reaped tremendous benefit. This book shows you how to resolve most of the common diseases, using electro-acupressure and other lifestyle changes. To the extent that you follow them, you will be amazed how healthy you can become.

Good Luck and Good Health.

Robert S. Redfern
Personal Email To: robert@goodhealth.nu
UK Help Line phone: 0870-225-2530
USA Help Line phone: 1800-455-9155

Other books and publications:

Turning A Blind Eye – 10 Steps to Your Natural Eye Health
The Miracle Enzyme – Is Serrapeptase
Various cutting edge newsletters with the latest on Natural Health

THE DOCTOR

Dr Julian Kenyon

Dr Julian Kenyon, **MD MB ChB**. is a medical doctor involved full time in research and treatment using Complementary Medicine. He has over 20 years experience in this field and has published many relevant books and papers, including contributions to papers in 'The Lancet' and 'The British Medical Journal'.

Julian graduated in Medicine in 1970 at Liverpool University medical school. He began his career, spending a short time as House Physician, then House Surgeon at Broadgreen Hospital in Liverpool.

He went on to become a Lecturer in Embryology in the Liverpool University Department of Child Health in 1972. In that same year he obtained his primary FRCS and remained there for a further two years.

From 1974 - 76 Dr Kenyon was the Principal in General Practice in Crosby. During this period he had been become a keen student of Medical Alternatives and established his own private practice in 1976.

In 1978 Julian gained an MD for his thesis on the development of the human tympanum and he was Honorary Specialist in the Pain Relief Foundation Clinic at Walton Hospital, Liverpool from 1980 -1982.

Julian was Founder-Chairman of the British Medical Acupuncture Society in 1980 and established The Centre for The Study of Complementary Medicine in Southampton in 1982. From this Centre, with a colleague and a staff of 42, he treats, conducts research and runs a number of teaching courses for doctors on a range of techniques within complementary medicine. He has published widely on the subject of acupuncture, homeopathy and clinical ecology.

In 1976, Dr Kenyon designed the world's first electro-acupuncture device. This was followed in 1982 by the E.P.S., which was sold mainly to the medical and veterinary professions world-wide.

INTRODUCTION By Robert Redfern

This book can be used with finger acupressure (which I used on my four grandchildren to stop any suffering from teething) or acupuncture, but I strongly recommend using an electro-acupuncture instrument, or micro-current stimulator. These are battery operated devices that pass a square-waveform, with a low intensity electric current, directly onto meridian points by means of an electric probe and can provide 100% accuracy. This stimulation gives fast relief of many conditions, as well as boosting your body's healing and regeneration system. *Warning: We do not recommend the use of an instrument that has an electrical output greater than 20 micro amps. Do not use a device that has an output of greater than 50 micro amps, or does not provide biphasic (alternating) waveform. If in doubt, telephone the Helpline number shown below.*

The purpose of this manual is threefold:

1. It will give scientific backing and support as to why small electric currents can be used in treating illness and relieving pain.
2. To briefly explain the science of acupuncture, from a traditional and scientific viewpoint.
3. To explain how and where to treat a wide range of common pains and other conditions.

A certain amount of acquired skill is needed and a good result depends upon correct usage; however, most people can master the basics in an hour or so.

Caution

For your own well-being and to ensure that the correct condition is treated, you should always obtain a diagnosis from your Doctor before commencing treatment. For your health's sake, we recommend you consult a doctor who practises Natural Healthcare.

It should be said that, to our knowledge, there have never been any problems with electro-acupuncture, but for safety's sake, please consider the following:

1. HEART PACEMAKERS - If an in-dwelling cardiac pacemaker is used, electro-acupuncture should only be used if the output is 20 micro amps or less.

2. PREGNANCY - During the first three months of pregnancy, please call the Helpline for guidance on the use of electro-acupuncture.

If you have any specific concerns, please ask your medical advisor to fax any questions directly to us, as they are unlikely to know the answer.

HELPLINE

Tel: +44 (0) 870 225 2530
Fax: +44 (0) 870 122 8538

USA & Canada Tel: 1-800 455 9155 Fax: 1-858 225 3959

HOW TO USE THIS BOOK

1. Find the Page
Refer to the condition you wish to treat, using the index at the end of this manual. Turn to the appropriate page and find the points to treat.

2. Switch the Instrument On
Switch the instrument on and ensure that all settings are as shown in the manufacturer's instructions.

3. Hold the Instrument Correctly
All Electro-acupuncture units have a conductor grip or pad, which must be held by the fingers of the person being treated, as the grip acts as one end of the circuit, the other end being the probe applied to the point.
If the instrument is held by a partner or a therapist, physical contact must be maintained between therapist and patient, using the palm of the hand in order to complete the circuit.
If possible, the person being treated should hold and control the machine and they, or the therapist or partner, can hold the probe.

4. Locate the Points
There are three different types of acupuncture points to be treated.
1. Points as recommended in the user guide.
2. Points as detected in the painful areas (Ah-Shi).
3. Points as shown on the ear.

Electro-acupuncture units have a built in volt meter. This detects acupuncture points as areas of high electrical conductivity relative to the surrounding skin. Draw or rub the probe gently, but firmly across the skin when detecting an acupuncture point. Do not jump around with the tip. Once a point has been located the instrument's indication system will confirm the location (te indication system varies with each manufacturer, but a light and/or an audio buzzer system are the most common).
Each condition that Electro-acupuncture may be used to treat is described with both written and visual details for each point to be used. In painful conditions, it is important to treat all three types of points. Each diagram describes where the points are located on the body. With the diagrams and the point detection system on Electro-acupuncture equipment, you should have no difficulty locating, with sufficient accuracy, the majority of points.

5. Treat the Points
Once the point is located, activate the treatment mode of your unit while leaving the probe on the same treatment point. Treat for 30-60 seconds (your unit's instructions should give a recommended time), then stop the unit and move to treat the next point in exactly the same way.

TREATMENT FREQUENCY
Initially the treatment should be repeated two to four times a day until the symptoms have gone, then treat once a day for up to thirty days for chronic problems. After the condition improves the interval between treatments can be extended and eventually terminated. Treatment may be resumed in the same way if the condition recurs. This is common in certain chronic conditions such as osteoarthritis. It may be many months before appreciable pain and discomfort returns, but the condition is likely to respond just as well to a second or third course of treatment.

IMPORTANT: Very occasionally, an apparent worsening of the condition is observed for a day or so, before a rapid improvement. This is a positive and common response. It shows that the treatment is working and the benefits should be noticed within a day or so.

If the condition does not respond, please ring the helpline or email help@dovehealth.com

AURICULAR TREATMENT (EAR ACUPUNCTURE)

The Chinese discovered that an ailment anywhere on the body can, in many cases, be treated effectively and quickly by applying treatment to points on the outer ear. Recent research has shown an apparent representation of the body on the outer ear, in an upside-down fashion, (see illustration).

As well as treating the body points, treat the ear points as follows:

1. Locate the problem in the index.
2. Find the corresponding site on the ear (refer to the illustration).
3. Treat the point (a definite reaction will be felt on the correct point).

In some cases relief is almost instantaneous. Great accuracy in locating the point is required, however, as the ear is small in relation to the body.

Thus: Using the unit's remote probe

Use the ear that is on the same side as the problem, (i.e. the right ear for right-sided problems, left ear for left-sided). If your problem is situated in the midline, (such as some cases of back pain) use the right ear if you are right-handed or the left ear if you are left-handed. (If in doubt treat both sides).

You will appreciate that searching the ear with the probe is not easy. There is, as is usually the case, a knack. In this instance a mirror is used. Searching for points using the probe with the aid of a mirror should be done slowly and with care. With practice it will become easier.
To steady the probe, rest the insulated part of the probe (not the metal tip) on your finger.

Please note: The auricular treatment points are shown for each ailment. However, due to space constraints, they may not be as accurate as we would ideally like. **Always refer to the detailed ear chart shown on page 10.2**

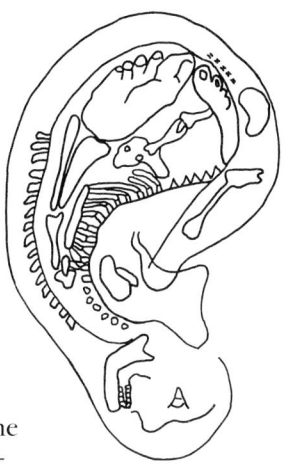

THE TREATMENT OF SPECIFIC DISORDERS

This section is divided into the following parts:
1. Painful disorders
2. Ear, nose and throat problems
3. Heart and circulatory disorders
4. Abdominal problems
5. Skin disorders
6. Chest diseases
7. Genito-urinary problems
8. Miscellaneous disorders
9. Sports and industrial injuries

The index is located at the back of this manual. Ailments are listed either under their common medical name, i.e. Sinusitis, or under the affected area, i.e. Back Pain.

For Example: For someone suffering from arthritis in the knee, looking in the index, the reference is under Knee Pain, page 1.17, as shown below.

Headache (Migraine) Temporal	1.4	Constipation	4.5
Headache (Migraine) Vertex	1.5	Diarrhoea	4.5
Hip Pain	1.16	Duodenal Ulcer	4.14
Intercostal Neuralgia	1.19	Flatulence	4.1
Jaw Pain	1.6	Gallbladder Colic	4.9
Knee Pain	1.17	Gallbladder Disease	4.8
Neck Pain	1.9	Haemorrhoids	4.4

Turn to the appropriate page. You will find a brief description of the ailment, along with the recommended treatment points - as shown. Use all the points listed - the order in which they are given is not important. Measurements are given in 'Fingers' or 'Thumbs' - see page 7 for further information on measurement.
If you are treating an ailment that is 'handed' e.g. your right knee, then treat the points on the same side of your body. If, however, the ailment is not 'handed' i.e. Laryngitis, then treat both left and right sides of the body.
If your condition is not listed - be creative. Look for a condition that relates to the same part of your body, or similar symptoms, and treat accordingly. No harm can be done when stimulating any of the points.

Knee pain - arthritis

In older people this is often due to arthritis of the knee, and in younger people, damage to the Cartilages in the knee joint is generally the culprit. Occasionally these Cartilages are torn due to a twisting injury. The knee can sometimes lock when the torn cartilage sticks in the joint making removal of the cartilage (or a part of it) the most likely remedy. Generally though, the use of Electro-Acupuncture is highly effective in treating knee pain.

P O I N T S

B40 This lies directly behind the knee joint in the centre of the crease.

SP9 This lies just below the inside of the kneecap and below the top of the tibia. This point is usually tender when pressed with a finger tip.

Stress and Pain - For long term conditions it may be that a level of stress has built up and the Anxiety and Stress points may be helpful for a few weeks as part of the treatment program.

This book makes no claims to cure any disorder mentioned; it merely shows simple ways in which these conditions may benefit. In some cases this will result in cure and in others it may only help. Bear in mind that correct diagnosis is important in serious or persistent conditions. If you are unsure as to the cause of your pain, seek the opinion of a doctor before commencing treatment.
REMEMBER... pain is a warning sign given by the body, so it must be heeded. In chronic cases, the pain can cease to perform its usual alert function. This makes treatment even more important

THE TREATMENT OF PAIN

Pain is perhaps the most common of all complaints and can be divided into:

1. Acute (having been present for only a short time: say less than 2 weeks duration)
2. Chronic (lasting more than 2 weeks).

Pain occurs in many parts and for many reasons. This makes diagnosis important. When one knows where and why the pain occurs (such as an Arthritic joint) one can begin treatment. If no diagnosis has been made however, your most urgent need is to seek advice and determine what treatment is required.

SPORTS AND INDUSTRIAL INJURIES, SPRAINS AND STRAINS

These are common and often acutely painful conditions. The cause is usually obvious and treatment can be applied immediately, provided always that the possibility of any injury to the bone (such as a fracture) has been ruled out by an appropriate investigation. Turn to the index for the part of the body affected. Electro-acupuncture is an ideal way of self-treatment. Treating such injuries in the early stages is of considerable importance. It serves to ensure that the condition does not develop into a chronic problem.

MIGRAINES AND HEADACHES

These can be treated regularly to prevent them starting in the first place. Consider other methods of prevention, including diet (see page 0.1) and breathing exercises if tension is a major part.

CHILDREN - It is important that children's ailments, especially headaches, are diagnosed as soon as possible by an appropriate physician.

ARTHRITIS - OSTEO-ARTHRITIS, RHEUMATOID ARTHRITIS

These are perhaps the most common cause of chronic pain. There are two main types of arthritis: Osteoarthritis, which in lay terms is due to wear and tear of the joint, and rheumatoid arthritis which is a form of arthritis whereby the joints have become inflamed. In general Osteoarthritic pain will respond faster to Electro-acupuncture treatment than rheumatoid arthritis which needs many treatments as well as diet change.

To treat Arthritis - Simply turn to the pain section and use the points shown for the part of your body.

BACK PAIN

Back pain is a common reason for time lost from work. It is usually due to narrowed inter-vertebral discs in the lower part of the spine. Sometimes this is associated with osteoarthritis of the spine. Electro-acupuncture is a useful way of treating this pain and should reduce time away from work. Both general back pain and sciatica are covered in the index. The back can be divided into three distinct areas:

Upper Back

> This is known as the cervical region and when treating Vertebrae problems in this area you should refer to the section in the index for Neck Pain.

Middle Back

> This is the thoracic region and when treating Vertebrae problems in this area, you should refer to the section on Thoracic pain.

Lower Back

> This is the lumbar region and when treating problems in this area, you should refer to the section on Lumbar pain.

When using Electro-acupuncture to treat back problems you should always remember the following three points:

1. Always treat local tender points which the Chinese call "Ah Shi" (literally translated this means "ouch") points. These can be found either with the probe (see earlier) or by pressing deeply with a finger tip over the painful area and using Electro-acupuncture to treat the points which are tender to such examination.

2. In acute conditions treat daily; in some instances it is beneficial to treat hourly to begin with. If discomfort returns within a short period after treatment, repeat the treatment as often as necessary.

3. In chronic conditions treat daily until the condition improves, then two or perhaps three times weekly. Intervals between treatments can be increased as the condition further improves.

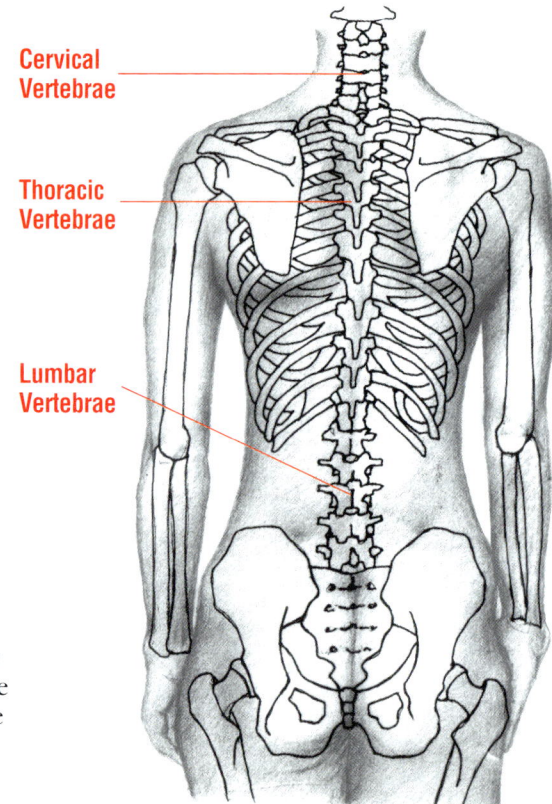

UNITS OF MEASUREMENT

There is a very simple, accurate unit of measurement used in acupuncture, called the 'CUN'. It is the width of the thumb joint - as shown in the diagram below. The width of the index finger is also used in conjunction with the thumb; for example, 3 thumbs are equal to four fingers.

The measurements are always accurate for each individual. Obviously, **it is essential that the measurements are those of the person being treated.**

Throughout this manual, to avoid any confusion, measurements are always given in either 'Thumbs' or 'Fingers'.

'Cun' - Thumb Finger 3 Thumbs
..

      'Cun' - Thumb   **Finger**   **3 Thumbs**

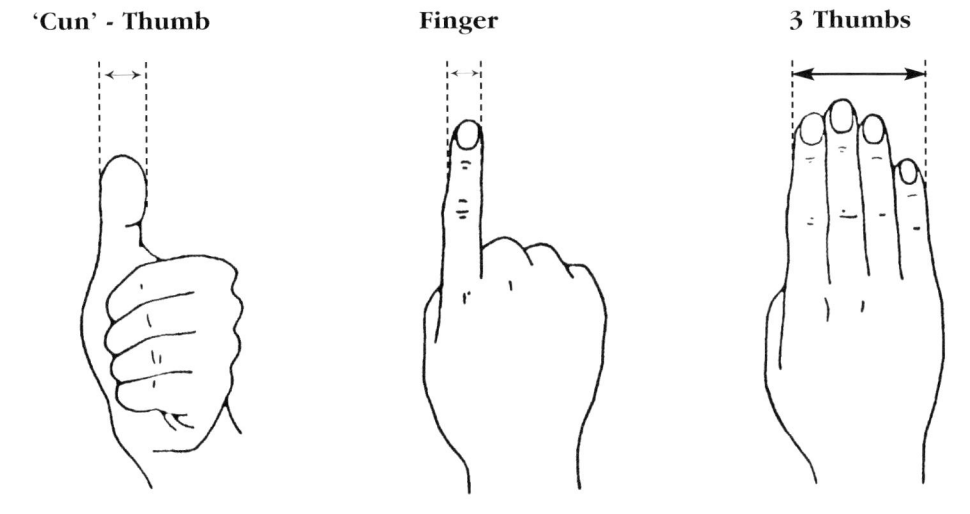

Make your own 'Body Ruler'

The easiest way to ensure that you measure points correctly, is to make your own personal 'Body Ruler'. This is a very simple process and whilst only taking a few minutes to produce, will greatly increase the speed and accuracy with which you locate your treatment points.

Take a piece of card and mark five fingers width along one edge - use the 1st joint of the index finger for each measurement, as shown above then mark three thumb divisions along the end of the card and four along its side.

Use your 'ruler' to locate the points as shown in the User's Guide. The ruler will be far more accurate than simply guessing with your fingers. If you treat more than one person, remember to make a separate 'ruler' for each individual.

LOCATING KEY POINTS

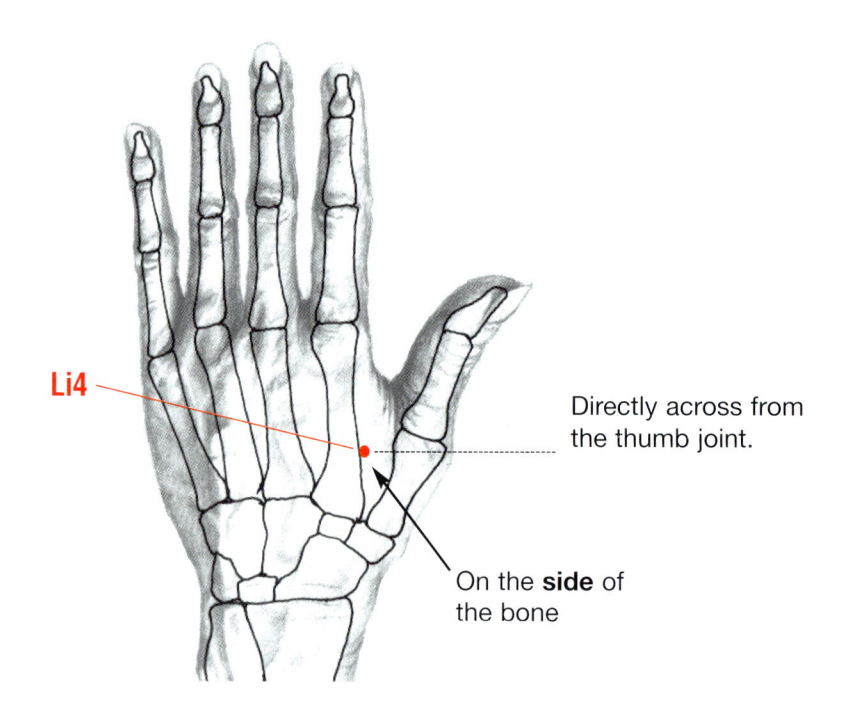

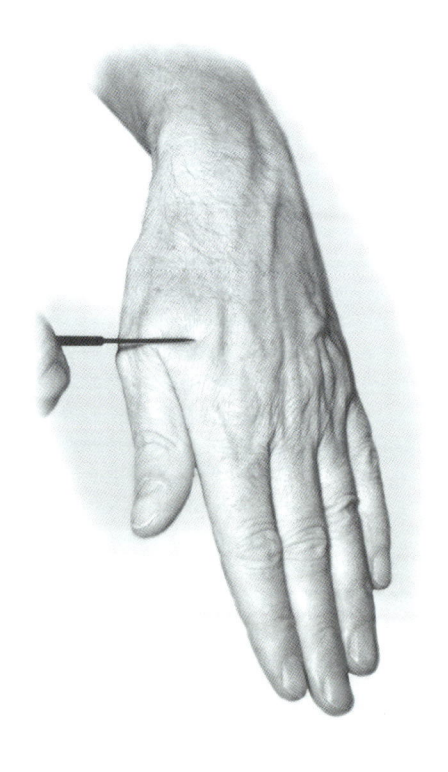

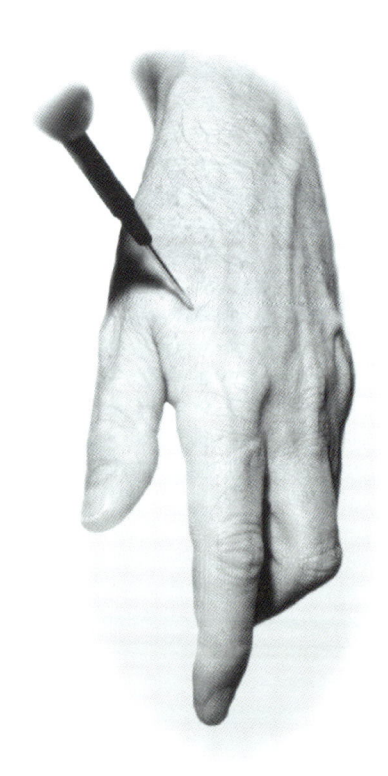

Li4

Directly across from the thumb joint.

On the **side** of the bone

8

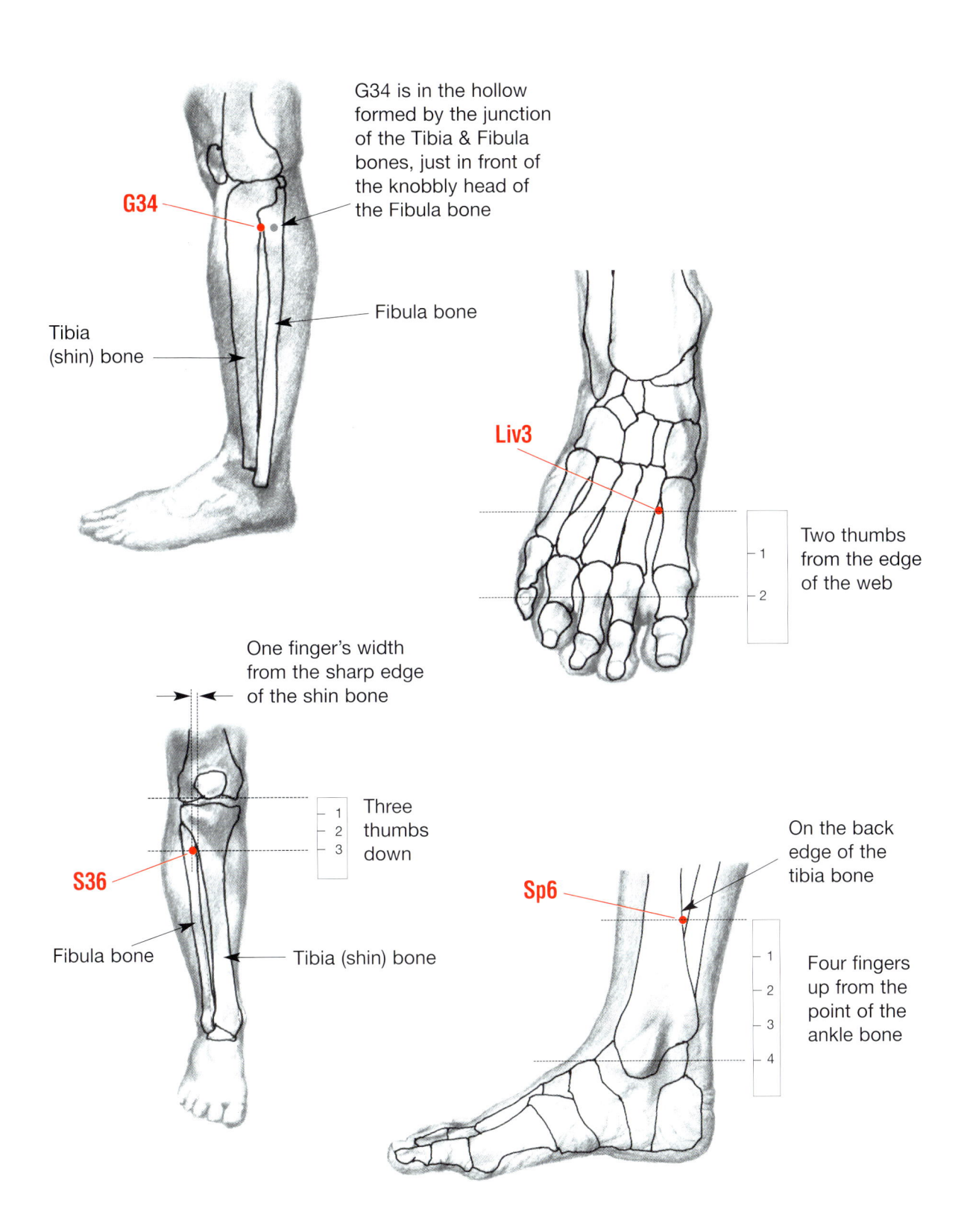

G34 is in the hollow formed by the junction of the Tibia & Fibula bones, just in front of the knobbly head of the Fibula bone

Tibia (shin) bone

Fibula bone

Liv3

Two thumbs from the edge of the web

One finger's width from the sharp edge of the shin bone

Three thumbs down

S36

Fibula bone

Tibia (shin) bone

On the back edge of the tibia bone

Sp6

Four fingers up from the point of the ankle bone

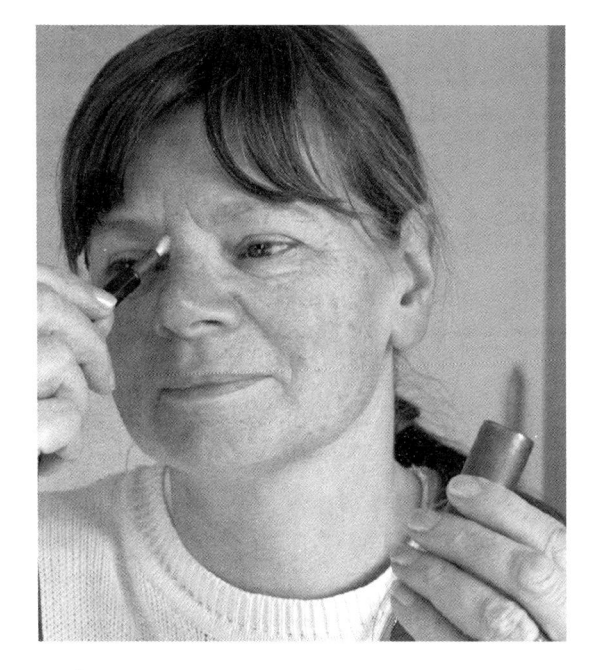

HOW TO TREAT EYES

Cotton Bud Instructions

The cotton bud probe provides a comfortable means of treating the eye points shown on the following pages.

Directions for Use:

1. Twist Cotton Bud plug into the extension socket on Device, ensuring that the cotton is in contact with the metal inner.
2. The person being treated holds the copper tube earth.
3. Switch Device On.
4. Set Timer switch to Manual.
5. Dip Cotton Bud in a small dish of saline solution (salt water or small saline dropper bottle from the chemists) made with sea salt.
6. Touch the wet cotton bud to the copper earth and you should get a high-pitched sound if a good contact is made.
7. If good contact, set timer switch to Constant.
8. Treat general points around the eye as per instructions for 30 seconds on each point.
9. Treat other points shown on specific points page for 30 seconds.
10. Each eye point should create a retinal flashing (or away from eyes a small tingle). If the sensation is too strong around the eyes, slide the Intensity switch down to suit.
11. Treat once per day minimum and twice preferably.
12. You cannot over-treat.
13. When renewing the cotton bud, cut the tip off close to the start of the cotton.
    The cotton bud probe and Device can be used to treat all the eye conditions listed in the book 'Ten Steps to Your Natural Eye Health'. The extra points shown on page four of this instruction leaflet are an extract from the book - full details of points to treat for the other eye conditions are detailed in the book.
    If you are unsure of any of the above, or would like further information, you can call the Helpline on page 1 at the front of the book for Support.

HOW TO TREAT EYES

Basic Eye Points to Stimulate For All Eye Conditions - *See also Page 8.20*

Treat the ring of 10 points shown in Fig. 1. There are 7 just on the edge of the eye socket and three around the eyebrow (see description below). It may be slightly easier to moisten all of these points with saliva or saline eye drops before starting.
Note: These instructions relate to using the metal probe, but the points are correct for the cotton bud as well.

SELF TREATMENT

Sit at a table with the device flat on the table, gripped in the left hand with your fingers placed as shown in Fig. 2, Fig. 4 and the quickstart guide. Do not lift the device off the table, as it is easier to keep your fingers on the black grip and to control the sliding switches with it flat on the table.

IMPORTANT - your fingers must stay in good contact with the black grip. If your finger is dry then moisten it with saliva or saline eye drops.

Hold the remote probe in your right hand as shown in Fig. 2 and Fig. 3 and slide the tip over the skin until it is in one of the positions shown in Fig. 1 and you have located a point that gives a high pitched sound. Test that this point gives a sting and or a flashing when you touch the treatment button on the top. Turn the intensity down to a low comfortable setting and treat the point for 15-30 seconds, depending upon your time available. REMEMBER, hold the probe perpendicular to the skin at all times and keep it pressed gently on to the point while you are stimulating.

N.B. For those with very thin or sensitive skin there is a cotton bud probe that can be used in place of the gold metal probe. Call the help line for information.

POINT 1 — Is on the bony edge of the eye socket, central with the centre of the eye.

POINT 2 — Is on the bony edge of the eye approximately halfway to the outer eye corner from Point 1.

POINT 3 — Is on the bony edge of the eye approx. 1/2" from the outer edge of the eye.

POINT 4 — Is on the bony edge of the socket directly above point 2.

POINT 5 — Is on the bony edge of the eye socket directly above point 1.

POINT 6 — Is on the bony edge of the eye approx. 1/2" from the inner corner of the eye and point 5.

POINT 7 — Is on the bony edge of the eye socket directly below point 6.

POINT 8 — Is on the centre of the eyebrowdirectly above point 5.

POINT 9 — Is slightly above the inner end of the eybrow.

POINT 10 — Is slightly below the inner end of the eyebrow.

HOW TO TREAT EYES

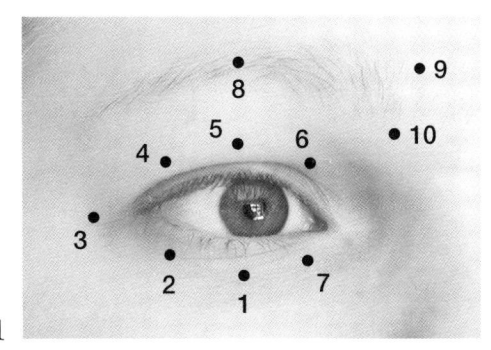

Fig. 1

Fig. 2

Fig. 3

Using the cotton bud probe as shown on page 11 is the preferred method for treating around the eyes.

Fig. 4

THE HISTORY AND THEORY OF TRADITIONAL ACUPUNCTURE

Electro-acupuncture utilises traditional acupuncture principles for its success.

A brief introduction to acupuncture is necessary to facilitate an understanding of the subject. You will then gain ability of how to use modern electro-acupuncture devices with confidence and to best effect. Acupuncture is an ancient system of treatment. It is part of the discipline of traditional Chinese medicine. This embraces many other forms of healing, quite apart from acupuncture, for example Chinese herbal medicine. Acupuncture is not, nor has it ever been, a complete system of medicine in its own right. It is, however, effective in many conditions which have often not responded to conventional approaches.

Acupuncture's main use is in treating chronic and painful conditions such as arthritis, headaches and migraines. After dental caries (tooth decay) and the common cold, these are the most common afflictions of the human race. Its effectiveness has enabled acupuncture to survive against, at times, enormous odds. It was banned by law in China at the beginning of this century but continued to be practised as folk medicine. Interest by Western doctors in acupuncture was stimulated by President Nixon's visit to China in 1972. Since that time medical interest in the subject has grown apace, underpinned by a number of important discoveries pointing to the effectiveness of Acupuncture.

The ancient Chinese hypothesized that energy circulated in the body via specific channels, which they called meridians. They considered that the balance and transmission of this energy from side to side, top to bottom and from the inside to the outside of the body was of great importance. They expressed this idea using their doctrine of Yin and Yang, which considers that everything is an amalgam of opposites (the opposites being called Yin or Yang). Yang was associated with activity, fire, the sunny side of the hill or the male principle and Yin was associated with physical substance, water, the dark side of the hill or the female principle. The balance between these two opposites was considered to be constantly fluctuating, in other words it was a dynamic balance. If one was out of balance, in an energetic sense, the principle of treatment would be to re-establish that balance.

The Chinese had an essentially vitalistic approach to the body and its physiology in keeping with many ancient systems of medicine. It is interesting to reflect that modern Western medicine is the only such system ever to have existed without a vitalistic approach to health and disease.

The Chinese developed a highly complex and sophisticated system of empirical laws based on countless observations of illness and response to treatment. These laws resulted in a number of ground rules aimed at guiding a doctor to the improvement of his patient's condition. The astonishing fact is that the application of these apparently odd-sounding laws does appear to work in a highly significant proportion of patients. It can clearly be surmised that if it did not work, acupuncture would not have been adopted within both Western and Eastern cultures to such a degree.

The Chinese believed that in addition to being in balance, the energy or life force (which the Chinese called chi) had to be able to circulate freely around the meridians. If a break occurred anywhere in this circulation, illness would result. An example is backache, which is viewed by the Chinese as a blockage in the "chi" circulating in the bladder meridian (this runs over the back as shown in the following diagram). The remedy was, put in the simplest of terms, to insert a needle at the point of discomfort, thus encouraging flow to re-establish itself. Interestingly enough this relatively crude approach does work in a sufficient number of cases to create a curious, rather than passing interest.

Each meridian refers to a particular organ, and the energy flowing through that meridian can be taken as indicating the functional state of that organ. Inserting a needle into a point on the liver meridian for instance could be expected to affect the function of the liver, the effect would depend on the actual point used and the state of the patient at the time of treatment

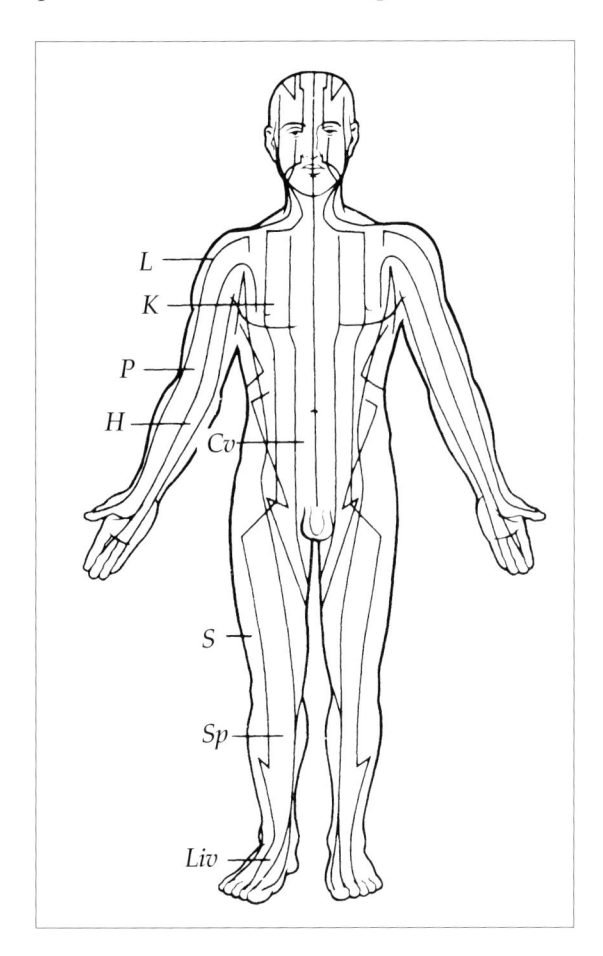

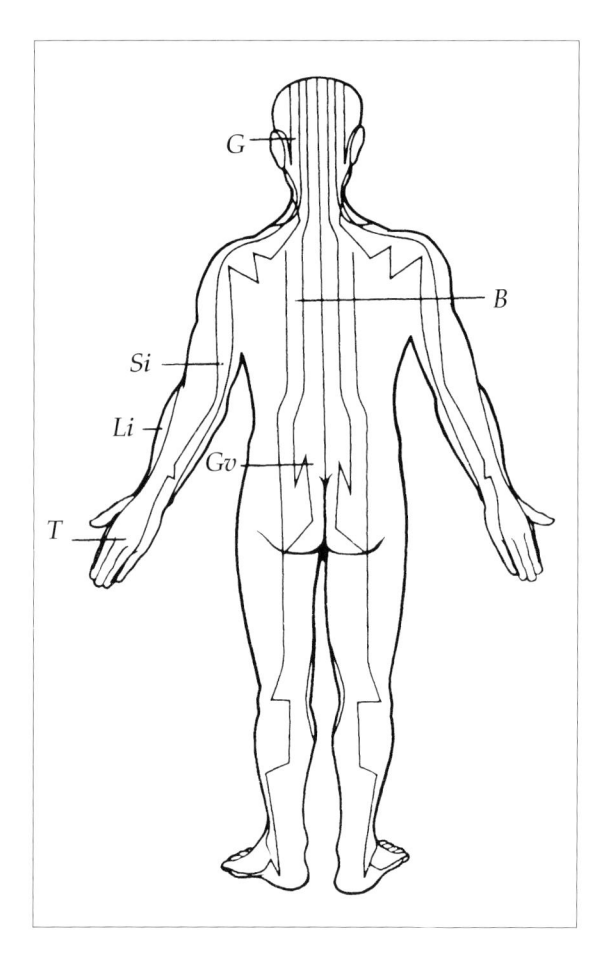

A number of standard abbreviations are used in the treatment section and on the charts. They are listed in the following table. There are twelve paired meridians, six running over the arms and onto the torso, the rest down the legs and onto the trunk. There are two unpaired meridians, one running down the front mid-line and one down the back mid-line.

Abbreviations for the leg meridians: The six paired arm meridians   Unpaired mid-line meridians

Abbreviations for the leg meridians:

G	=	Gall bladder
B	=	Urinary bladder
K	=	Kidney
Liv	=	Liver
S	=	Stomach
Sp	=	Spleen

The six paired arm meridians:

Li	=	Large intestine
Si	=	Small intestine
H	=	Heart
P	=	Pericardium
T	=	Triplewarmer
L	=	Lung

Unpaired mid-line meridians:

| Cv | = | Conception vessel |
| Gv | = | Governor vessel |

Electro-acupuncture allows you, without the use of needles, to stimulate points at which the energy flow is blocked. Gently apply the tip of the instrument probe to the points which hurt. We call these "trigger points", the Chinese call them "Ah-Shi" (practically translated "ouch") points.

Electro-acupuncture technique can be as effective as traditional needle acupuncture. It will work in the vast majority of cases. On no account however should you insert acupuncture needles into yourself. Leave this to a qualified practitioner.

HOW DOES ACUPUNCTURE WORK?

There are three currently favoured explanations. The gate control theory of pain, the neuro-endocrine theory and the semi-conductor theory.

The gate control theory of pain.

Nerve fibres are like large bundles of various sized cables, some thick and some thin. The thin fibres transmit the sensation of pain, while the thick ones carry the sensation of touch. It has been found, by experiment, that if impulse transmission in the thick (touch) fibre is increased, conduction in the thin (pain) fibre is selectively blocked. This is by closing a gate, consisting of specific nerve cells, in the spinal cord. This provides a useful method of controlling pain. Anything that increases transmission in the touch fibres, such as rubbing an injured knee, will help relieve some of the pain. This theory relates more to the use of TENS machines, as they can use up to 3000 times more current than a 20microamp stimulator. Acupuncture has been found to increase transmission in the thick (touch) fibres markedly. Electro-acupuncture achieves the same result, to some extent, although the intensity of stimulation is low. It is nevertheless a significant factor, explaining some of the treatment success using Electro-acupuncture.

Neuro-endocrine theory

One of the most recent and exciting discoveries in connection with acupuncture is the finding that needling an acupuncture point causes the body to release its own natural pain killer called endorphin (a protein molecule with very powerful pain killing capabilities). Endorphin is released by many parts of the nervous system and is related to the glandular or endocrine system, hence the term neuro-endocrine. It has been found that the release of endorphin is only a part of the explanation for some of the successes of Electro-acupuncture.

Semi-conductor theory

An information and control system using direct current (DC) analogue electrical signals, which runs in connection with the nervous system, has been proposed by Robert Becker - a retired Professor of Orthopaedic Surgery working in New York State - to explain how acupuncture might work. His hypothesis is based on work with limb regeneration in amphibians and on the phenomenon of the current of injury. Becker's hypothesis leads to a whole range of theoretical assumptions regarding acupuncture points.

Becker proposed that the signals in the DC system are carried via the neuroglia which are cells surrounding nerve fibres. Currents known to be produced by injury are said to be produced by this glial system, which is associated with growth and repair. For example, if an injury is created and there is no current of injury, then no growth or repair occurs.

Also electrical currents and associated fields have been shown to be fundamental to development in both plants and animals. Becker described a number of spectacular examples, including the regeneration of amputated limbs in newts, and finger-tips in children.

The integration of the glial system with acupuncture was proposed by Becker with acupuncture points acting like booster stations along the meridians, which are lines connecting acupuncture points, and these meridian lines act as transmission lines for these DC signals.

Acupuncture points along meridians do show specific electrical properties, and changes in these characteristics can be used for diagnosis. Acupuncture points appear to have little or no electrical activity when the tissue or organ which they represent is healthy.
When an injury takes place, or disease occurs, a current is produced local to that damage. At the same time, the properties of the related acupuncture point change, and there are also electrical changes in the acupuncture points in relationship to the surrounding skin

Acupuncture points are usually negative relative to the surrounding skin, with a value of -0.05 milli volts being fairly average. Higher negative values represent increased electrical activity in the corresponding anatomical area with readings of -0.25 milli volts. In acute conditions, this level can go up to as high as -0.75 milli volts. In extreme cases readings over -1 milli volts are usually associated with severe pain.

In other situations a high positive value is found, particularly with infections, psoriasis, asthma and allergies, and readings of +0.5 milli volts are not unusual. A low permanent positive value such as 0.001 milli volts is present in some chronic conditions such as in chronic osteo-arthritis.

What this means is that it is possible to detect acupuncture points looking at voltage change. However, the most common method used to find acupuncture points is looking for areas of high conductance or low resistance (these both mean the same thing). This is what is used in the majority of electro-acupuncture instruments - a sensitive skin resistance meter being built in to the unit.

The fact that semi-conductor properties are present in acupuncture points can be shown by taking the reading over an acupuncture point with a simple voltmeter. If the electrodes are reversed, and if ionic conduction was solely responsible, then the reading would remain the same but would have a negative to positive. In practice this rarely happens and the second measurement with the electrodes the other way round is often different. This indicates a partial, or in some cases total, semi-conductor effect.

What is found is that if a bi-polar electrical current is driven through a semi conductive tissue then normal conductive properties will be restored, the stored charge in the damaged area will be discharged and the resultant symptoms will disappear, often with sufficient treatment this can result in a complete disappearance of the problem.

In conclusion, therefore, acupuncture points only become electrically active when a dysfunction is present in the body. The size and shapes of acupuncture points appear to vary considerably.

Electrical measurements reveal them in some cases to be zones within which a number of highly localized points may exist, and in other situations they appear to be highly localized points even localized within a small number of millimetres.

This simple biophysical model of acupuncture can be confirmed by any reasonably committed investigator, using a simple multi-meter. This confirms the semi-conductor properties of acupuncture points and their related tissue. It also provides a scientific basis for the use of a biphasic current of stimulation. Essentially what an acupuncture point is expressing when it becomes active (in other words where disease is present), is it is trying to resolve biophysically the electrical abnormality produced by the injury or disease in the affected tissue. The use of a biphasic current over the affected point facilitates this process, which in turn leads to a return to normal health.

This theory, therefore, has the beauty of having considerable scientific evidence, and of its being able to be confirmed by simple experiments, which can be carried out by anybody of reasonable intelligence using a multimeter.

Dr Julian Kenyon MD, Southampton, UK., February, 1995.

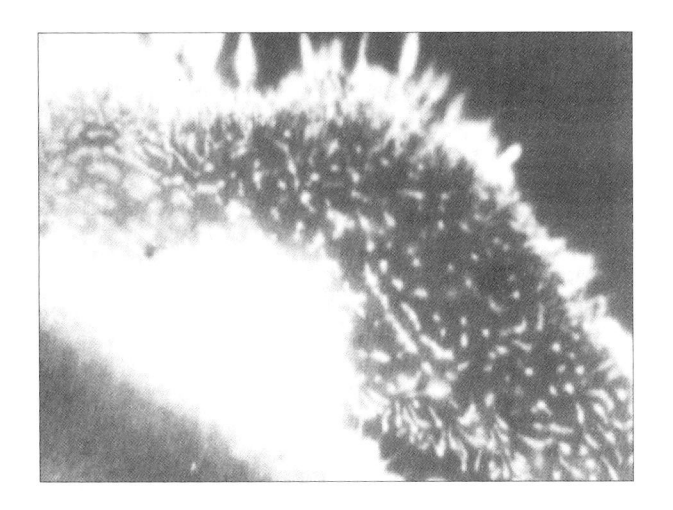

To assist with the location of Acupuncture points, Electro-acupuncture units usually have a built-in detection facility with audio and visual read-outs. They should also provide a physical sensation, which will only be felt when 100% accuracy is achieved. With the aid of sophisticated photographic technology, the points appear like electrical pores on the skin. If the point is viewed from the side, (in other words with the camera looking along the skin) a halo consisting of charged particles (called ions) can be seen. In some cases mostly negative ions and in other cases mainly positive. (see illustration)

GENERAL HEALTH PLAN

Introduction

To achieve full, vital health we believe that any recovery regime needs a continuing health plan as well as the stimulation of the healing system through the acupuncture points. To this end we recommend a step-by-step recovery plan that leaves our bodies strong and able to cope with the demands of our hectic lifestyles.

Step 1 - Cleanse and Heal

This first step is designed to cleanse our bodies of the toxins and deposits that have accumulated as a result of processed foods that have become normal in our busy lifestyles. There are three specific products:

CLEANSE - a powerful herbal formulation that cleanses the blood, organs, small intestine and colon.
This should be done annually.

OXYPLUS - a combination of aloe-Vera and oxygen, which helps heal the colon and acts as an anti-fungal cleanser. This should be done annually.

SERRAPEPTASE – an anti-inflammatory enzyme, stops inflammation and clears out the dead tissue from around the body and joints.

CURCUMIN – antiviral, antifungal, anti-inflammatory, antispasmodic, anti-tumor etc

Step 2 - Replenish the Immune System

The second step is to ensure that our immune systems are replenished. There are two specific products:

COLLOIDAL SILVER - a natural antibiotic that can kill up to 650 different bacteria, viruses, and fungi. This compares to the 5-6 bacteria (only) that ordinary manufactured antibiotics can kill. Colloidal Silver has no known side effects and has been used for over 100 years. It can be used as a first line of defence against any infection - taken under the tongue, swallowed, sprayed into the ear or eyes, or inhaled into the lungs.

PROBIOTIC FRIENDLY FLORA - many people do not realise that their natural first line of defence against bacteria is the friendly flora that should live in the small and large intestine. Unfortunately, there are many reasons why this is destroyed and it is imperative that we restore it as soon as possible. The obvious benefits are felt by those who suffer digestive disorders, skin problems and immune system problems. Every child and adult will benefit in the long run and should consider replenishing annually.

Step 3 - Rebuild through Nutrition

The third step is to ensure that our bodies receive the full range of essential vitamins and minerals that are sadly lacking from our regular diets. There are three specific products, which should be taken regularly:

ORGANIC MINERALS - this contains approximately seventy-seven plant derived colloidal minerals and provides all the essential trace minerals required in our diet, in a highly absorbable form.

DIGESTIVE ENZYMES - a natural combination of the enzymes required by our bodies when digesting food. This replaces the enzymes in our food which are destroyed by heat during the cooking process.

COLLOIDAL VITAMINS & MINERALS - a combination of colloidal vitamins which are absorbed by the body almost ten times greater than some other formulations giving almost 100% absorption.

Foods to avoid: • all starchy carbohydrates • sugar • microwaved foods • processed foods • cooked meats • milk • cheeses • more than 2 cups of coffee per day • any cooked or processed foods.
Foods to include: • lots of vegetables • avocado • brown rice • olive oil • lentils, • pulses • seeds and sproutlings • salads • tofu • beans • vegetable juices • free range eggs • veggie burgers • sweet potatoes • wild fish • free range poultry • sprouted wheat bread

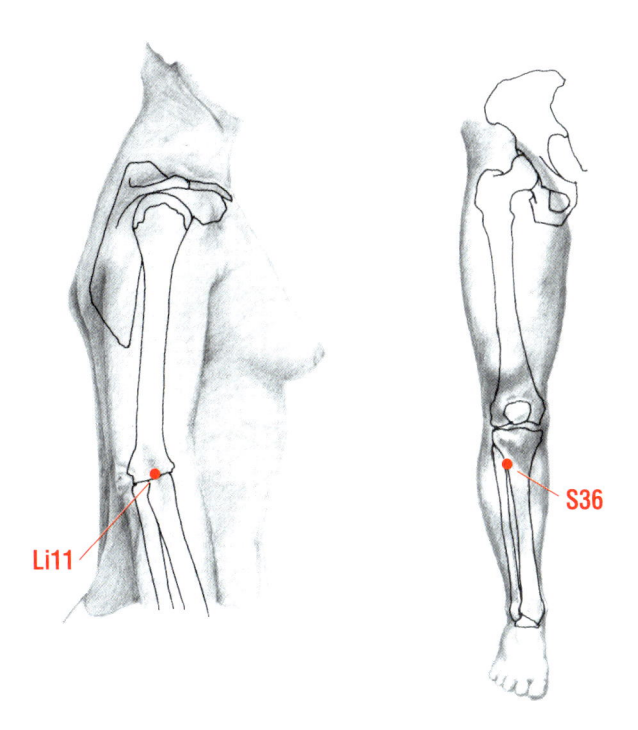

ANTI - AGEING & GOOD HEALTH

Anti - Ageing & Good Health

Electro-Acupuncture, used regularly, can be an effective part of a healthy lifestyle. A balanced diet, appropriate vitamin and mineral supplements and regular exercise are also essential to maintain your body in optimum condition.

POINTS

Liv3 — This lies in between the tendons of the big toe and the first toe, two thumb's width towards the top of the foot from the web.

Sp6 — This lies one hand's width (four fingers) up from the inner ankle joint. It lies just behind the tibia bone at this point.

S36 — This lies three thumb's width below the joint under the kneecap lying on the outer side of the knee. One finger's width back from the sharp edge of the shin bone.

Li4 — This lies on the side of the bone which runs from the forefinger knuckle down towards the wrist. See page 8 for a detailed description of this point.

Li11 — This lies 2cm beyond the end of the outer elbow crease with the arm bent.

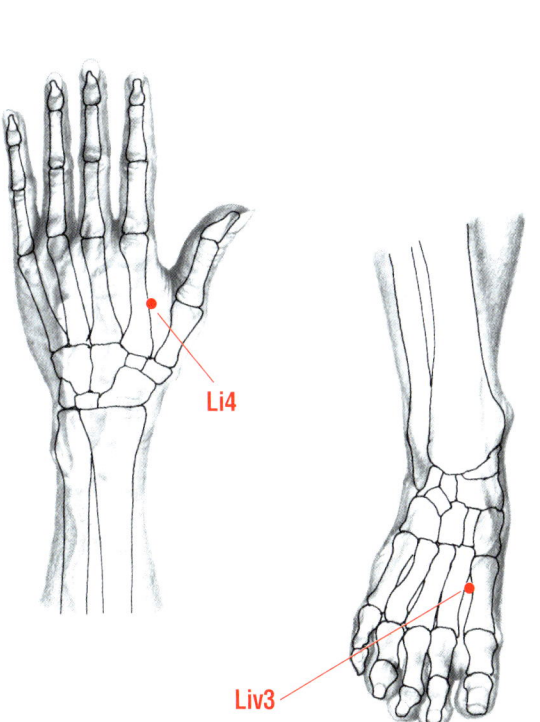

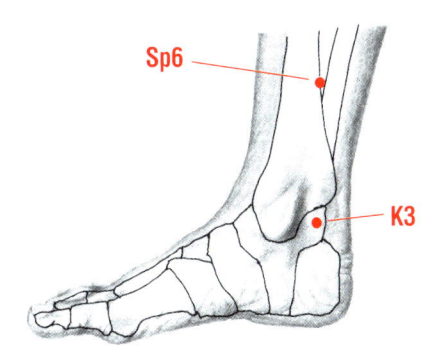

1. PAINFUL DISORDERS

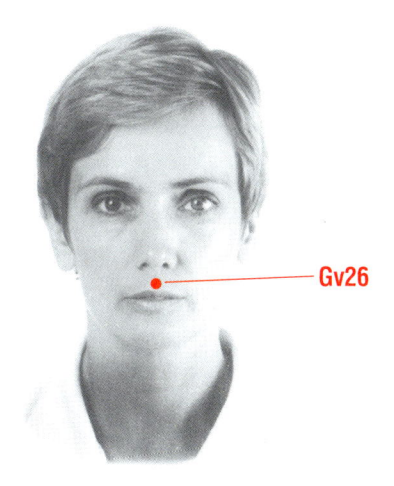

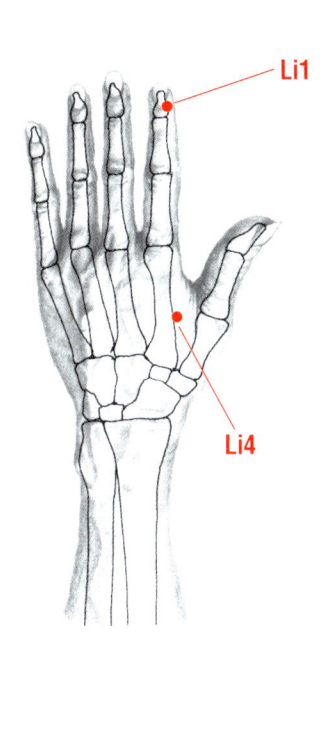

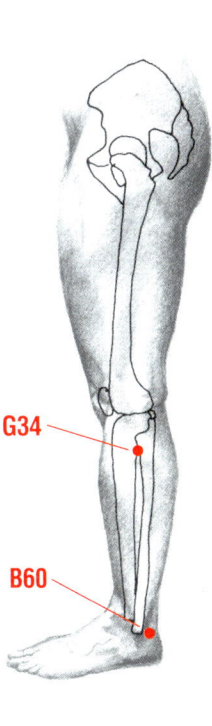

Pain - Not Otherwise Specifically Covered

Some points are useful in the relief of pain that is difficult to diagnose or in a general sense

POINTS

B60 — This lies midway between the tip of the outer ankle bone and the achilles tendon (in the hollow).

G34 — This is just below and in front of the knobbly head of the fibula, which is the bone just below the outer side of knee. This point is in a slight depression and is sometimes tender when pressed with a finger tip.

Gv26 — This is at the junction of the upper third and lower two thirds of a line joining the nose and the middle of the upper lip.

Li1 — This is situated a quarter of a finger from the corner of the index finger nail on the thumb side.

Li4 — This lies on the side of the bone which runs from the forefinger knuckle down towards the wrist. See page 8 for a detailed description of this point.

Ah Shi — Any local tender acupuncture points to be found in the area of pain that give a reaction when stimulated

> **Warning:** Headaches, especially in children should be immediately checked by your physician.

1.1

1. PAINFUL DISORDERS

Headache (Migraine) Frontal

These points can be used for any headache occurring over the frontal region of the head (forehead). Migraine is a particular type of headache, often lasting many hours and accompanied by sensations of flashing lights, nausea and vomiting. A migraine should be treated using the points indicated as soon as any warning signs (such as flashing lights, etc.) appear. Do not wait for the headache to start, simply treat each point for 60 seconds. During a migraine attack you can repeat the treatment as often as you feel necessary. ***Always treat the local tender (Ah shi) points*** as well as the ear points and consider the Sinusitis treatment. A balanced diet including appropriate vitamin and mineral supplements can be of great value - see page 0.1.

Warning: Headaches, especially in children should be immediately checked by your physician.

Fully established migraines can be difficult to stop, often requiring many treatments over a few hours. Once the migraine is gone, commence preventative treatment. Over a period of months, preventative treatments will be required progressively less often.

POINTS

B2 — This lies just beneath the inner end of the eyebrow. **IT IS NOT LOCATED AT THE INNER END OF THE EYE,** and in no case stimulate this area.

G14 — This lies one thumb's width above the mid point of the eyebrow.

Li4 — This lies on the side of the bone which runs from the forefinger knuckle down towards the wrist. See page 8 for a detailed description of this point.

Liv3 — This lies in between the tendons of the big toe and the first toe, two thumb's width towards the top of the foot from the web.

S36 — This lies three thumb's width below the joint under the kneecap lying on the outer side of the knee. One finger's width back from the sharp edge of the shin bone.

Yintang — This lies directly between the eyebrows, just above the bridge of the nose.

Ah Shi — Any local tender acupuncture points to be found in the area of pain that give a reaction when stimulated

Ear — Ear point

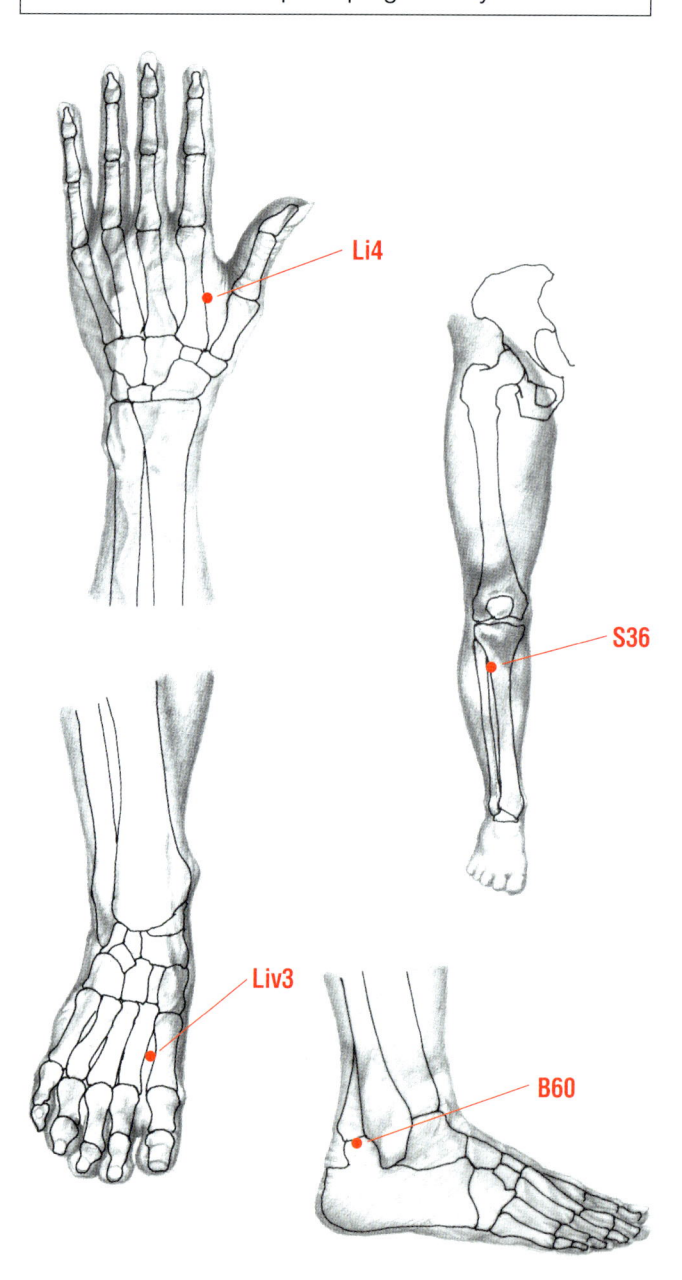

1. PAINFUL DISORDERS

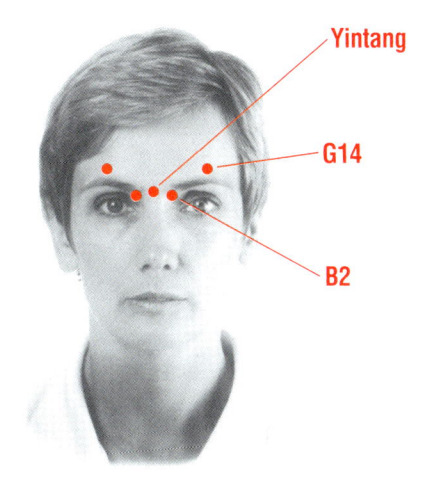

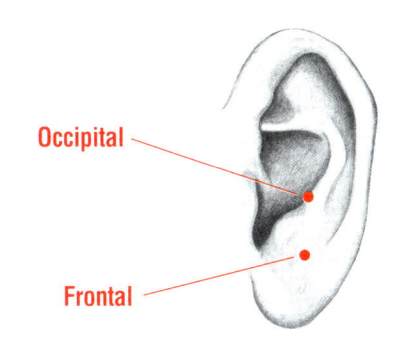

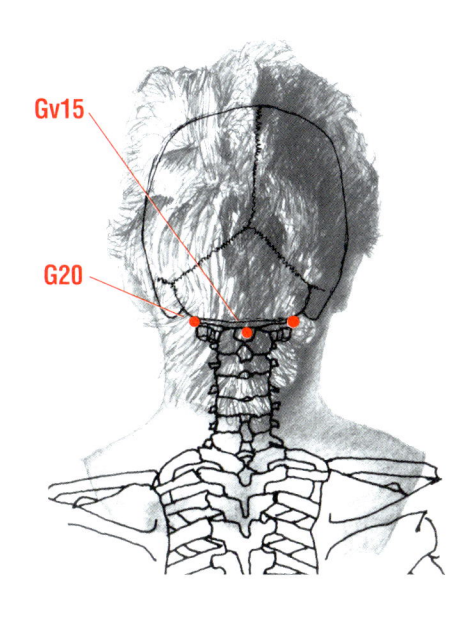

Headache (Migraine) Occipital

This is a headache occurring over the back of the head. Many patients with occipital headaches suffer accompanying neck problems. It is well worth referring to the section on neck pain and treating the points shown in addition to the *local tender (Ah shi) points*.

POINTS

B60 — This lies midway between the tip of the outer ankle bone and the achilles tendon (in the hollow).

G20 — Just below the skull bone and outside the muscle bulge.

Gv15 — This lies right at the top of the spine just below the small knob of bone in the centre of the mid line at the back of the skull.

Li4 — This lies on the side of the bone which runs from the forefinger knuckle down towards the wrist. See page 8 for a detailed description of this point.

S36 — This lies three thumb's width below the joint under the kneecap lying on the outer side of the knee. One finger's width back from the sharp edge of the shin bone.

Ah Shi — Any local tender acupuncture points to be found in the area of pain that give a reaction when stimulated

Ear — Ear point

1. PAINFUL DISORDERS

Headache (Migraine) Temporal

This is headache occurring on the side of the head. Always treat **local tender (Ah shi) points.** *If neck pain, treat neck points as well.*

POINTS

G20 — Just below the skull bone and outside the muscle bulge.

G34 — This is just below and in front of the knobbly head of the fibula, which is the bone just below the outer side of knee. This point is in a slight depression and is sometimes tender when pressed with a finger tip.

Li4 — This lies on the side of the bone which runs from the forefinger knuckle down towards the wrist. See page 8 for a detailed description of this point.

S36 — This lies three thumb's width below the joint under the kneecap lying on the outer side of the knee. One finger's width back from the sharp edge of the shin bone.

T5 — This lies on the back of the wrist, two thumb's width towards the elbow from the wrist crease.

Taiyang — This lies one thumb's width behind the outer edge of the eye. It lies in the centre of the temples.

Ah Shi — Any local tender acupuncture points to be found in the area of pain that give a reaction when stimulated

Ear — Ear point

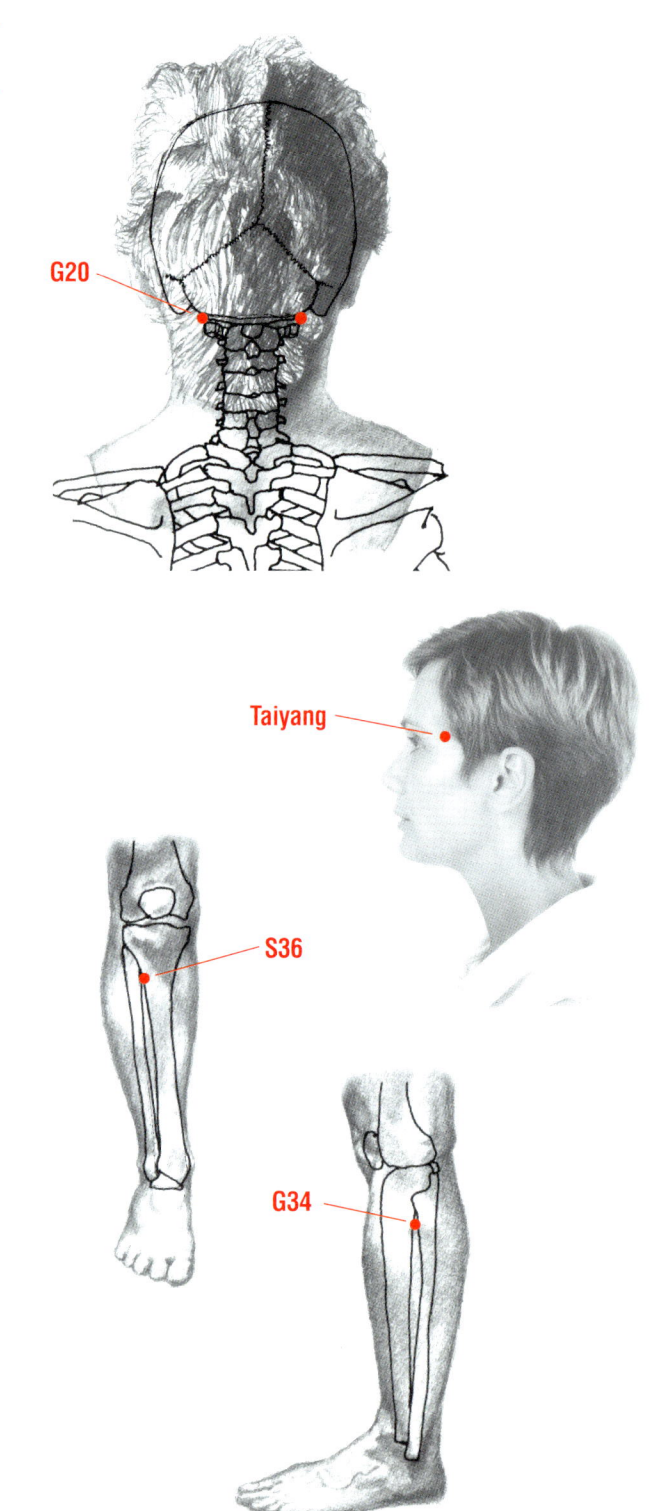

1.4

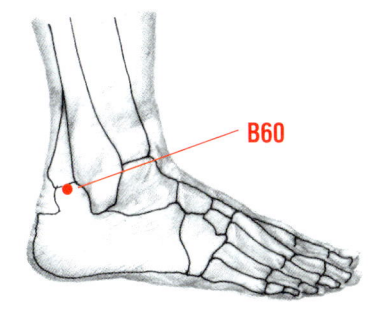

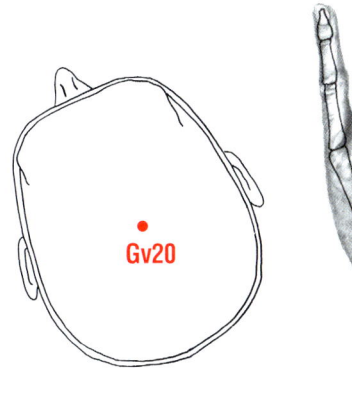

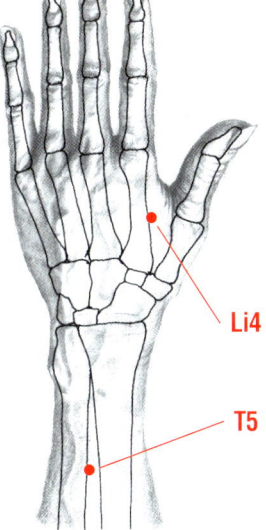

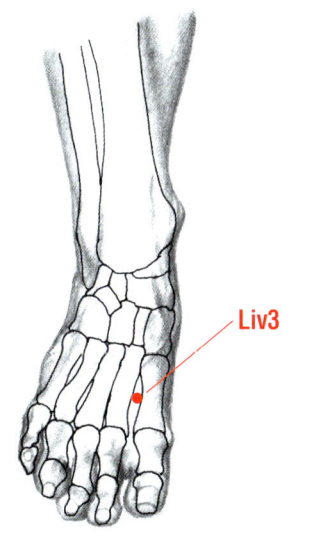

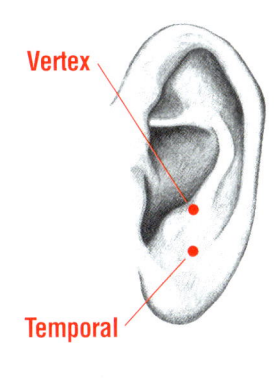

1. PAINFUL DISORDERS

Headache (Migraine) Vertex

This is a headache occurring on the top of the head. Always treat *local tender (Ah shi) tender points*.

P O I N T S

B60 — This lies midway between the tip of the outer ankle bone and the achilles tendon (in the hollow).

Gv20 — This point lies right at the top of the head where two imaginary lines cross, one drawn from the top of one ear to the top of the other ear, the other line drawn from the top of the nose right over the top of the skull to the back of the skull. Where these lines cross is Gv20.

Li4 — This lies on the side of the bone which runs from the forefinger knuckle down towards the wrist. See page 8 for a detailed description of this point.

Liv3 — This lies in between the tendons of the big toe and the first toe, two thumb's width towards the top of the foot from the web.

S36 — This lies three thumb's width below the joint under the kneecap lying on the outer side of the knee. One finger's width back from the sharp edge of the shin bone.

Ah Shi — Any local tender acupuncture points to be found in the area of pain that give a reaction when stimulated

Ear — Ear point

1. PAINFUL DISORDERS

Jaw Pain - arthritis - TMJ

This is sometimes accompanied by temporomandibular arthritis. Treatment with Electro-Acupuncture is often highly effective.

POINTS

Li4 — This lies on the side of the bone which runs from the forefinger knuckle down towards the wrist. See page 8 for a detailed description of this point.

S7 — This lies just below the mid point of the cheek bone, over the front part of the top end of the jaw bone.

Si19 — This is immediately over the jaw joint between the jaw and the skull, just in front of the small piece of cartilage, which forms the front part of the ear.

Ear — Ear point

Toothache (lower jaw)

Only use Electro-Acupuncture as a stop-gap "first aid" measure prior to seeing the dentist, it is not intended as a substitute for proper dental care.

POINTS

Li4 — This lies on the side of the bone which runs from the forefinger knuckle down towards the wrist. See page 8 for a detailed description of this point.

Ear — Ear point

Ah Shi — Any local tender acupuncture points to be found in the area of pain that give a reaction when stimulated

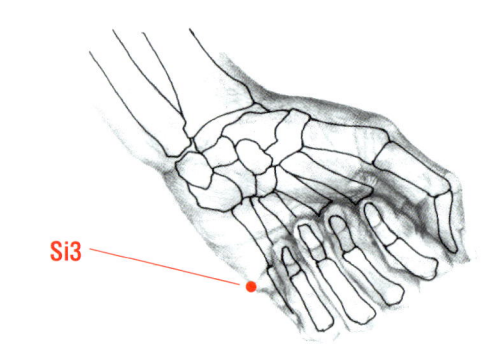

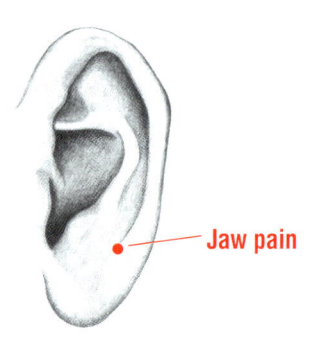

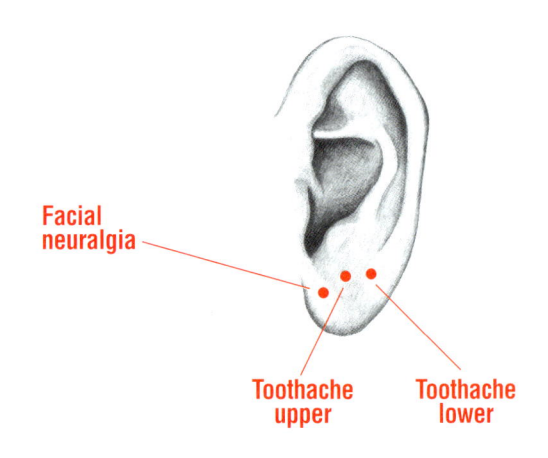

1.6

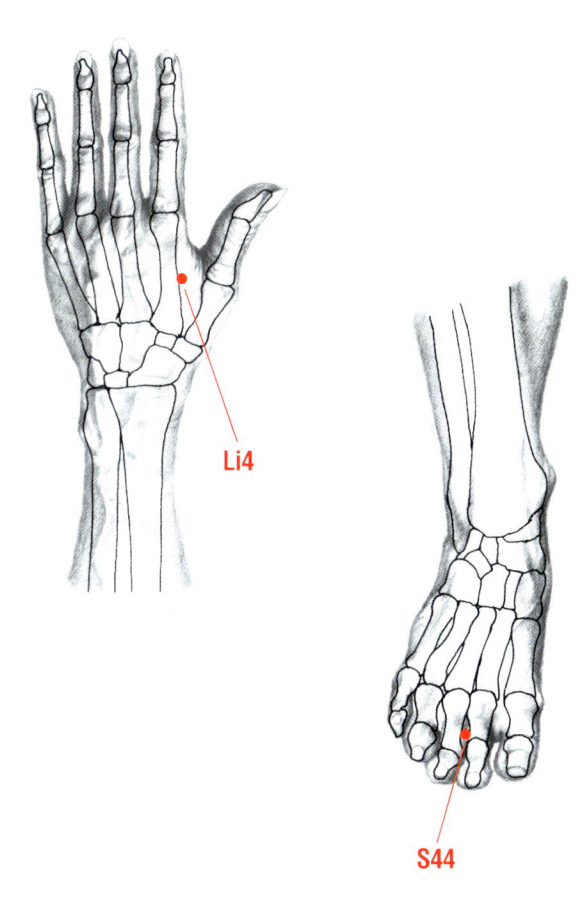

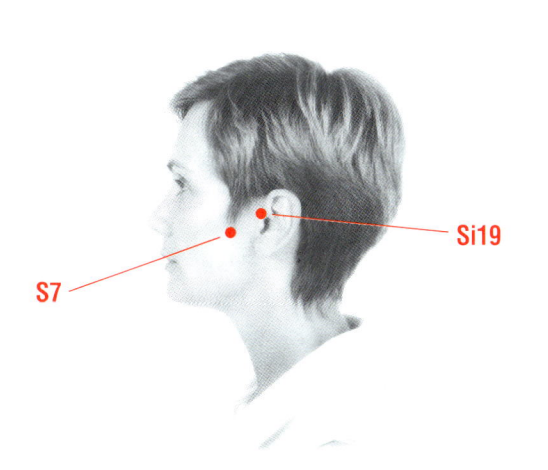

1. PAINFUL DISORDERS

Toothache (upper jaw)

The same comments apply as toothache in the lower jaw.

POINTS

Li4 — Description as shown opposite, under the heading of Jaw Pain

S44 — This lies in the web between the second and third toes.

Ear — Ear point

Ah Shi — Any local tender acupuncture points to be found in the area of pain that give a reaction when stimulated

Facial Neuralgia (Tic Doloreux)

This condition is also sometimes called trigeminal neuralgia. It is characterised by a severe stabbing, often lancing, pain which can occur in various parts of the face. In some cases its severity can even make eating and talking difficult.

POINTS

Li4 — Description as shown opposite, under the heading of Jaw Pain

Si3 — With the fist clenched, this lies at the end of the main crease of the palm at the junction of the red and white skin (It is easier to locate unclenched).

Si19 — This is immediately over the jaw joint between the jaw and the skull, just in front of the small piece of cartilage, which forms the front part of the ear.

Ear — Ear point

Ah Shi — The local tender points should be used for treating the condition. Use only the points in the area where the pain actually occurs.

1. PAINFUL DISORDERS

Ear Pain

Earache can arise from a variety of causes, if it is an infection, with a discharge, antibiotics are probably not needed if treated early enough with Electro-Acupuncture. It can often be resolved without resorting to medication. Treat with colloidal silver - place drops in the ear and take ½ teaspoon under the tongue. If after 24 hours of treatment there is no improvement, consult a doctor.

POINTS

Li4 — This lies on the side of the bone which runs from the forefinger knuckle down towards the wrist. See page 8 for a detailed description of this point.

Si3 — With the fist clenched, this lies at the end of the main crease of the palm at the junction of the red and white skin (It is easier to locate unclenched).

Si19 — This is immediately over the jaw joint between the jaw and the skull, just in front of the small piece of cartilage, which forms the front part of the ear.

T5 — This lies on the back of the wrist, two thumb's width towards the elbow from the wrist crease.

T17 — This point lies in the hollow behind the earlobe between the mastoid bone and the angle of the jaw.

Ear — Ear point

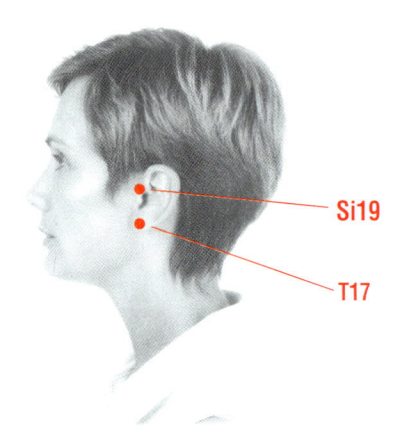

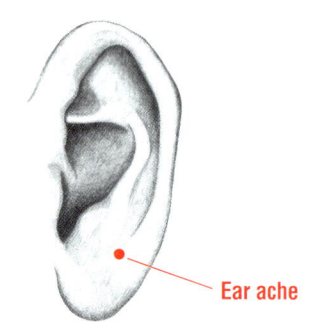

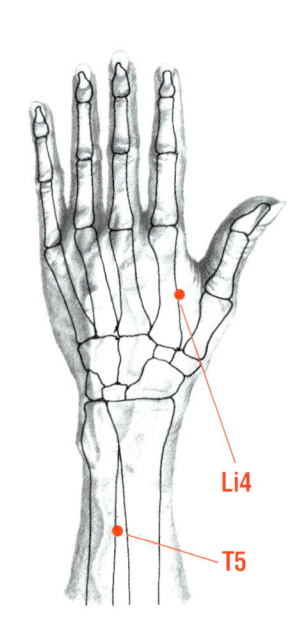

1. PAINFUL DISORDERS

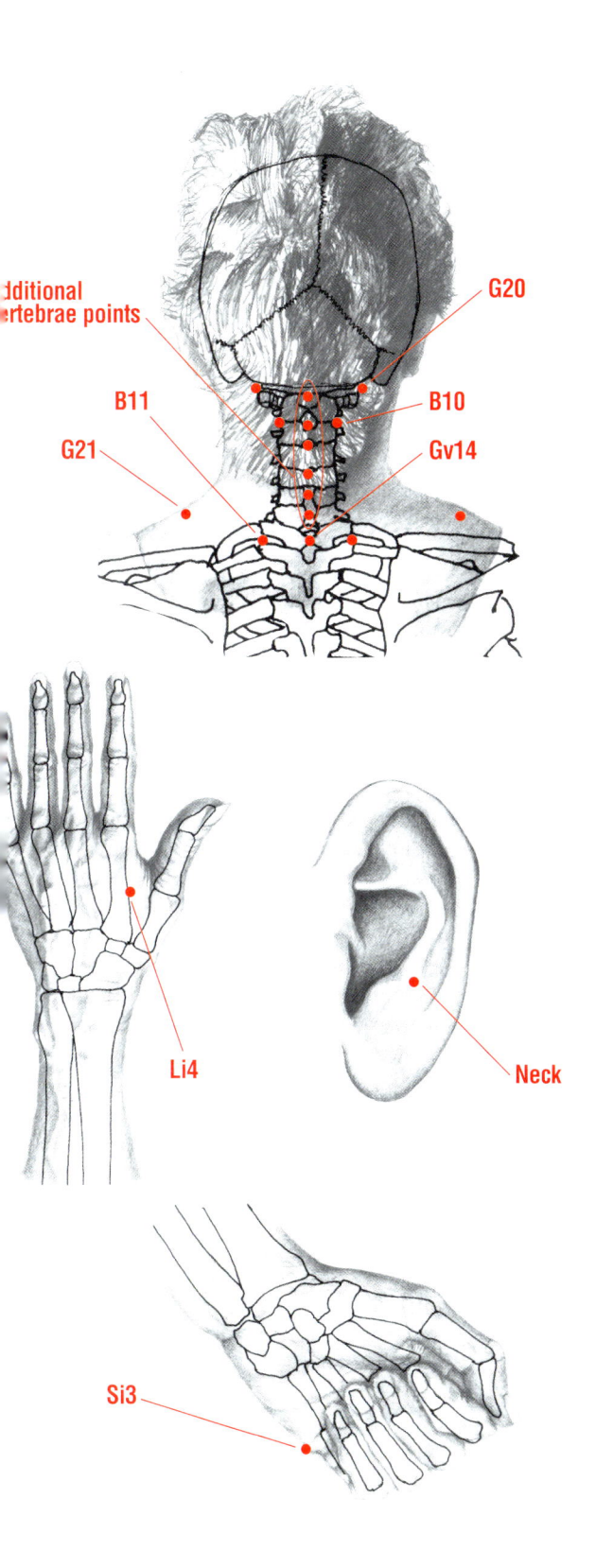

Neck Pain - arthritis - stiffness

Neck pain is most commonly due to arthritis, sometimes called cervical spondylosis. A qualified osteopathic or chiropractic opinion is often helpful in the treatment of this problem. Electro-Acupuncture however, can be a highly effective method of treatment.

POINTS

G20 — Just below the skull bone and outside the muscle bulge.

G21 — This lies halfway between the knob of bone in the centre at the bottom of the neck and the tip of the shoulder, in the fleshy mass of muscle passing over the shoulder.

Gv14 — This lies just below the most prominent knob of bone at the base of the neck in the mid-line.

Li4 — This lies on the side of the bone which runs from the forefinger knuckle down towards the wrist. See page 8 for a detailed description of this point.

Si3 — With the fist clenched, this lies at the end of the main crease of the palm at the junction of the red and white skin (It is easier to locate unclenched).

B10 — This lies one and a half thumb's width to each side of the centre of the spine at the level of the first cervical vertebra.

B11 — This lies one and a half thumb's width to each side of the centre of the spine at the level of the first thoracic vertebra.

Ah Shi — Any local tender acupuncture points to be found in the area of pain that give a reaction when stimulated

Ear — Ear point

1. PAINFUL DISORDERS

Shoulder pain - frozen - arthritis

This is a common problem and should be treated vigorously. If shoulder pain is left for more than a month then a frozen shoulder may ensue. Stiffness of the joint and pain become troublesome features. In a chronically painful and stiff shoulder physiotherapy is a usual approach to treatment. Now Electro-Acupuncture is an alternative option for treating the pain.

POINTS

B57 — This lies in the centre of the back of the calf, just where the fleshy mass of muscle narrows down into tendon.

G21 — This lies halfway between the knob of bone in the centre at the bottom of the neck and the tip of the shoulder, in the fleshy mass of muscle passing over the shoulder.

Li11 — This lies 2cm beyond the end of the outer elbow crease with the arm bent.

Li15 — This lies just in front of the shoulder joint, in a depression which is produced when the arm is lifted above the head, it can be tender with finger tip pressure.

S38 — This lies exactly halfway down the lower leg, two finger's width away from the mid-line measured from the ridge of bone running down the front of the shin.

T14 — This lies in a depression behind the shoulder joint, which is produced again by putting the arm above the head.

Ah Shi — Any local tender acupuncture points to be found in the area of pain that give a reaction when stimulated

Ear — Ear point

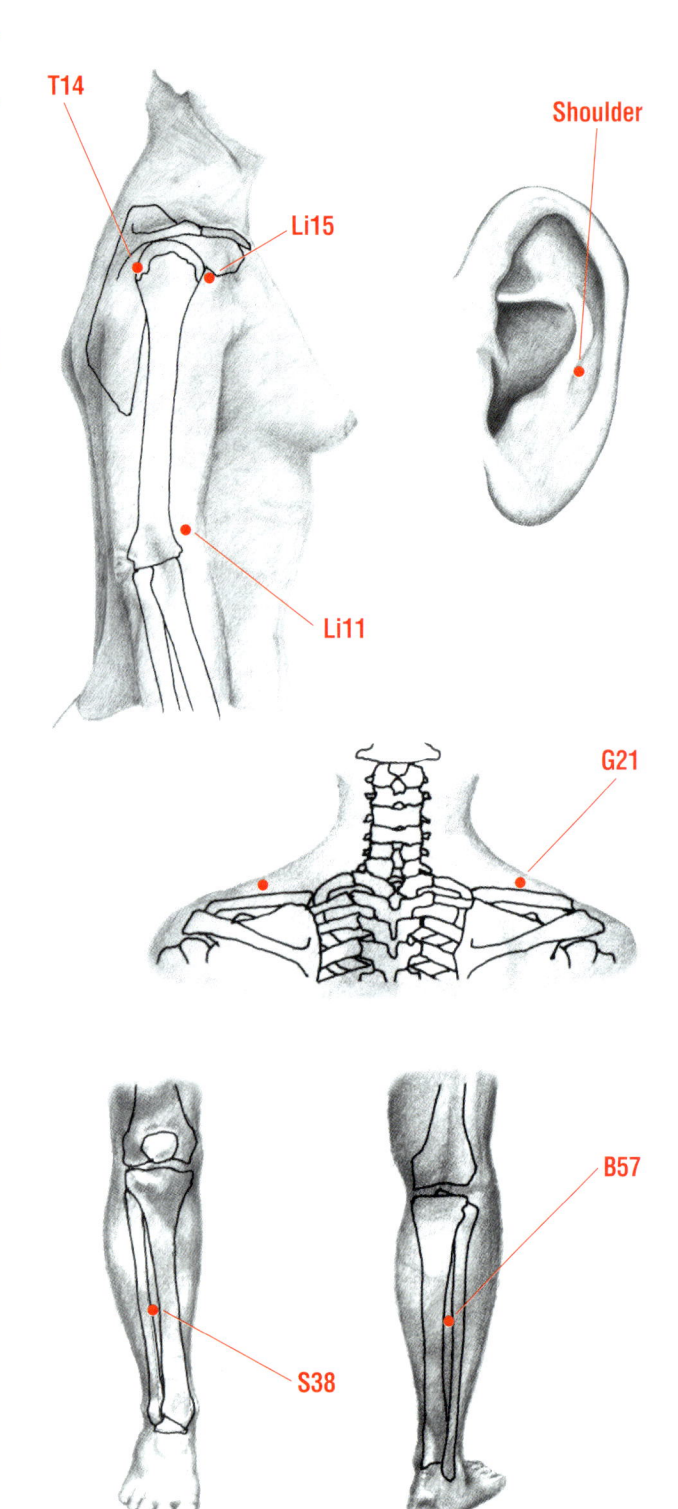

1.10

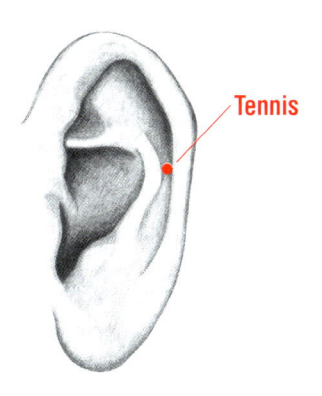

1. PAINFUL DISORDERS

Tennis Elbow - arthritis

This is due to inflammation of the muscle at the point where it joins the bone at the outer edge of the Humerus.

POINTS

G34 This is just below and in front of the knobbly head of the fibula, which is the bone just below the outer side of knee. This point is in a slight depression and is sometimes tender when pressed with a finger tip.

Li11 This lies 2cm beyond the end of the outer elbow crease with the arm bent.

Ah Shi Any local tender acupuncture points to be found in the area of pain that give a reaction when stimulated

Ear Ear point

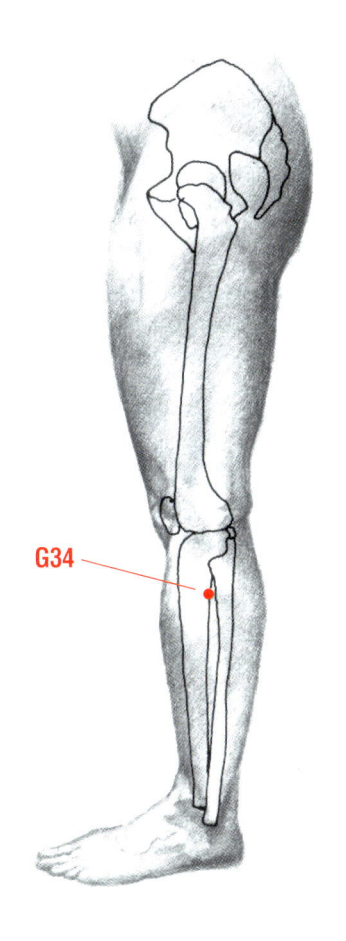

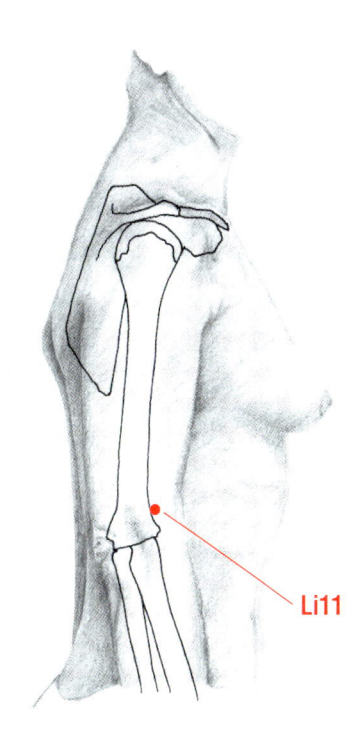

1. PAINFUL DISORDERS

Hand, Fingers - pain arthritis

The most common hand pain is due to Osteo-arthritis, injury or, when it is acute or chronic, rheumatoid arthritis.

POINTS

Li4 — This lies on the side of the bone which runs from the forefinger knuckle down towards the wrist. See page 8 for a detailed description of this point.

Li5 — This lies in a depression right at the very base of the thumb, almost at the wrist joint, the depression being much more obvious when the thumb is spread away from the index finger.

Finger points — At the end of the creases on each side of the finger joint and the joint creases top and bottom.

Knuckle points — With the fist clenched these lie half a finger width back towards the wrist.

Extra hand points — These lie in the centre of the web between the fingers.

Ah Shi — Any local tender acupuncture points to be found in the area of pain that give a reaction when stimulated

Ear — Ear point

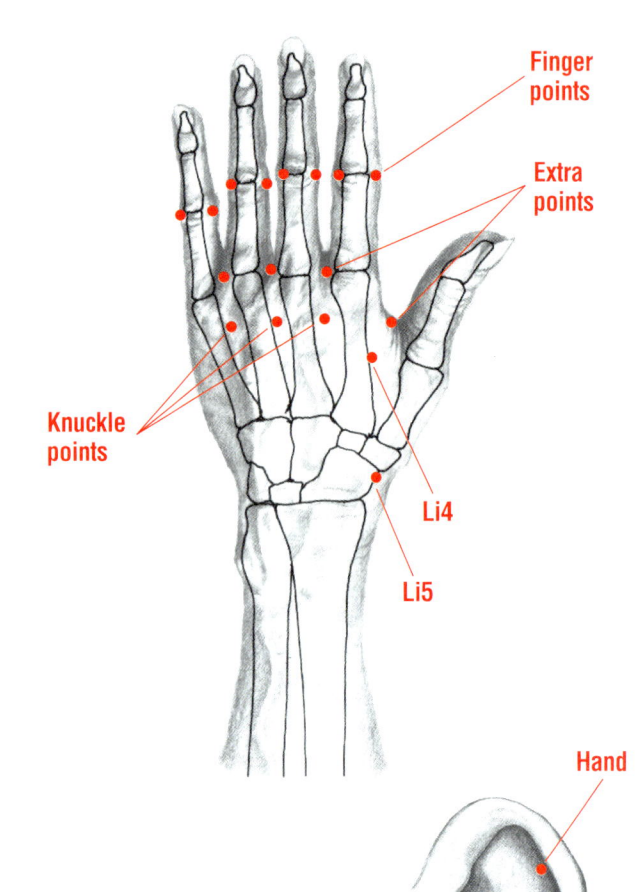

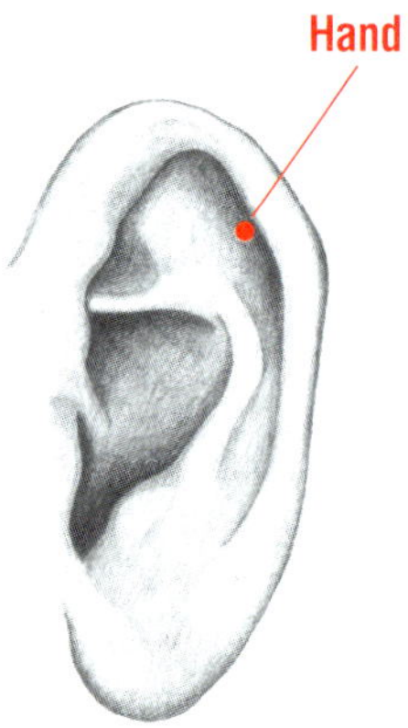

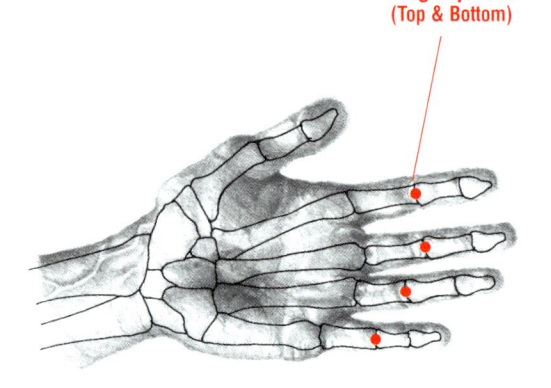

1.12

1. PAINFUL DISORDERS

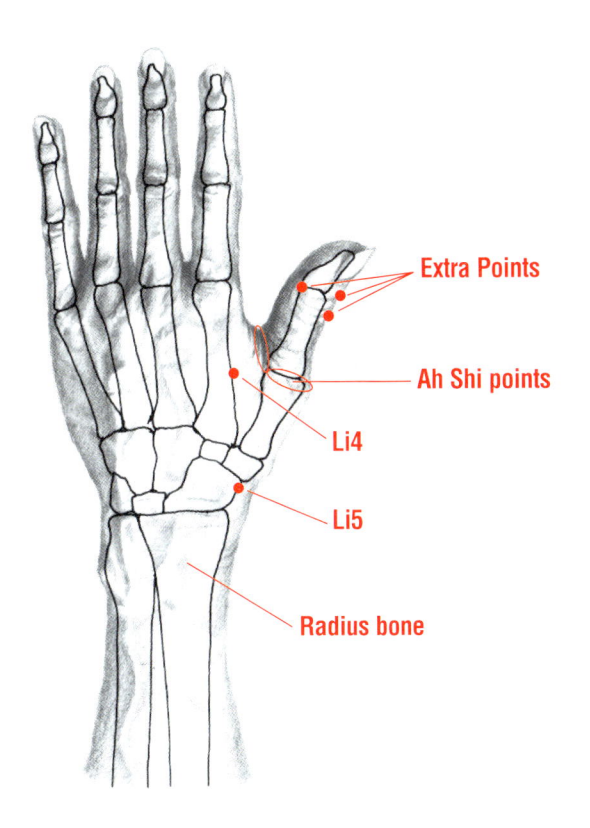

Thumb pain - arthritis

The most common thumb pain is due to Osteo-arthritis, injury or, when it is acute or chronic, rheumatoid arthritis.

POINTS

L9 This is situated at the end of the radius bone, by the thumb, on the palm side, in the depression just before the wrist crease.

L10 This is situated on the palm side of the thumb, one finger's width from the thumb knuckle, towards the wrist.

L11 This is situated on the outer side of the nail bed of the thumb.

Li4 This lies on the side of the bone which runs from the forefinger knuckle down towards the wrist. See page 8 for a detailed description of this point.

Li5 This lies in a depression right at the very base of the thumb, almost at the wrist joint, the depression being much more obvious when the thumb is spread away from the index finger.

Ah Shi Any local tender acupuncture points to be found in the area of pain that give a reaction when stimulated - particularly on the line of creases as shown.

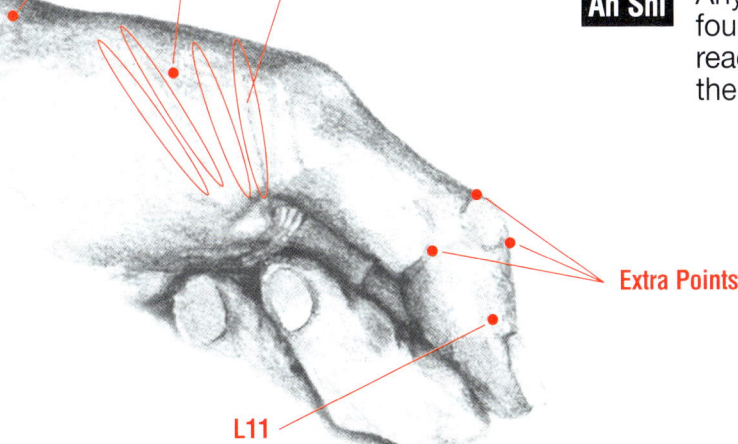

1. PAINFUL DISORDERS

Wrist pain - Carpal Tunnel Syndrome

This is most often due to strain caused by excessive use. It can occasionally be due to arthritis (most commonly rheumatoid arthritis). Carpal tunnel syndrome is a condition that is due to compression of the median nerve which passes deep to the front surface of the wrist. When compressed this gives rise to painful tingling sensations in the thumb, index, middle and part of the ring finger. Electro-Acupuncture is an effective way of treating this and the most important points to use are P6 & P7. Also take 100mg vitamin B6 daily.

POINTS

Li5 This lies in a depression right at the very base of the thumb, almost at the wrist joint, the depression being much more obvious when the thumb is spread away from the index finger.

P6 This lies two thumb's width up from the palm wrist crease towards the elbow, directly in the centre between the two tendons.

P7 This lies in the centre of the wrist crease palm side of hand.

Si5 This lies on the edge of the wrist joint crease on the little finger side of the hand.

T4 This lies on the back of the wrist, one finger's width towards the elbow from the wrist crease and next to the small prominent bone.

Ear Ear point

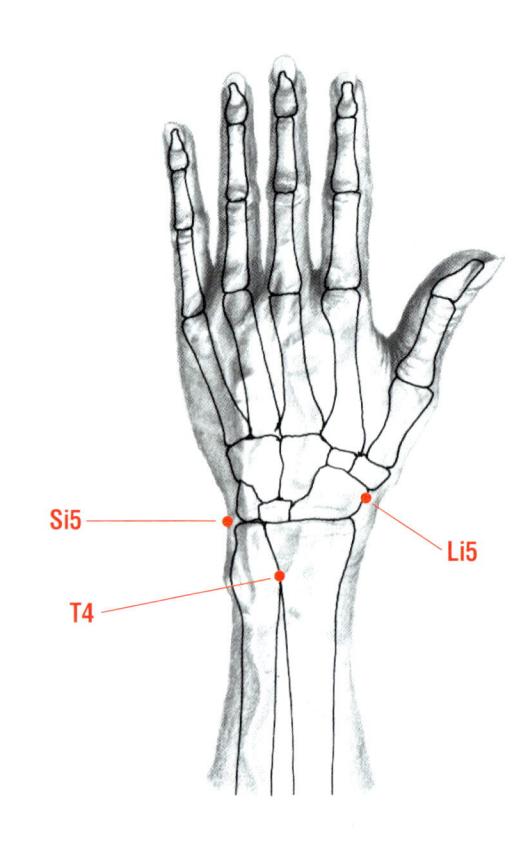

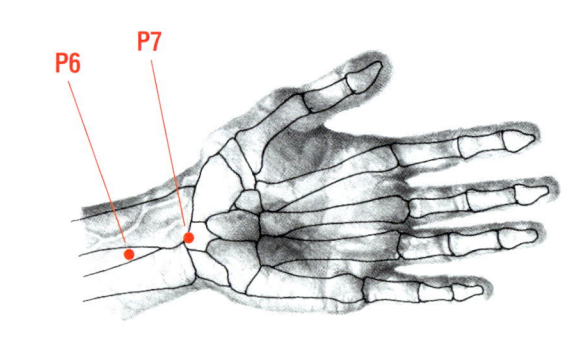

1. PAINFUL DISORDERS

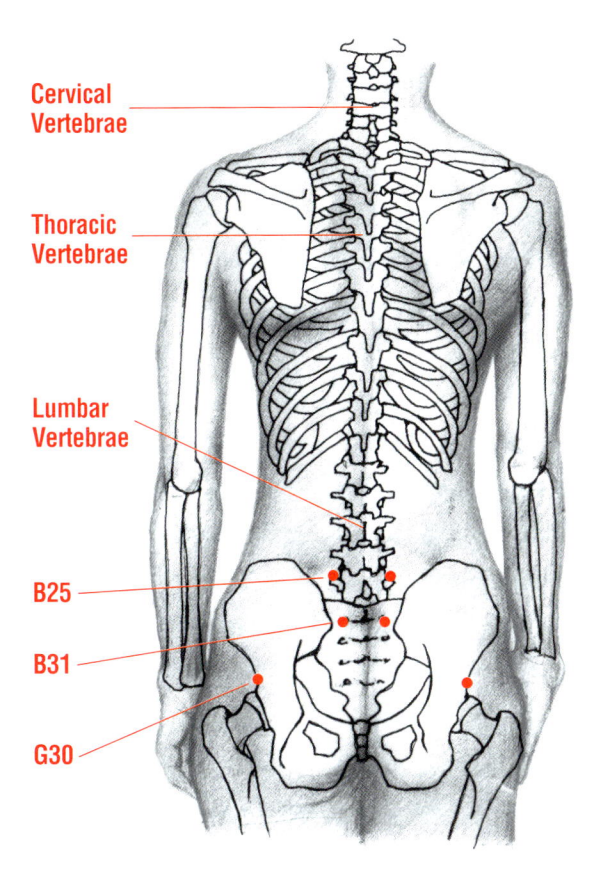

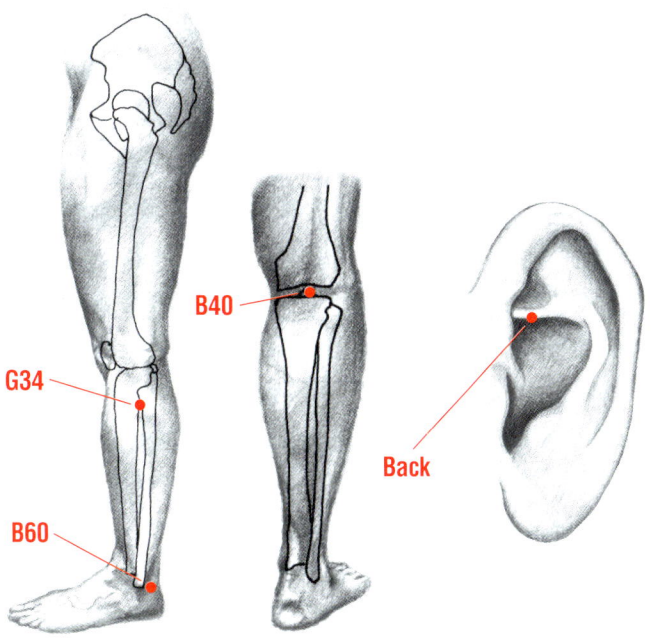

Back pain - Lower

This is most commonly due to narrowed discs in the lower lumbar spine. Occasionally the cause can be a prolapsed intervertebral disc and in these cases the pain often extends into the leg. If this does not respond satisfactorily to treatment a competent osteopathic, chiropractic or orthopaedic opinion should be sought. Electro-Acupuncture is successful at relieving chronic low back pain in many cases. For *Upper back* - also treat thoracic points, page 9.14 points B12 - B19.

POINTS

B25 — This lies one thumb's width above the sacral bone, one and a half thumb's width away from the mid-line.

B31 — This lies at the top of the sacral bone one and a half thumb's width away from the mid-line.

B40 — This lies directly behind the knee joint in the centre of the crease.

B60 — This lies midway between the tip of the outer ankle bone and the achilles tendon (in the hollow).

G30 — This lies in the upper, outer part of the buttock muscle. It is usually tender on deep finger tip pressure.

G34 — This is just below and in front of the knobbly head of the fibula, which is the bone just below the outer side of knee. This point is in a slight depression and is sometimes tender when pressed with a finger tip.

Ah Shi — Any local tender acupuncture points to be found in the area of pain that give a reaction when stimulated

Ear — Ear point

Please ensure that you use your 'body ruler' to locate the points - particularly B25 and B31

1. PAINFUL DISORDERS

Hip pain - arthritis

This is most commonly due to arthritis in the hip. Only if Electro-Acupuncture treatment is unsuccessful should a competent orthopaedic opinion be sought.

POINTS

G29 This lies halfway between the bony knob found at the top and front of the rim of the pelvis and the bony mass formed by the top of the hip bone, which is situated at the top of the thigh.

G30 This lies in the upper, outer part of the buttock muscle. It is usually tender on deep finger tip pressure.

G34 This is just below and in front of the knobbly head of the fibula, which is the bone just below the outer side of knee. This point is in a slight depression and can be tender when pressed with a finger tip.

S31 This lies on the level of the pubic bone just below the bony knob found at the top and front of the pelvis

S36 This lies three thumb's width below the joint under the kneecap lying on the outer side of the knee. One finger's width back from the sharp edge of the shin bone.

Ah Shi Any local tender acupuncture points to be found in the area of pain that give a reaction when stimulated

Ear Ear point

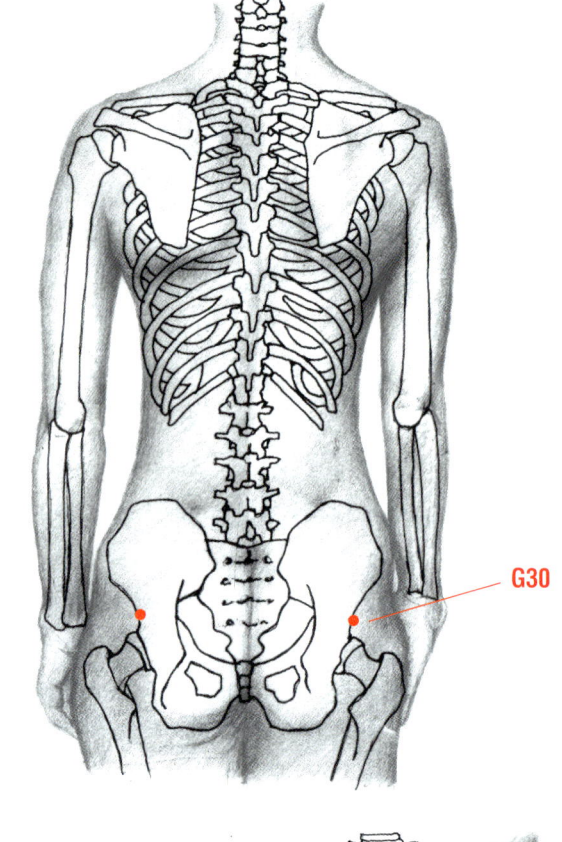

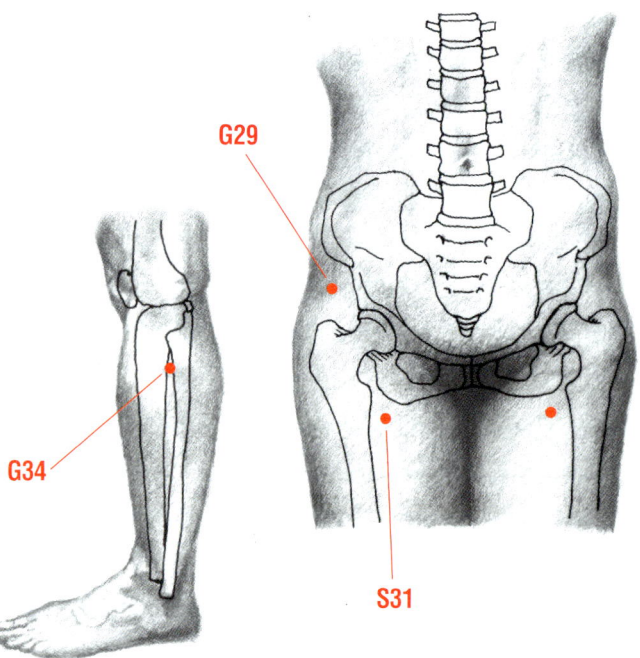

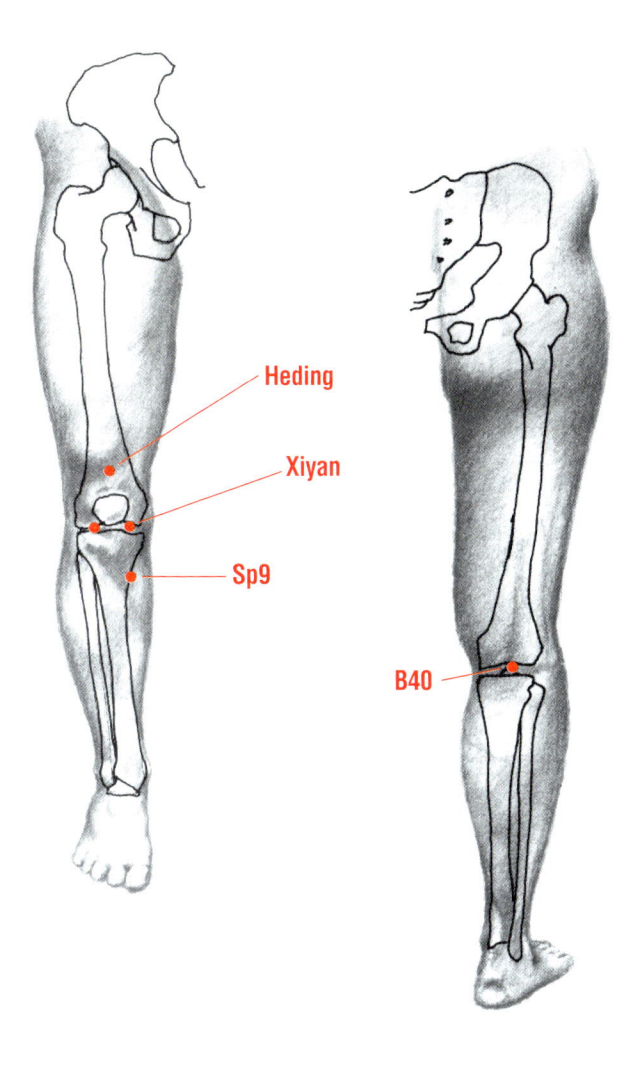

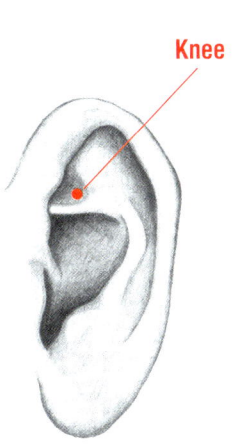

1. PAINFUL DISORDERS

Knee pain - arthritis

In older people this is often due to arthritis of the knee, and in younger people, damage to the Cartilages in the knee joint is generally the culprit. Occasionally these Cartilages are torn due to a twisting injury. The knee can sometimes lock when the torn cartilage sticks in the joint making removal of the cartilage (or a part of it) the most likely remedy. Generally though, the use of Electro-Acupuncture is highly effective in treating knee pain.

POINTS

Xiyan — These points lie in the depressions formed on either side of the ligament just beneath the knee-cap. These depressions become obvious when the knee is slightly bent.

B40 — This lies directly behind the knee joint in the centre of the crease.

G34 — This is just below and in front of the knobbly head of the fibula, which is the bone just below the outer side of knee. This point is in a slight depression and can be tender when pressed with a finger.

S36 — This lies three thumb's width below the joint under the kneecap lying on the outer side of the knee. One finger's width back from the sharp edge of the shin bone.

Sp9 — This lies just below the inside of the kneecap and below the top of the tibia. This point is usually tender when pressed with a finger tip.

Heding — Lies two finger's width above the kneecap in the centre line.

Ah Shi — Any local tender acupuncture points to be found in the area of pain that give a reaction when stimulated

Ear — Ear point

1. PAINFUL DISORDERS

Ankle pain - arthritis

When acute, pain is often due to a sprain. A chronic pain may indicate arthritis.

POINTS

- **B60** — This lies midway between the tip of the outer ankle bone and the achilles tendon (in the hollow).
- **G40** — This lies just in front of the knob of bone on the outside ankle bone.
- **K3** — This lies midway between the tip of the inner ankle bone and the achilles tendon (in the hollow)
- **S41** — This lies directly over the middle point of the front of the foot joint.
- **Sp5** — This lies just in front of the knob of bone on the inside ankle bone.
- **Ah Shi** — Any local tender acupuncture points to be found in the area of pain that give a reaction when stimulated
- **Ear** — Ear point

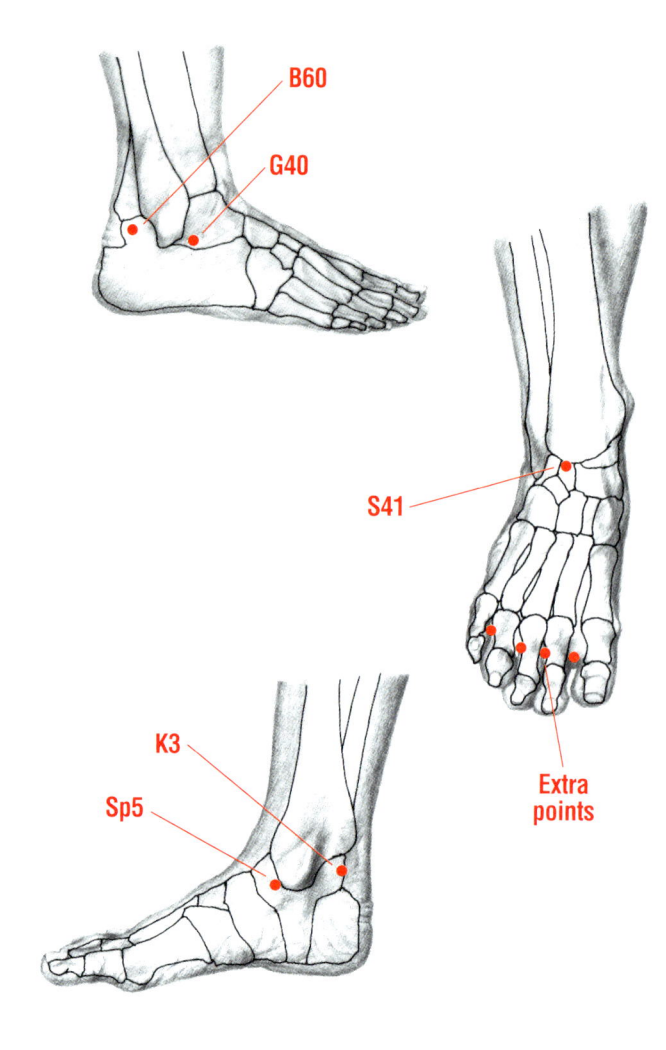

Foot pain - arthritis

This can be due to strain, but could also be caused by arthritis. For Bunion pain see page 9.32

POINTS

- **Extra foot points** — These lie at the web point between each toe.
- **Liv3** — This lies in between the tendons of the big toe and the first toe, two thumb's width towards the top of the foot from the web.
- **Ah Shi** — Any local tender acupuncture points to be found in the area of pain that give a reaction when stimulated
- **Ear** — Ear point

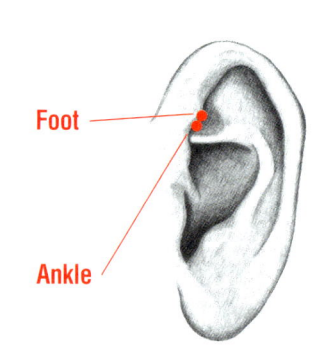

1. PAINFUL DISORDERS

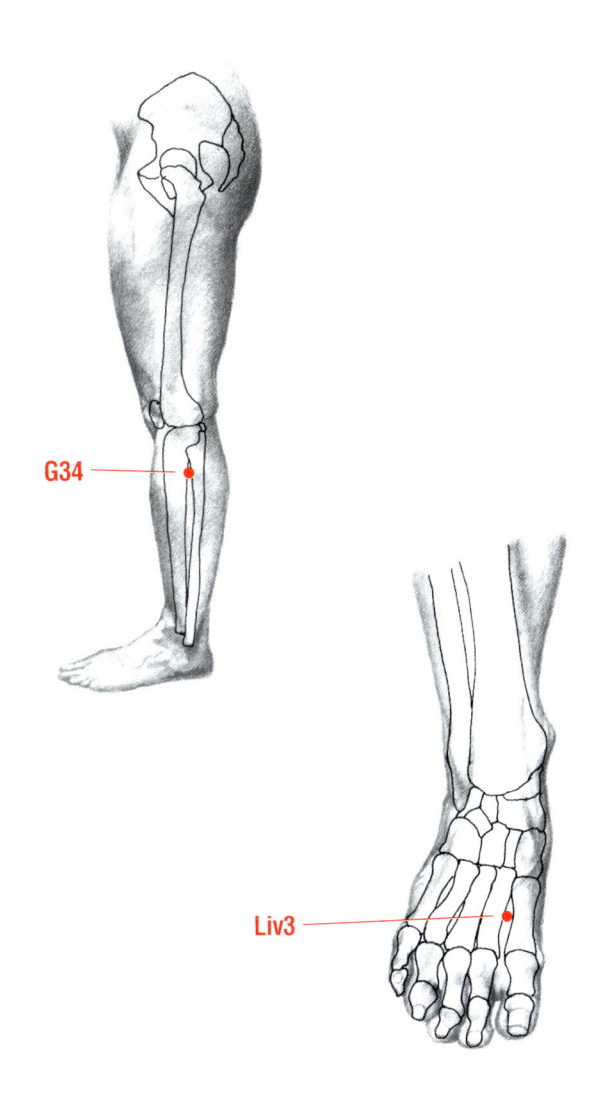

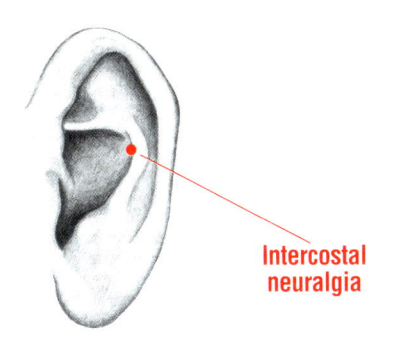

Repetitive Strain Injuries

Increasing intensity of industrial, computer, typewriter, and sports activities has led to wider recognition of over-use injuries (generally known as repetitive strain injuries). Over-use relates to repetitive, usually stereotyped, performance of limited movement patterns. These are generally highly specific for the activity concerned e.g. typing, tennis, kicking, using a screwdriver. The first principle of treatment is to rest and to avoid the repetitive action which caused the pain.

POINTS

Refer to the index, then treat according to the instructions for the part of the body where treatment is required e.g. wrist, elbow, neck etc., and with particular attention to all local tender (Ah-Shi) points. For example, Carpal Tunnel page 9.9.

Intercostal neuralgia

This is due to irritation of the Intercostal nerves. These originate from the spine at the back and pass around either side of the chest just below each rib. They can cause pain and breathing difficulty.

Accurate diagnosis is very important because this symptom occurring on the left side of the body could signify angina (heart pain). It could also indicate pleurisy on either side. Treatment for both of these ailments involves other important measures and therefore Electro-Acupuncture on its own is not the most appropriate form of treatment for either condition.

POINTS

G34 — This is just below and in front of the knobbly head of the fibula, - the bone just below the outer side of knee. This point is in a slight depression and is sometimes tender when pressed with a finger tip.

Liv3 — This lies in between the tendons of the big toe and the first toe, two thumb's width towards the top of the foot from the web.

Ear — Ear point

1.19

1. PAINFUL DISORDERS

Sciatica

This is pain radiated down the sciatic nerve which runs down the back of the leg onto the outer aspect of the foot. Sciatica does not always mean that there is a prolapsed intervertebral disc (a so-called "slipped disc") present. The majority of cases of sciatica respond well to a conservative approach as exemplified by Electro-Acupuncture. A very small proportion may require surgery.

POINTS

B31 This lies at the top of the sacral bone one and a half thumb's width away from the mid-line.

B32 This lies one finger's width below B31.

B33 This lies one finger's width below B32.

B37 This lies in the centre of the back of the thigh.

B40 This lies directly behind the knee joint in the centre of the crease.

G30 This lies in the upper, outer part of the buttock muscle. It is usually tender on deep finger tip pressure.

G34 This is just below and in front of the knobbly head of the fibula, which is the bone just below the outer side of knee. This point is in a slight depression and is often tender when pressed with a finger.

S36 This lies three thumb's width below the joint under the kneecap lying on the outer side of the knee. One finger's width back from the sharp edge of the shin bone.

Ah Shi Any local tender acupuncture points to be found in the area of pain that give a reaction when stimulated

Ear Ear point

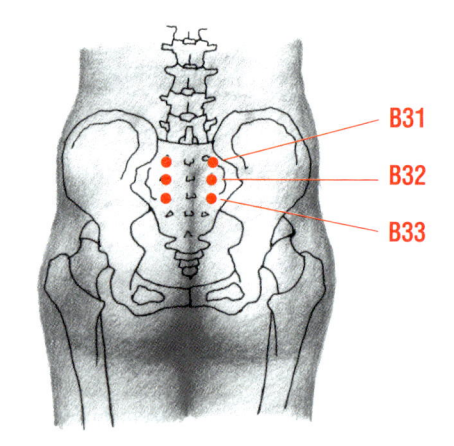

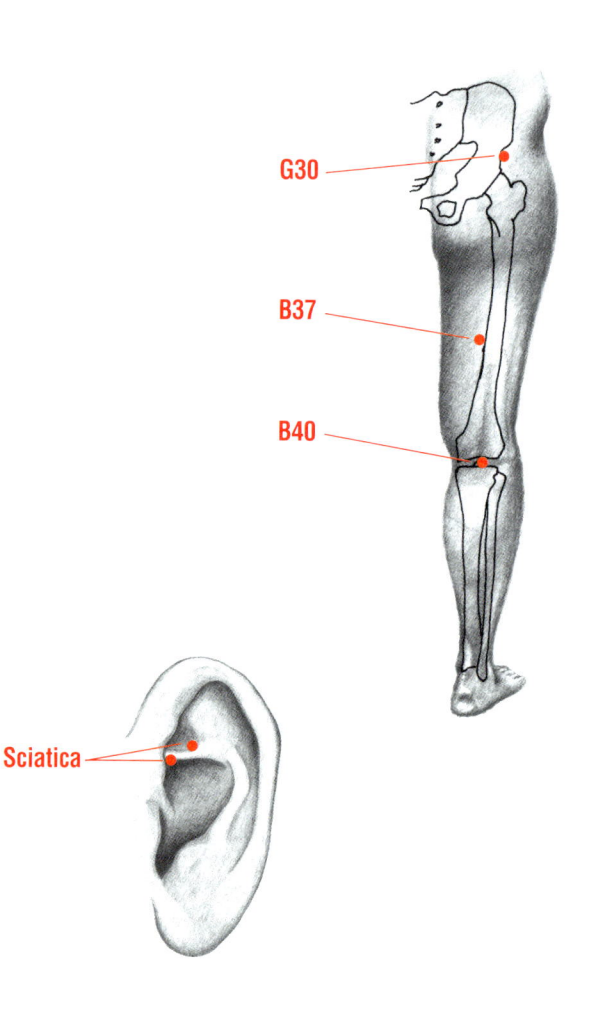

1. PAINFUL DISORDERS

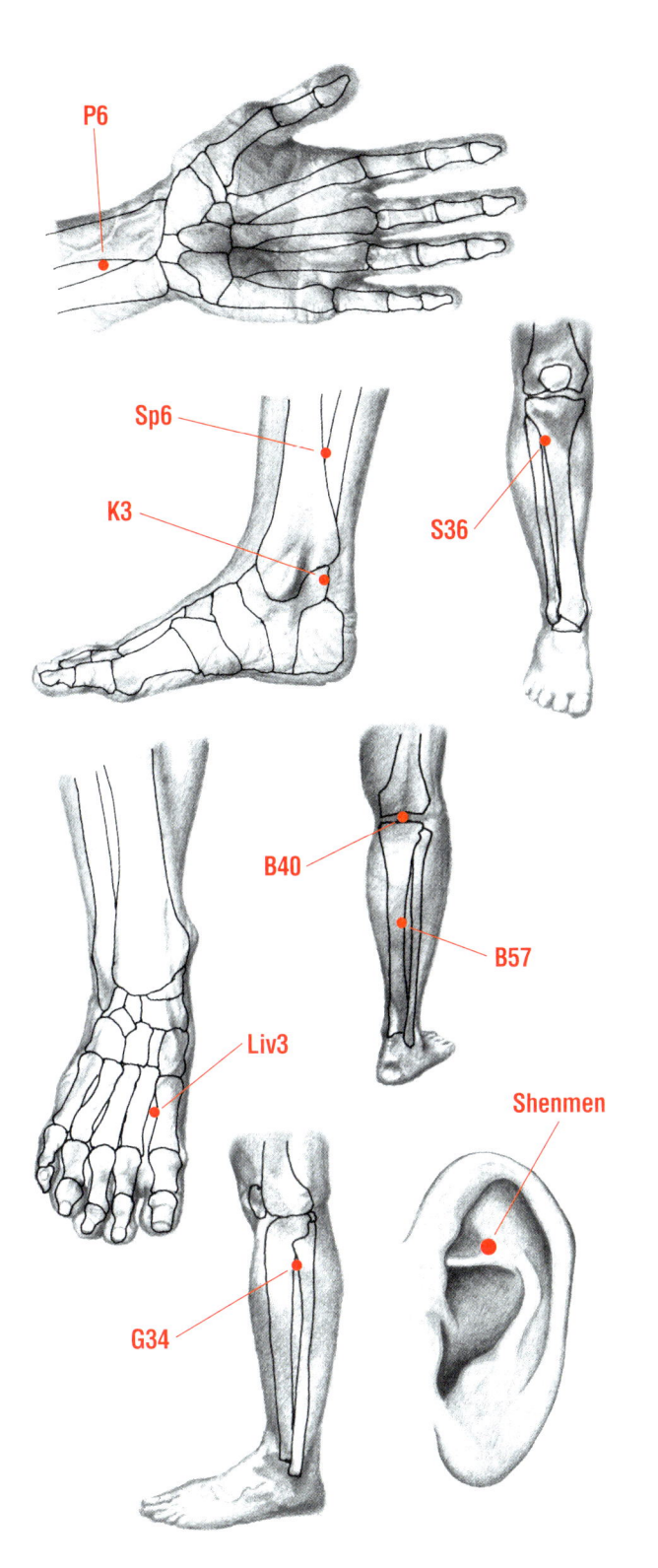

General Leg Pain - Varicose veins - Tired Legs

Veins in the legs become swollen and twisted. The condition is increasingly common from the late teens onwards and, in women, it often begins at the time of pregnancy. Electro-Acupuncture can help in providing comfort from the symptoms.

POINTS

B40 This lies directly behind the knee joint in the centre of the crease.

B57 This lies in the centre of the back of the calf, just where the fleshy mass of muscle narrows down into tendon.

G34 This is just below and in front of the knobbly head of the fibula, which is the bone just below the outer side of knee. This point is in a slight depression and is sometimes tender when pressed with a finger tip.

K3 This lies midway between the tip of the inner ankle bone and the achilles tendon.

Liv3 This lies in between the tendons of the big toe and the first toe, two thumb's width towards the top of the foot from the web.

S36 This lies three thumb's width below the joint under the kneecap lying on the outer side of the knee. One finger's width back from the sharp edge of the shin bone.

Sp6 This lies one hand's width (four fingers) up from the inner ankle joint. It lies just behind the tibia bone at this point.

P6 This lies two thumb's width up from the palm wrist crease towards the elbow, directly in the centre between the two tendons.

Ear Ear point

1.21

1. PAINFUL DISORDERS

Groin injury

Any swelling in the groin that recurs or persists for more than three days should be reported to your medical practitioner.

POINTS

G34 This is just below and in front of the knobbly head of the fibula, which is the bone just below the outer side of knee. This point is in a slight depression and is sometimes tender when pressed with a finger tip.

Li1 This is situated a quarter of a finger from the corner of the index finger nail on the thumb side.

Li4 This lies on the side of the bone which runs from the forefinger knuckle down towards the wrist. See page 8 for a detailed description of this point.

Liv8 On the inside of the knee in the hollow between the two tendons when the knee is bent.

Sp5 This lies just in front of the knob of bone on the inside ankle bone.

Ah Shi Any local tender acupuncture points to be found in the area of pain that give a reaction when stimulated

Ear Ear point

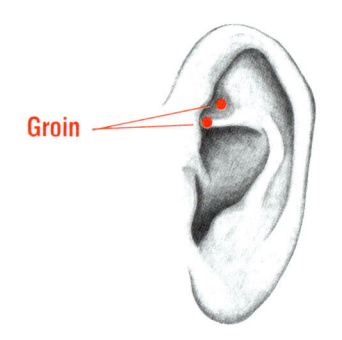

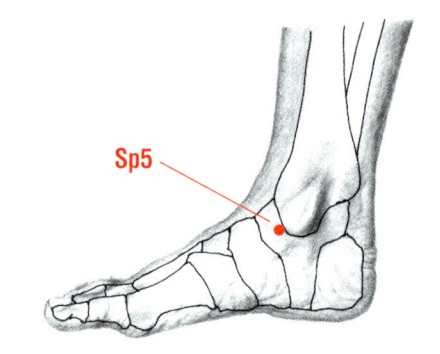

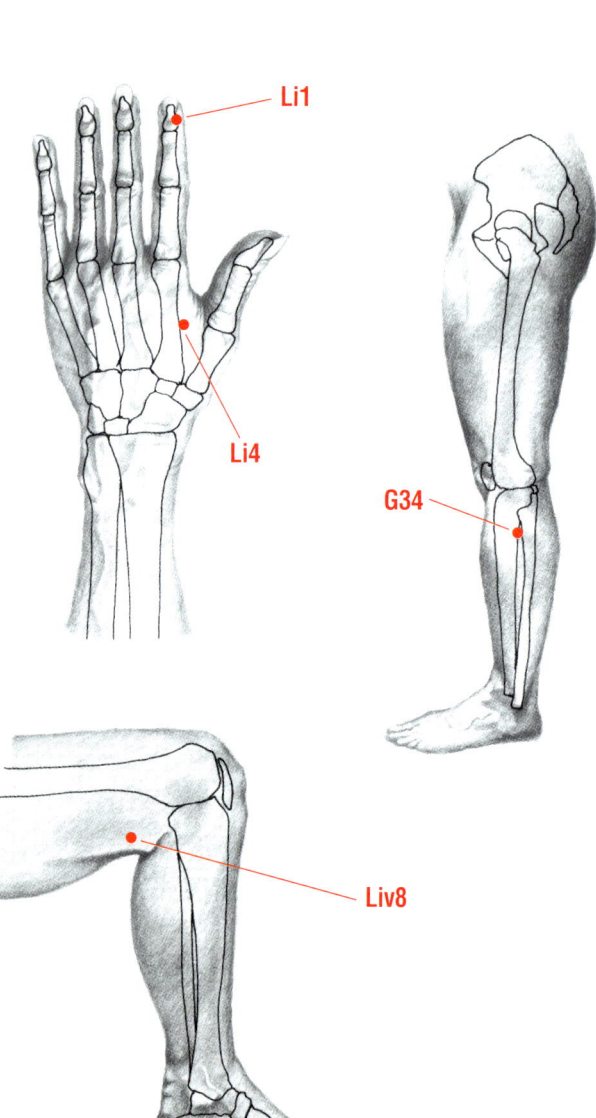

1. PAINFUL DISORDERS

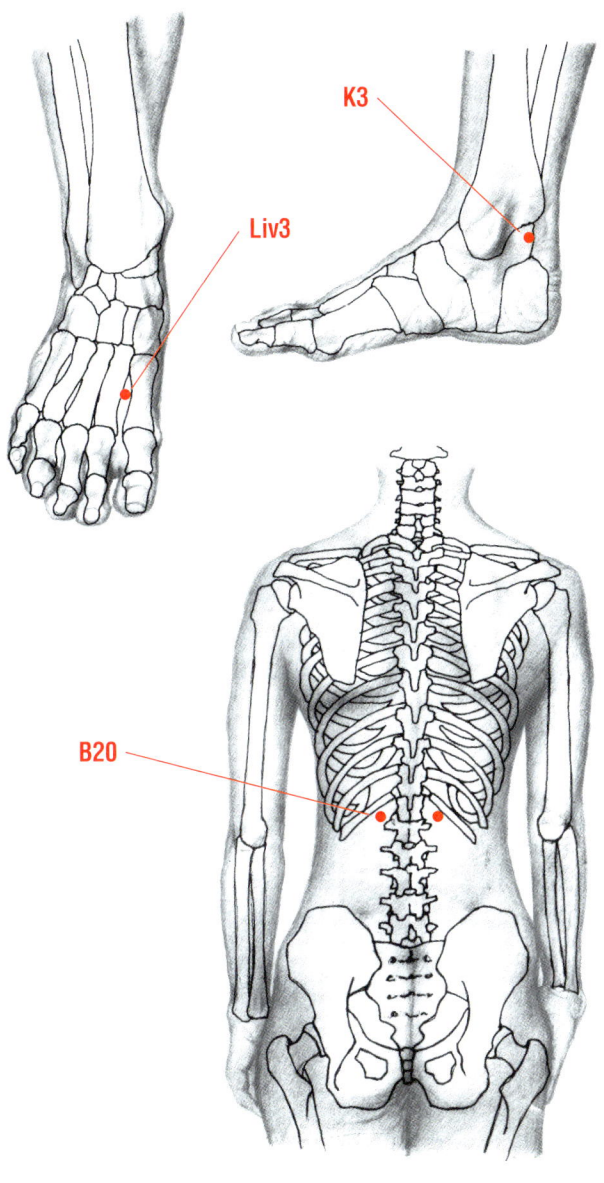

Shingles

This is an infection due to the herpes zoster virus (this is the same as the chicken pox virus). It results in a vesicular rash often present in a diagonal orientation running downward from the back towards the front. It is often situated somewhere over the chest or the abdomen and is a particularly painful condition.

Electro-Acupuncture can be regarded as an effective method of treatment. In some cases the pain from shingles can become chronic giving rise to a condition known as post-herpetic neuralgia. This is much more difficult to treat but Electro-Acupuncture is always a good option. To prevent the ailment becoming chronic, it is all the more essential to treat shingles vigorously in the acute stage.

Treat a number of points around the rash, which will involve many points if the rash is extensive, perhaps as many as 20 or 30. ***Do not treat in or on the rash itself***. Search for ear points choosing them according to the area affected as shown on the diagram in the section on ear acupuncture. Treat twice daily in the acute condition.

POINTS

Liv3 — This lies in between the tendons of the big toe and the first toe, two thumb's width towards the top of the foot from the web.

Renal (kidney) colic

This is pain due to the passage of a hard object (usually a kidney stone) down the urethra which is the tube passing from the kidney to the bladder. Pain is often severe and Electro-Acupuncture is often a useful method of treatment.

POINTS

B20 — This lies in the loin area, and is often tender in kidney problems. It lies one and a half thumb's width from the mid-line on each side.

K3 — This lies midway between the tip of the inner ankle bone and the achilles tendon (in the hollow)

Ear — Ear point - *particularly important*

1. PAINFUL DISORDERS

Dysmenorrhoea (painful periods) P.M.S.

This is a common problem and Electro-Acupuncture is often an effective method of treatment. Other measures may also be necessary, one of the useful approaches that can be applied at home is to take zinc and magnesium supplementation as well as Vitamin B6, G.L.A.

POINTS

B31 — This lies at the top of the sacral bone one and a half thumb's width away from the mid-line.

Cv6 — This lies one and a half thumb's width below the navel.

Liv3 — This lies in between the tendons of the big toe and the first toe, two thumb's width towards the top of the foot from the web.

S36 — This lies three thumb's width below the joint under the kneecap lying on the outer side of the knee. One finger's width back from the sharp edge of the shin bone.

Sp6 — This lies one hand's width (four fingers) up from the inner ankle joint. It lies just behind the tibia bone at this point.

Ear — Ear point

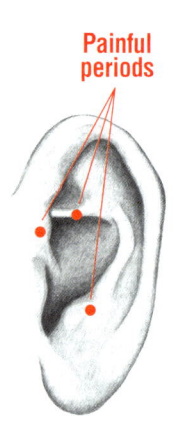

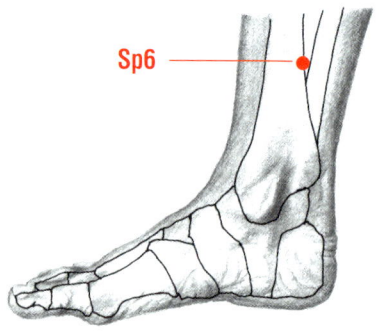

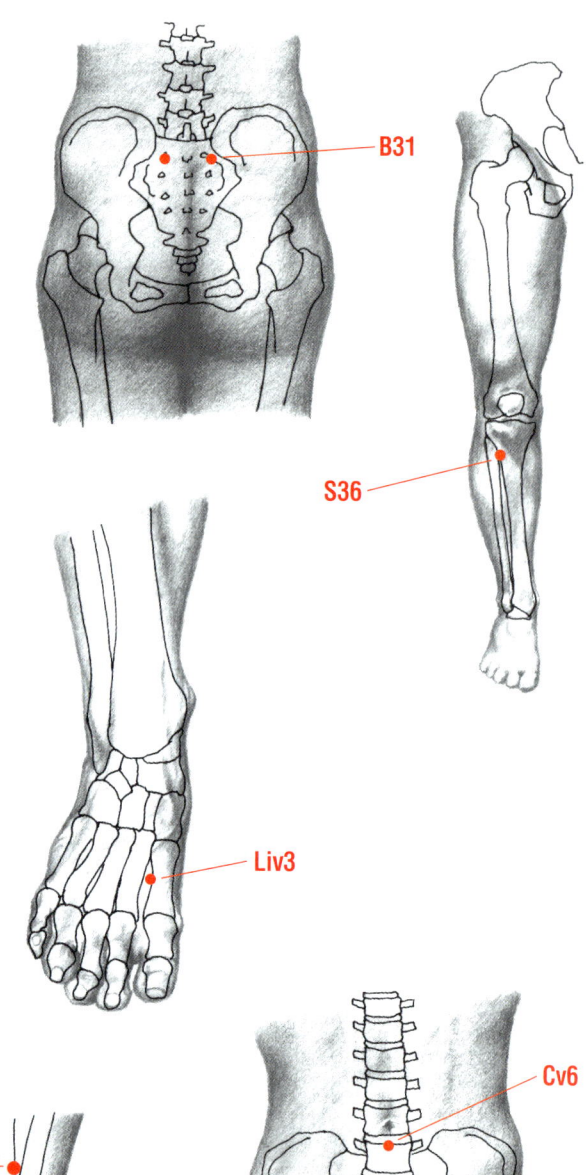

Painful periods

1.24

1. PAINFUL DISORDERS

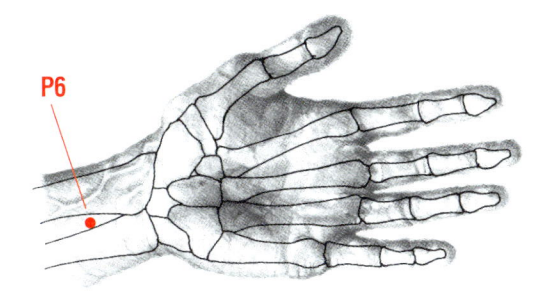

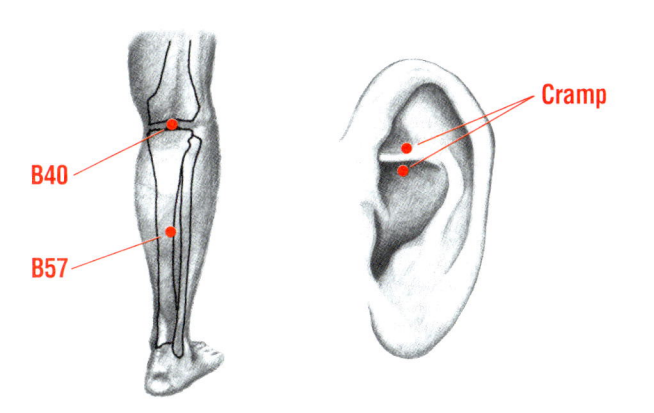

Cramp

Cramp is due to spasm in the blood vessels supplying the muscles of the leg, particularly the calf. Electro-Acupuncture can be used as a prevention and in many cases will actually prevent cramps from occurring. In the event of a cramp however, Electro-Acupuncture should be used immediately. Mineral deficiency is a common cause of cramp - a balanced diet including appropriate vitamin and mineral supplements can be of great value.

POINTS

B40 — This lies directly behind the knee joint in the centre of the crease.

B57 — This lies in the centre of the back of the calf, just where the fleshy mass of muscle narrows down into tendon.

P6 — This lies two thumb's width up from the palm wrist crease towards the elbow, directly in the centre between the two tendons.

Ear — Ear point

1. PAINFUL DISORDERS

Scoliosis - sideways curvature of the spine

Scoliosis, sideways curvature of the spine, may be structural, beginning in childhood or adolescence and increasing until growth stops; or the result of an attempt to relieve pain in the spine, caused for example by a slipped disc.

POINTS

Spine — The point at the centre of the spine and the points one and a half thumb's width either side of the centre. These are located between every vertebra. Treat all points in the area of curvature and those just above and below the area. See treatment method below.

Ear — Ear points - all points on the line of cartilage as shown in the diagram.

Treatment Method.

It is important to treat all three points (centre and each side) between <u>every vertebra in the area of the curvature and those just above and below</u>. This may seem a daunting prospect, but is essential. It is acceptable to treat each point for just ten seconds - this will reduce the time taken to treat the condition, but will not adversely affect the results. Using a body ruler (see page 7) will greatly simplify the process.

Similarly, treat every ear point that reacts, in the area relating to the curvature (cervical, thoracic, lumbar - see diagram).

This treatment protocol may seem very time-consuming but the results are well worth the effort.

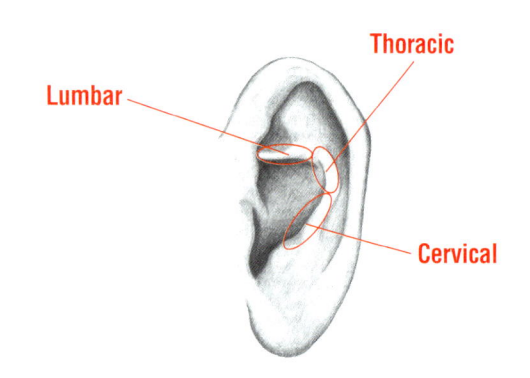

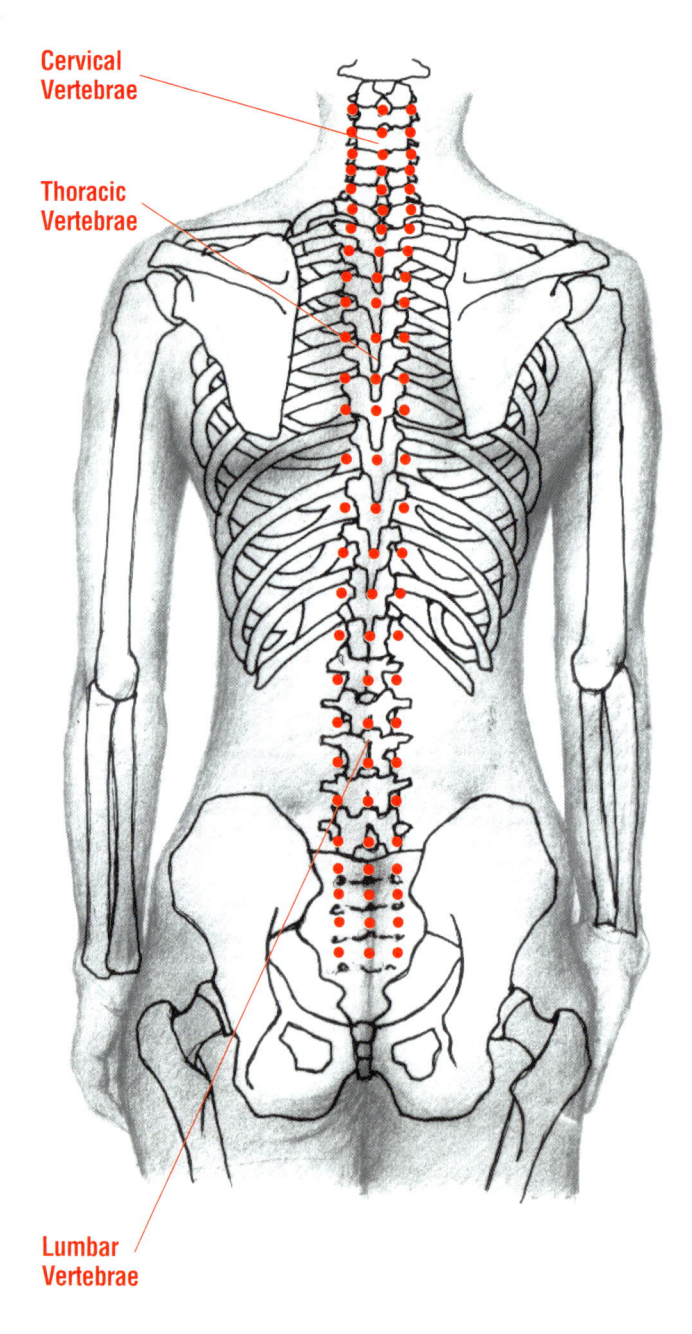

1. PAINFUL DISORDERS

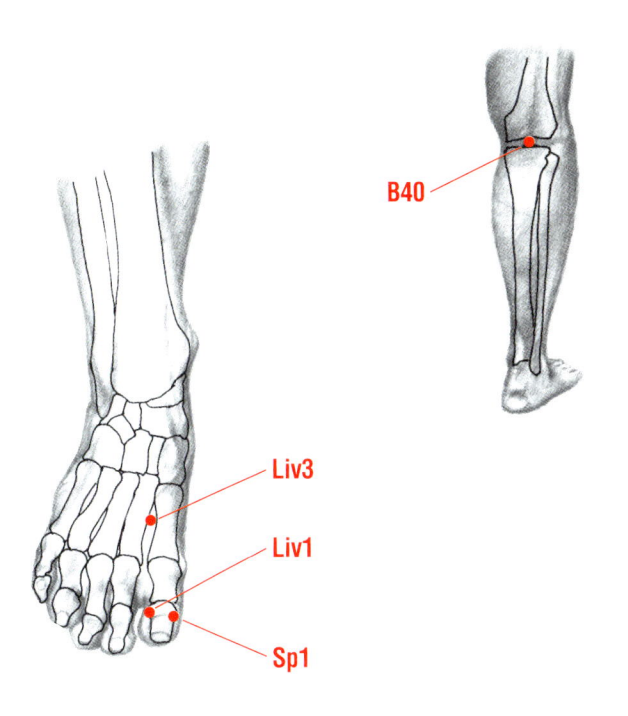

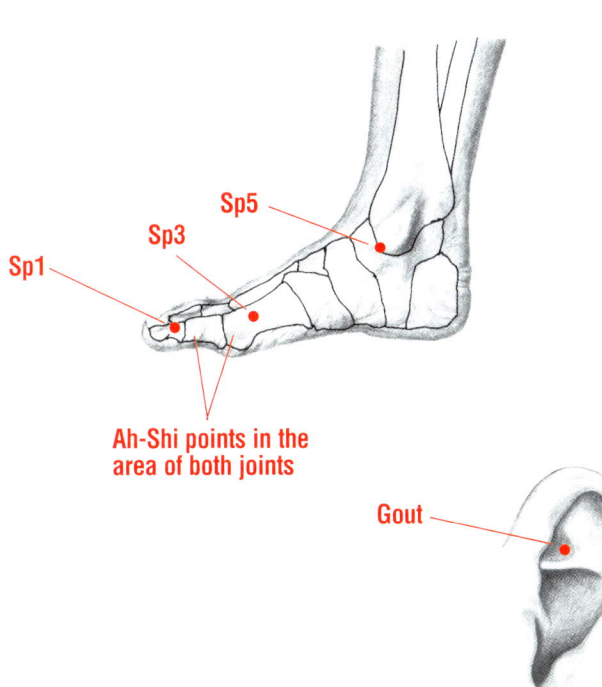

Gout & Pain in Big Toe

Gout is a disorder in which the chemical processes of the body are upset, resulting in excess uric-acid salts collecting in various organs. Men between the ages of 20 and 60 are the most susceptible to gout. The condition rarely affects women. The symptoms are the sudden onset of severe pain, swelling and tenderness of affected joints - for some reason the big toe joints are the most likely to be affected.

POINTS

B40 This lies directly behind the knee joint in the centre of the crease.

Liv1 This is situated on the inner side of the nail bed of the big toe.

Liv3 This lies between the tendons of the big toe and the first toe, two thumb's width towards the top of the foot from the web.

Sp1 This is situated on the outer side of the nail bed of the big toe.

Sp3 This is situated on the inside edge of the foot, two thumbs width towards the ankle from Sp1, in a depression, up against the large knob of bone.

Sp5 This lies just in front of the knob of bone on the inside ankle bone.

Ah Shi Any local tender acupuncture points to be found in the area of pain that give a reaction when stimulated - particularly around the area of the big-toe joints.

Ear Ear point

1. PAINFUL DISORDERS

Coccyx - Painful - Coccydynia

Pain in the coccyx (lowest segment of the spine) or surrounding area is usually caused by injury and either occurs when sitting or is made worse when sitting. This condition is more commen in women, in whom the coccyx is less well protected.

POINTS

B40 — This lies directly behind the knee joint in the centre of the crease.

B60 — This lies midway between the tip of the outer ankle bone and the achilles tendon (in the hollow).

G30 — This lies in the upper, outer part of the buttock muscle. It is usually tender on deep finger tip pressure.

G34 — This is just below and in front of the knobbly head of the fibula, which is the bone just below the outer side of knee. This point is in a slight depression and is sometimes tender when pressed with a finger tip.

Gv1 — This lies right at the base of the spine below the tip of the coccyx, midway towards the anus.

Ah Shi — Any local tender acupuncture points to be found in the area of pain that give a reaction when stimulated

Ear — Ear point.

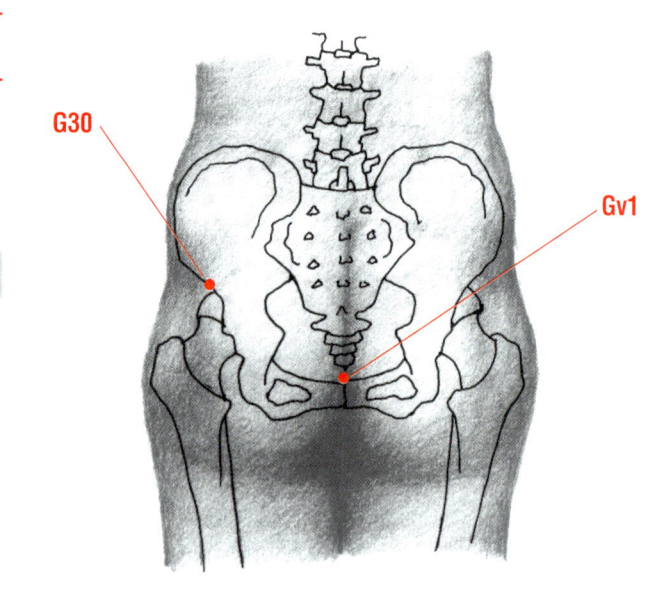

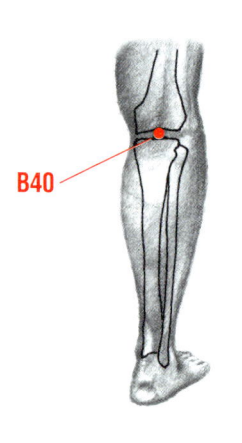

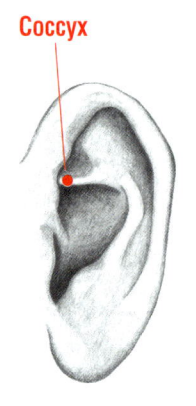

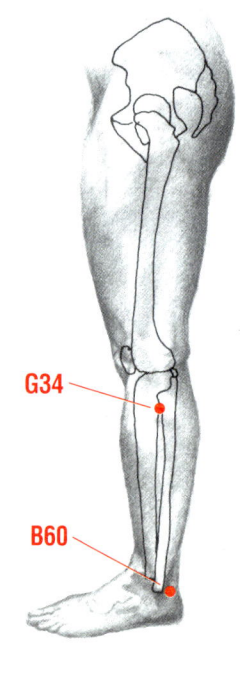

1.28

2. EAR, NOSE & THROAT PROBLEMS

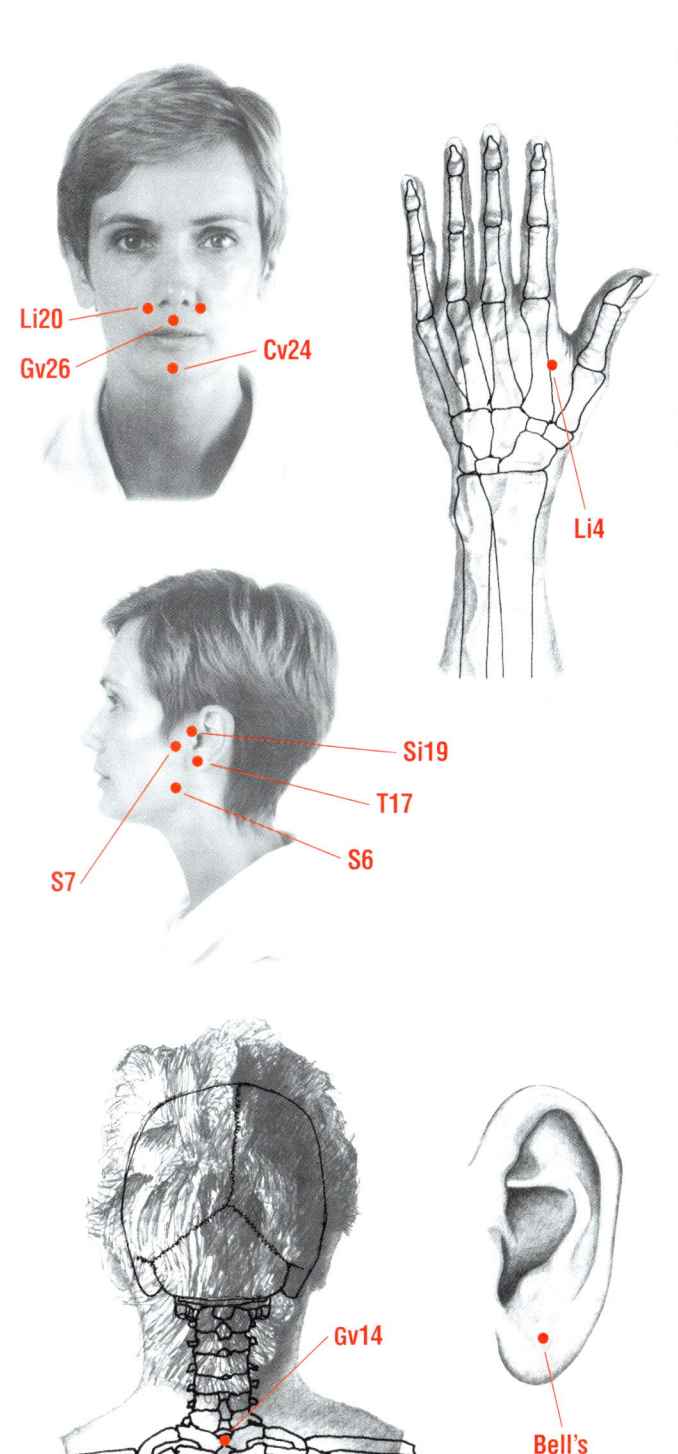

Facial Paralysis - Bell's Palsy

This condition causes the eyelid and the side to the mouth to droop on the affected side. These muscles become weakened as no nerve impulses are reaching them. It can, in some cases be due to a virus. Electro-Acupuncture can be very useful in treating the condition and should be used 2 or 3 times a day until the paralysis has completely gone.

POINTS

Cv24 — This is at the mid point of the line joining the point of the chin with the middle of the lower lip.

Gv14 — This lies just below the most prominent knob of bone at the base of the neck in the mid-line.

Gv26 — This is at the junction of the upper third and lower two thirds of a line joining the nose and the middle of the upper lip.

Li4 — This lies on the side of the bone which runs from the forefinger knuckle down towards the wrist. See page 8 for a detailed description of this point.

Li20 — This is a half finger's width to the side of the lower end of the nose.

S6 — This lies over the centre of the muscle bulge formed when the jaw is clenched.

S7 — This lies just below the mid point of the cheek bone, over the front part of the top end of the jaw bone.

Si19 — This is immediately over the jaw joint between the jaw and the skull, just in front of the small piece of cartilage, which forms the front part of the ear.

T17 — This point lies in the hollow behind the earlobe between the mastoid bone and the angle of the jaw.

Ear — Ear point

2. EAR, NOSE & THROAT PROBLEMS

Sinusitis

Sinusitis is very common and can occur either in the maxillary sinuses, which lie on both sides, deep in the face below the eyes, or the frontal sinuses, situated on either side of the bridge of the nose. People with sinusitis should consider other treatments to complement Electro-Acupuncture.

Additional approaches to be considered include diet, the avoidance of mucous producing foods such as milk, dairy products and red meat. Attention should be paid to bowel function. Even slight constipation, in those predisposed to sinusitis, can lead to troublesome chronic problems. The reason for this is that the colon is connected to the sinuses as the large intestine meridian ends on the sinuses and has a connection with the large intestine itself (i.e. the colon). Consider spraying colloidal silver into the nostrils to kill any possible infection.

If pain or tension, treat frontal headaches points page 1.2. Consider hay fever points on page 8.3.

POINTS

Li4 — This lies on the side of the bone which runs from the forefinger knuckle down towards the wrist. See page 8 for a detailed description of this point.

Li20 — This is a half finger's width to the side of the lower end of the nose.

Sp6 — This lies one hand's width (four fingers) up from the inner ankle joint. It lies just behind the tibia bone at this point.

Yintang — This lies directly between the eyebrows, just above the bridge of the nose.

Ah Shi — Any local tender acupuncture points to be found in the area of pain that give a reaction when stimulated

Ear — Ear point

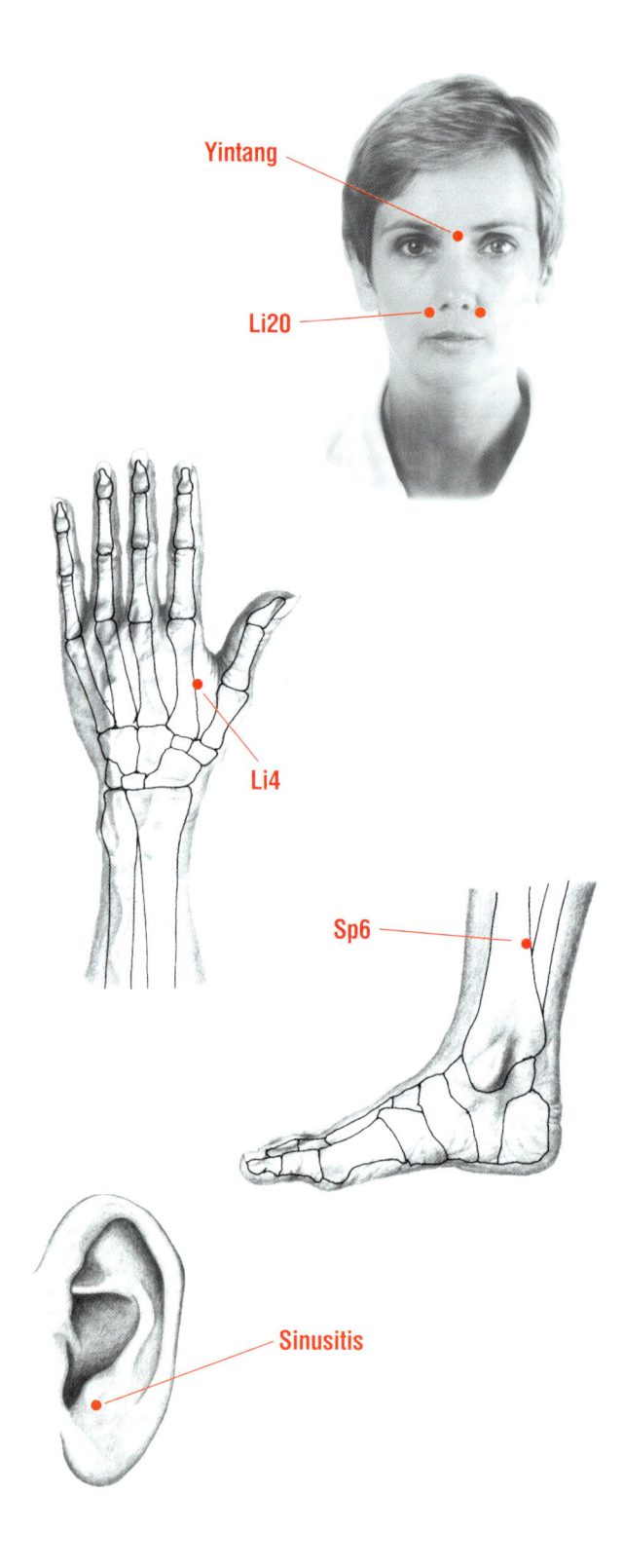

2. EAR, NOSE & THROAT PROBLEMS

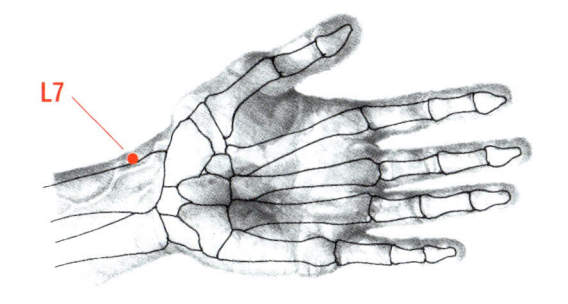

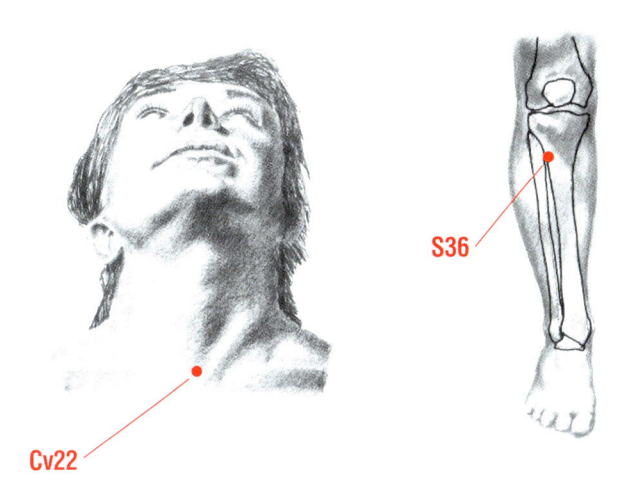

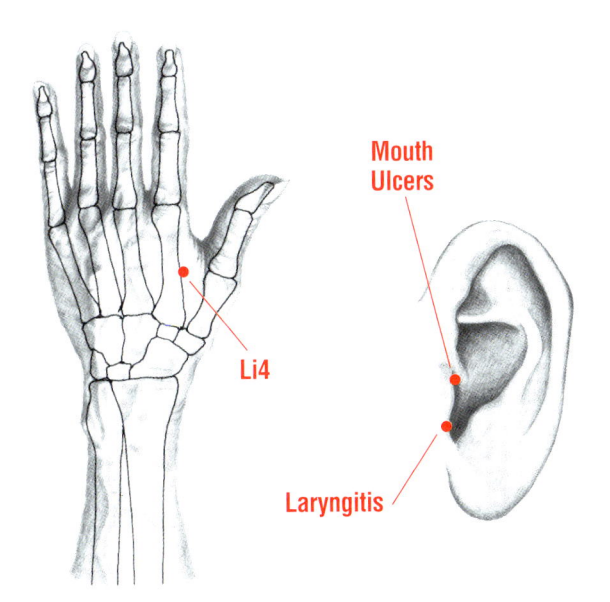

Laryngitis - 'sore throat'

Laryngitis is nearly always an acute problem that involves loss of voice and is often due to a viral infection. Colloidal silver has been shown to be highly effective - take 1/2 teaspoonful under the tongue. Chronic laryngitis should always be investigated by a qualified E.N.T specialist to rule out a more serious problem.

POINTS

Cv22 This lies in the hollow directly over the front of the larynx in the centre of the lower part of the neck.

L7 This lies one and a half thumb's width up from the inside wrist crease on the thumb side close to the radial pulse.

Li4 This lies on the side of the bone which runs from the forefinger knuckle down towards the wrist. See page 8 for a detailed description of this point.

Ear Ear point

Mouth Ulcers

Mouth ulcers are particularly common and troublesome, they are also often very painful. Colloidal silver has been shown to be highly effective - take 1/2 teaspoonful under the tongue.

POINTS

Li4 This lies on the side of the bone which runs from the forefinger knuckle down towards the wrist. See page 8 for a detailed description of this point.

Ear Ear point.

S36 This lies three thumb's width below the joint under the kneecap lying on the outer side of the knee. One finger's width back from the sharp edge of the shin bone.

2. EAR, NOSE & THROAT PROBLEMS

Tinnitus (ringing in the ears) - Menieres - Vertigo

Tinnitus is often perceived as a high-pitched whistling sound which is much more noticeable in quiet surroundings. It often accompanies degeneration of the hearing nerve, thus hearing loss is also sometimes experienced. It is a very difficult condition to treat, but Electro-Acupuncture offers relief in a considerable proportion of patients. This represents a substantial improvement on conventional approaches to the problem.

PRIMARY POINTS

Always treat the primary points. If time allows, also treat the secondary points.

G20 — Just below the skull bone and outside the muscle bulge.

K3 — This lies midway between the tip of the inner ankle bone and the achilles tendon (in the hollow)

Si3 — With the fist clenched, this lies at the end of the main crease of the palm at the junction of the red and white skin (It is easier to locate unclenched).

Si19 — This is immediately over the jaw joint between the jaw and the skull, just in front of the small piece of cartilage, which forms the front part of the ear.

T17 — This point lies in the hollow behind the earlobe between the mastoid bone and the angle of the jaw.

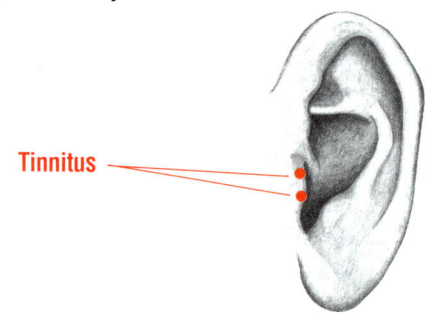

Continued on next page...

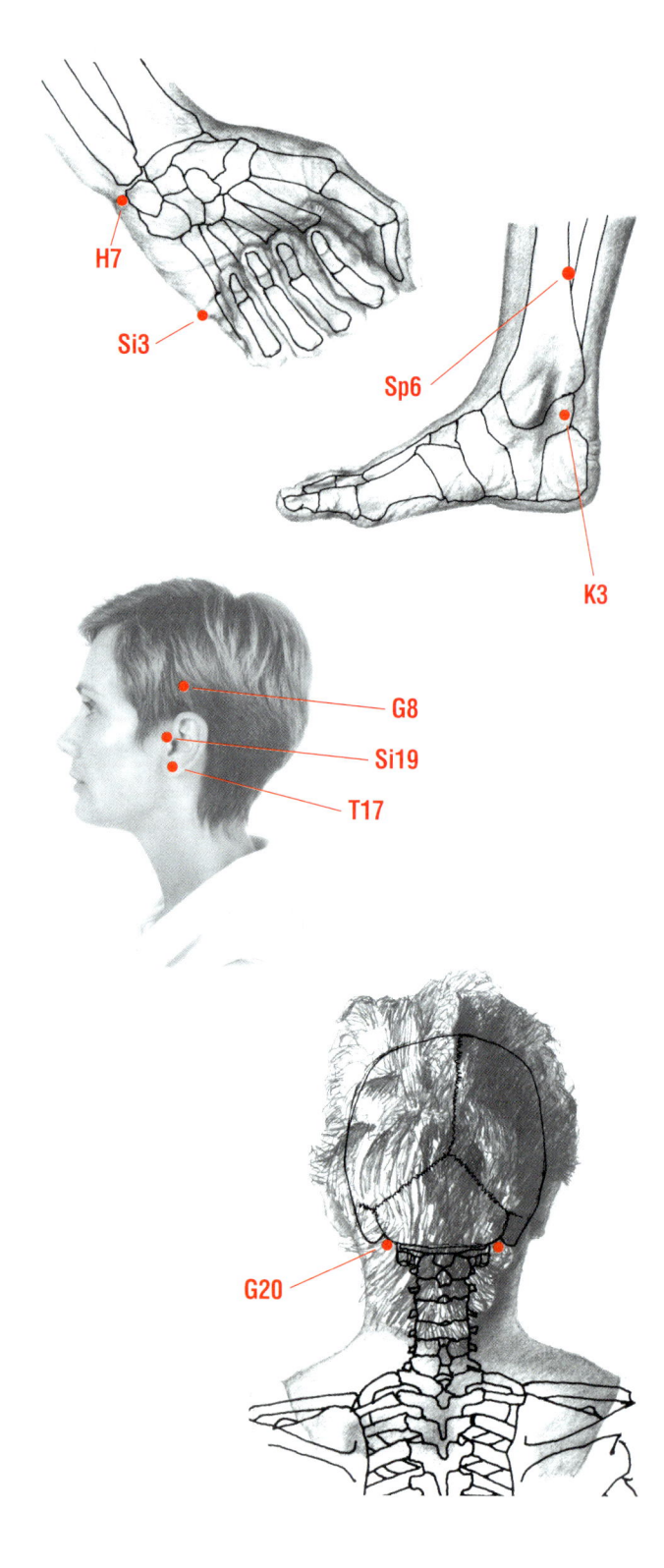

2. EAR, NOSE & THROAT PROBLEMS

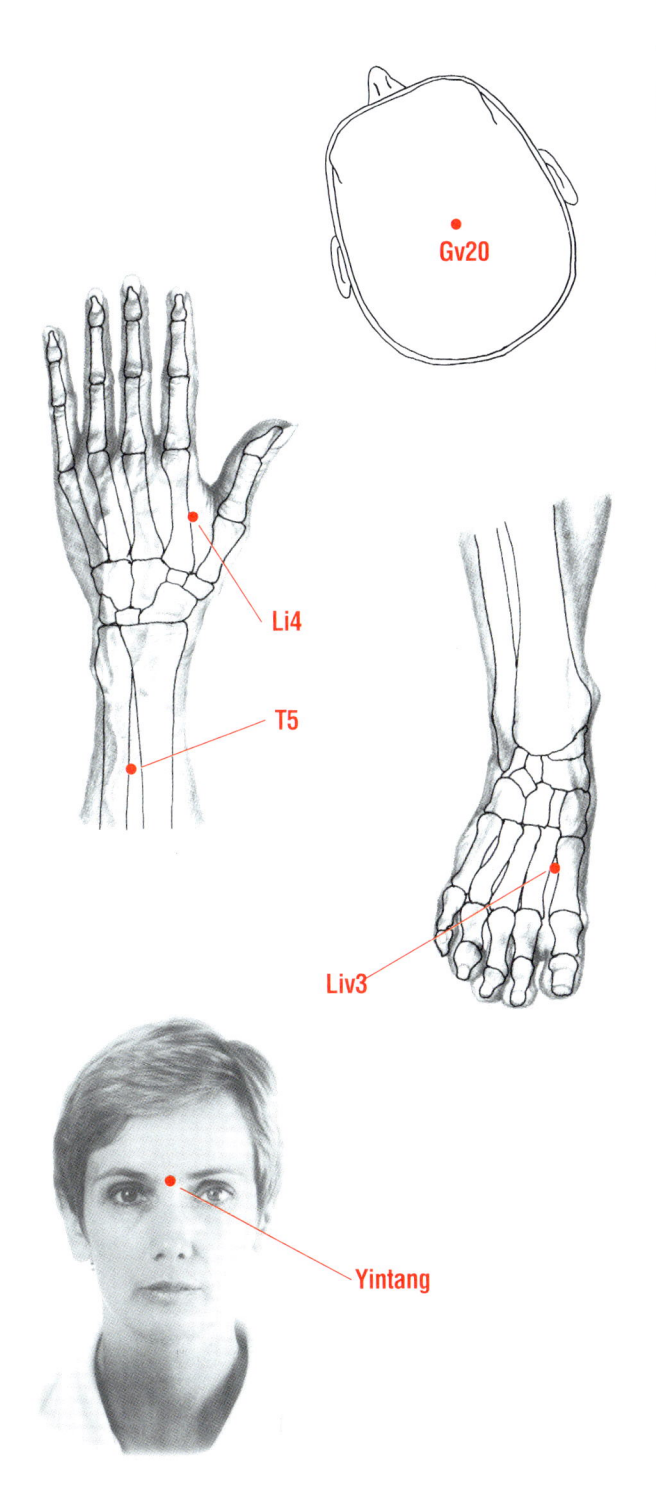

Tinnitus - *continued*

SECONDARY POINTS

Ear Ear points

G8 On the side of the skull, one thumb's width above the tip of the ear.

Gv20 This point lies right at the top of the head where two imaginary lines cross, one drawn from the top of one ear to the top of the other ear, the other line drawn from the top of the nose right over the top of the skull to the back of the skull. Where these lines cross is Gv20.

H7 This lies on the little finger side of the palm wrist crease just inside the small prominent bone.

Li4 This lies on the side of the bone which runs from the forefinger knuckle down towards the wrist. See page 8 for a detailed description of this point.

Liv3 This lies in between the tendons of the big toe and the first toe, two thumb's width towards the top of the foot from the web.

P6 This lies two thumb's width up from the palm wrist crease towards the elbow, directly in the centre between the two tendons.

Sp6 This lies one hand's width (four fingers) up from the inner ankle joint. It lies just behind the tibia bone at this point.

T5 This lies on the back of the wrist, two thumb's width towards the elbow from the wrist crease.

Yintang This lies directly between the eyebrows, just above the bridge of the nose.

2.5

2. EAR, NOSE & THROAT PROBLEMS

Nerve Deafness

Deafness may develop in one or both ears at any age There are two kinds of deafness: conductive deafness affecting the middle ear; and nerve deafness affecting the inner ear. Electro-Acupuncture has been shown to give an improvement in some cases.

POINTS

B62 This lies In the depression immediately below the outer ankle bone.

Gv20 This point lies right at the top of the head where two imaginary lines cross, one drawn from the top of one ear to the top of the other ear, the other line drawn from the top of the nose right over the top of the skull to the back of the skull. Where these lines cross is Gv20.

S36 This lies three thumb's width below the joint under the kneecap lying on the outer side of the knee. One finger's width back from the sharp edge of the shin bone.

Si19 This is immediately over the jaw joint between the jaw and the skull, just in front of the small piece of cartilage, which forms the front part of the ear.

T17 This point lies in the hollow behind the earlobe between the mastoid bone and the angle of the jaw.

T21 One finger above Si19

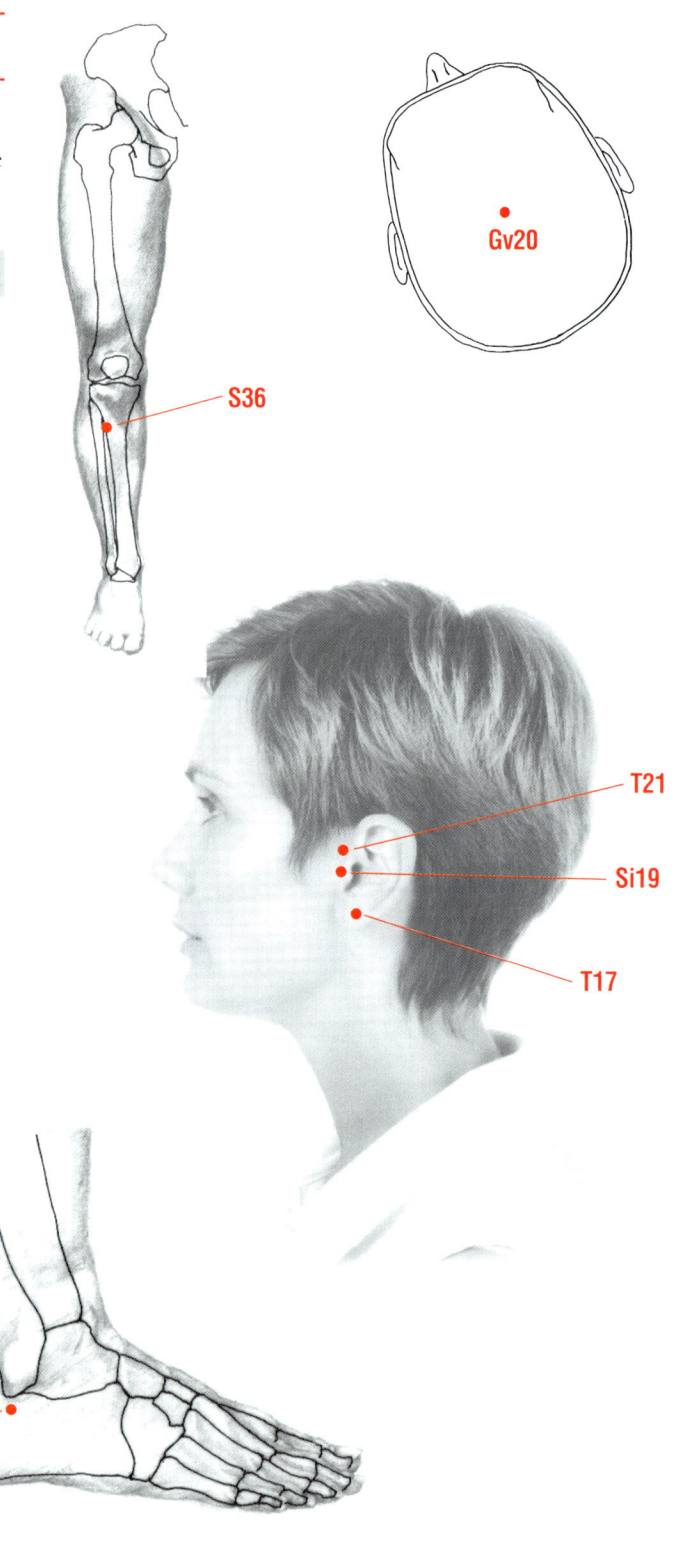

2. EAR, NOSE & THROAT PROBLEMS

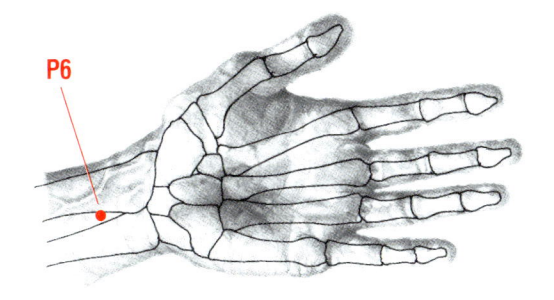

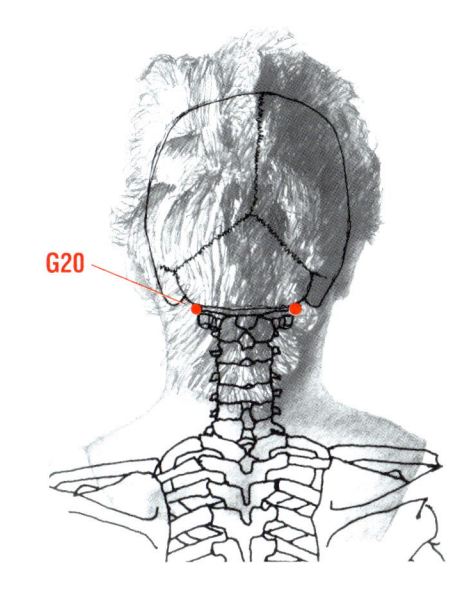

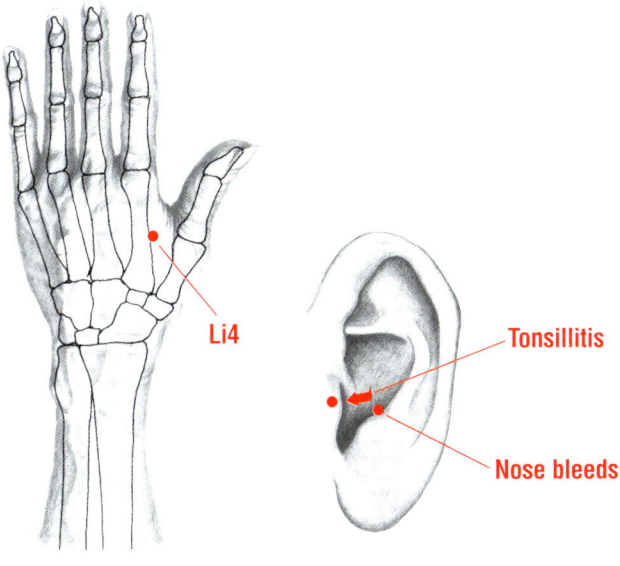

Nose bleeds (epistaxis)

Recurring nose bleeds are common in children and Electro-Acupuncture offers a method of reducing the duration of the nose bleed and so minimising blood loss.

POINTS

G20 Just below the skull bone and outside the muscle bulge.

Li4 This lies on the side of the bone which runs from the forefinger knuckle down towards the wrist. See page 8 for a detailed description of this point.

P6 This lies two thumb's width up from the palm wrist crease towards the elbow, directly in the centre between the two tendons.

Ear Ear point.

Tonsillitis

Tonsillitis, (or sore throat), is most often due to a viral infection. In some cases however, it can be due to bacteria. Colloidal silver has been shown to be highly effective - take 1/2 teaspoonful under the tongue. If no improvement follows treatment it is important to consult a doctor as a course of antibiotics may be required.

POINTS

Li4 This lies on the side of the bone which runs from the forefinger knuckle down towards the wrist. See page 8 for a detailed description of this point.

S36 This lies three thumb's width below the joint under the kneecap lying on the outer side of the knee. One finger's width back from the sharp edge of the shin bone.

Ear Ear point.

2. EAR, NOSE & THROAT PROBLEMS

Mumps

Mumps is a swelling of the salivary glands. This common infectious disease mostly affects children over the age of two, and occurs in epidemics every three or four years. Colloidal silver has been shown to be highly effective - take 1/2 teaspoonful under the tongue - see page 0.1.

POINTS

Li4 — This lies on the side of the bone which runs from the forefinger knuckle down towards the wrist. See page 8 for a detailed description of this point.

Li11 — This lies 2cm beyond the end of the outer elbow crease with the arm bent.

Liv3 — This lies between the tendons of the big toe and the first toe, two thumb's width towards the top of the foot from the web.

S6 — This lies over the centre of the muscle bulge formed when the jaw is clenched.

S7 — This lies just below the mid point of the cheek bone, over the front part of the top end of the jaw bone.

Sp6 — This lies one hand's width (four fingers) up from the inner ankle joint. It lies just behind the tibia bone at this point.

T5 — This lies on the back of the wrist, two thumb's width towards the elbow from the wrist crease.

T17 — This point lies in the hollow behind the earlobe between the mastoid bone and the angle of the jaw.

Ear — Ear points.

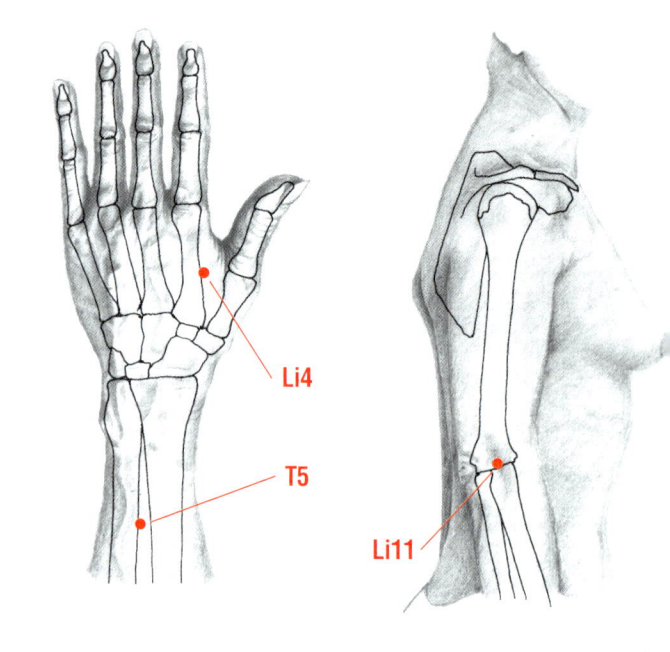

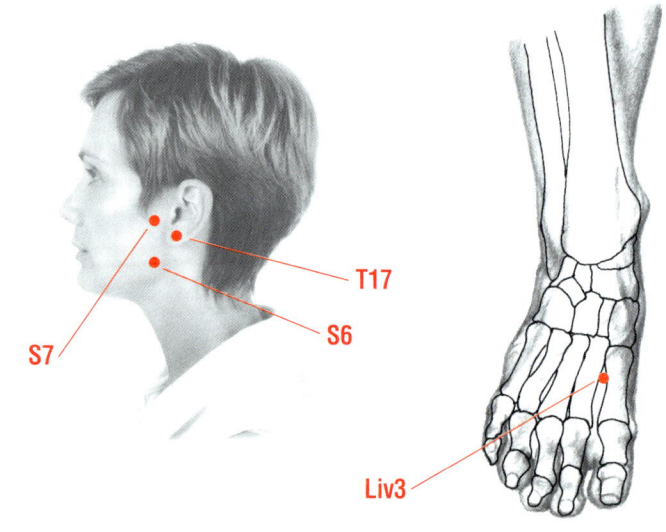

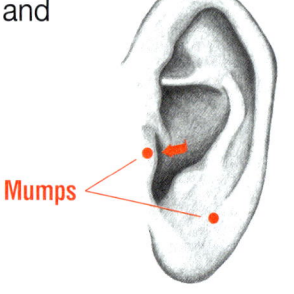

3. HEART & CIRCULATORY DISORDERS

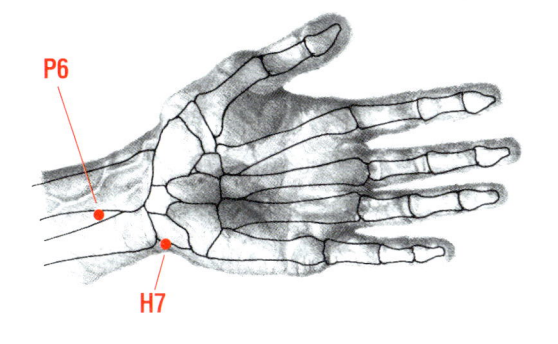

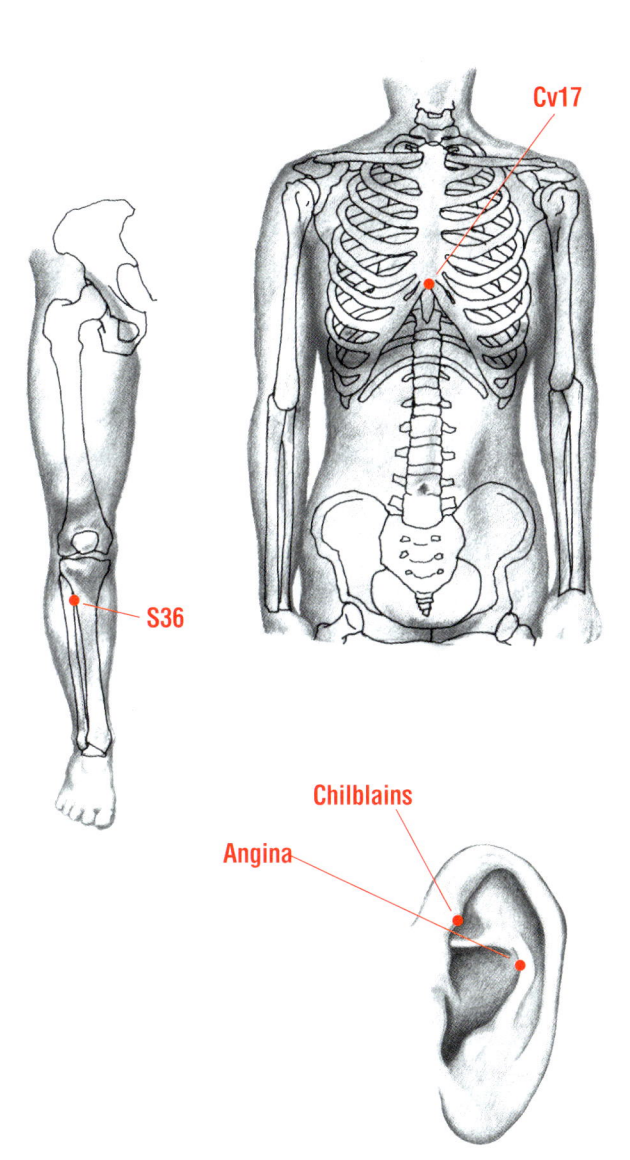

Angina

Angina is pain occurring on the left side of the chest and radiating down the left arm, and occasionally up into the left side of the jaw. It is due to a lack of blood supply to the heart muscle. Mineral deficiency is a common cause of angina - a balanced diet (avoid fatty foods such as red meats, milk and dairy products) including appropriate vitamin and mineral supplements can be of great value - see page 0.1. You should also pay attention to lifestyle and endeavour to limit stress and physical activity. Electro-Acupuncture can only be regarded as a symptomatic approach.

POINTS

Cv17 This lies in a depression at the centre of the front of the chest on a line joining both nipples.

H7 This lies on the little finger side of the palm wrist crease just inside the small prominent bone.

P6 This lies two thumb's width up from the palm wrist crease towards the elbow, in the centre between the two tendons.

Ear Ear point

Chilblains

These are relatively common in cold climates and Electro-Acupuncture offers a useful method of treatment.

POINTS

P6 This lies two thumb's width up from the palm wrist crease towards the elbow, in the centre between the two tendons.

S36 This lies three thumb's width below the joint under the kneecap lying on the outer side of the knee. One finger's width back from the sharp edge of the shin bone.

Ear Ear point

+ local tender (Ah shi) points around the chilblains.

3.1

3. HEART & CIRCULATORY DISORDERS

Circulation Improvement - Raynaud's

This may improve circulation problems. These can range from cold hands and feet, to more serious conditions where circulation is markedly interrupted, such as Raynaud's syndrome. This is a condition where the fingers and toes go white, sometimes blue and in severe cases almost black. If yours is a hand problem, treat the points for upper limb. If you suffer with the feet use the points for lower limb. In all cases also use Liver 3 and Pericardium 6 (Liv3 - P6).

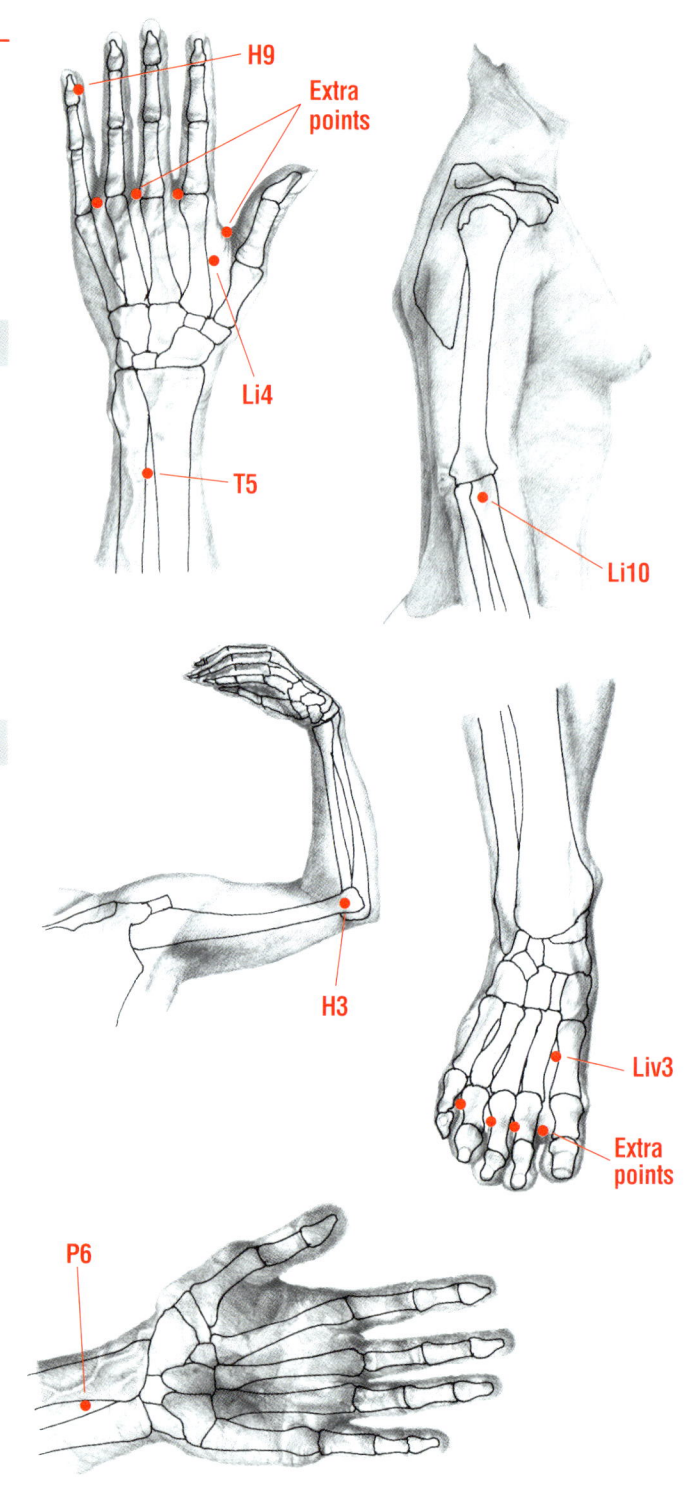

POINTS: ALL CASES

For all cases of poor circulation use Liv3, P6.

Liv3   This lies between the tendons of the big toe and the first toe, two thumb's width towards the top of the foot from the web.

P6   This lies two thumb's width up from the palm wrist crease towards the elbow, directly in the centre between the two tendons.

POINTS: UPPER LIMB

H3   This is at the end of the inner elbow crease.

H9   This is situated on the inner corner of the nail bed of the little finger next to the adjacent finger.

Li4   This lies on the side of the bone which runs from the forefinger knuckle down towards the wrist. See page 8 for a detailed description of this point.

Li10   This lies two finger's width below Li11 on a line towards the thumb.

T5   This lies on the back of the wrist, two thumb's width towards the elbow from the wrist crease.

Extra hand points   These lie in the centre of the web between the fingers.

Continued on next page...

3. HEART & CIRCULATORY DISORDERS

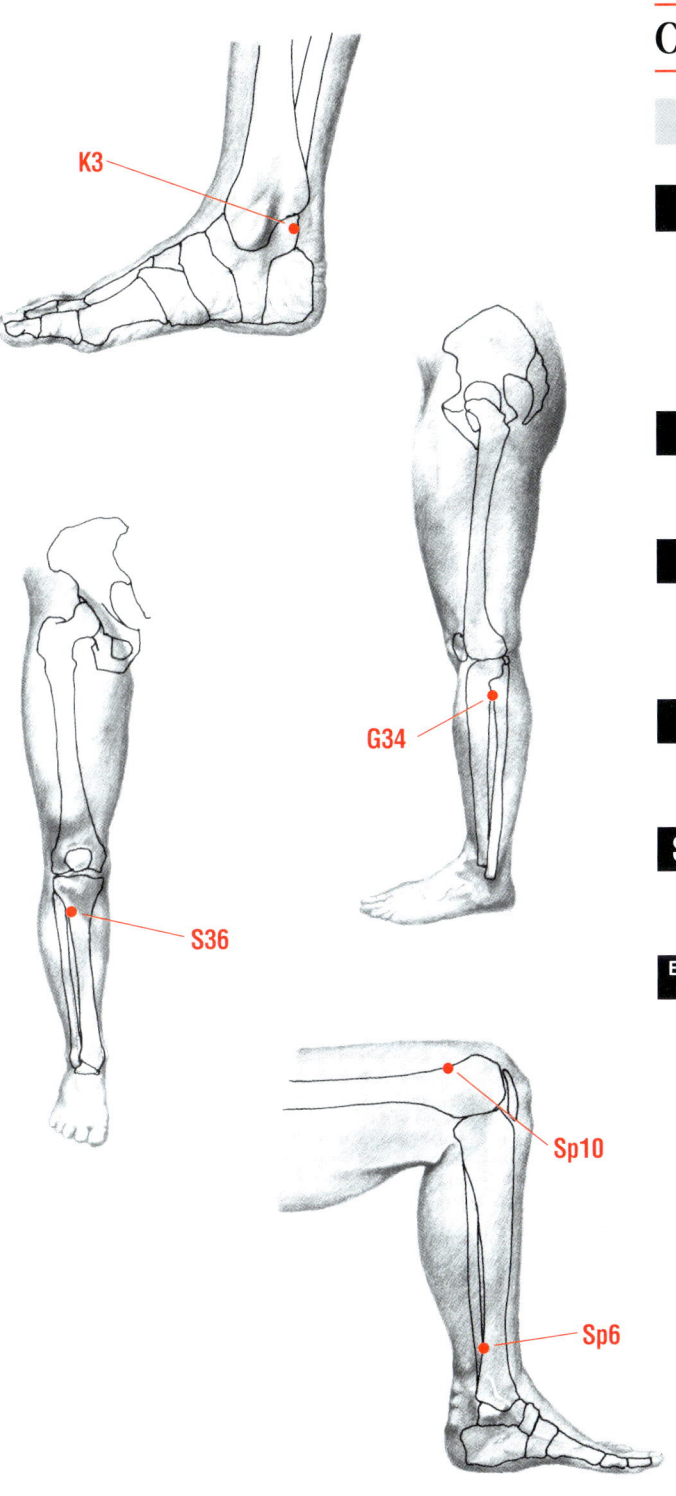

Circulation Improvement - Continued

POINTS: LOWER LIMB

G34 This is just below and in front of the knobbly head of the fibula, which is the bone just below the outer side of knee. This point is in a slight depression and is sometimes tender when pressed with a finger tip.

K3 This lies midway between the tip of the inner ankle bone and the achilles tendon (in the hollow)

S36 This lies three thumb's width below the joint under the kneecap lying on the outer side of the knee. One finger's width back from the sharp edge of the shin bone.

Sp6 This lies one hand's width (four fingers) up from the inner ankle joint. It lies just behind the tibia bone at this point.

SP10 This lies at the lower end of the muscular bulge, two fingers above the inside of the knee cap.

Extra foot points These lie at the web point between each toe.

3. HEART & CIRCULATORY DISORDERS

Low Blood Pressure (hypotension)

It is essential that HEALTHPOINT treatment is monitored by either taking the blood pressure yourself or seeing your doctor. Use Electro-Acupuncture and see your doctor.

POINTS

Cv6 This lies one and a half thumb's width below the navel.

Gv20 This point lies right at the top of the head where two imaginary lines cross, one drawn from the top of one ear to the top of the other ear, the other line drawn from the top of the nose right over the top of the skull to the back of the skull. Where these lines cross is Gv20.

H7 This lies on the little finger side of the palm wrist crease just inside the small prominent bone.

S36 This lies three thumb's width below the joint under the kneecap lying on the outer side of the knee. One finger's width back from the sharp edge of the shin bone.

Sp6 This lies one hand's width (four fingers) up from the inner ankle joint. It lies just behind the tibia bone at this point.

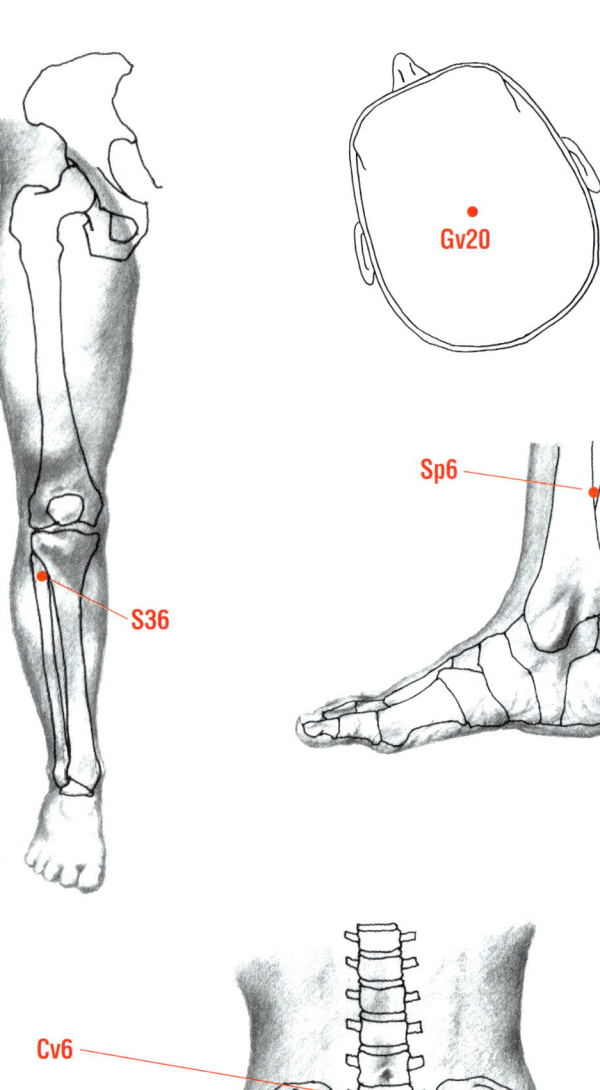

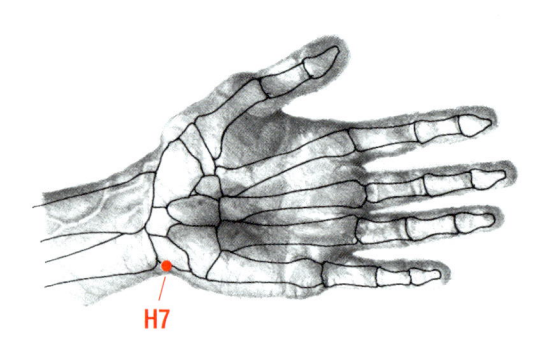

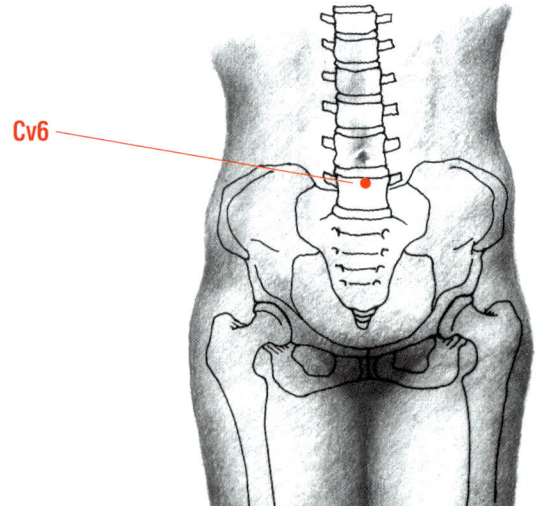

3. HEART & CIRCULATORY DISORDERS

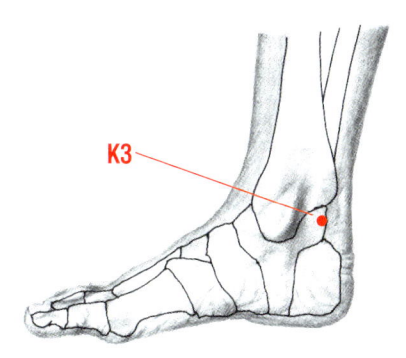

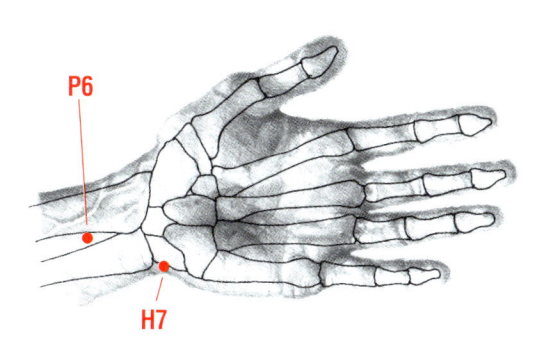

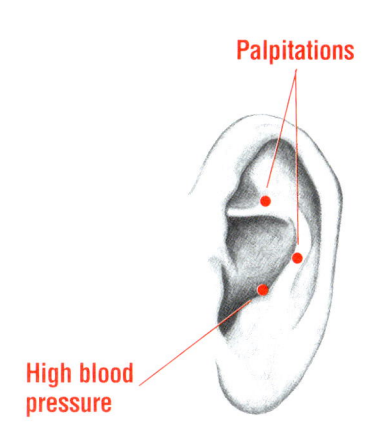

High Blood Pressure (hypertension)

Hypertension is common in the civilised world. Effective treatment is vital. Without it there is a risk of a stroke. It is therefore essential that treatment is monitored by either taking the blood pressure yourself or seeing your doctor. Use Electro-Acupuncture and see your doctor.

POINTS

K3 — This lies midway between the tip of the inner ankle bone and the achilles tendon (in the hollow)

P6 — This lies two thumb's width up from the palm wrist crease towards the elbow, directly in the centre between the two tendons.

S36 — This lies three thumb's width below the joint under the kneecap lying on the outer side of the knee. One finger's width back from the sharp edge of the shin bone.

Ear — Ear point - on the LEFT SIDE ONLY

Palpitations

Palpitations are caused by the heart beating irregularly. It often feels like a fluttering in the left side of the chest. Mineral deficiency is a common cause - a balanced diet including appropriate vitamin and mineral supplements can be of great value. In some cases palpitations are caused by reaction to coffee. It is therefore advisable for sufferers to avoid coffee completely in addition to using Electro-Acupuncture, as this can speed up improvements.

POINTS

H7 — This lies on the little finger side of the palm wrist crease just inside the small prominent bone.

P6 — As described above under Hypertension

Ear — Ear point

4. ABDOMINAL PROBLEMS

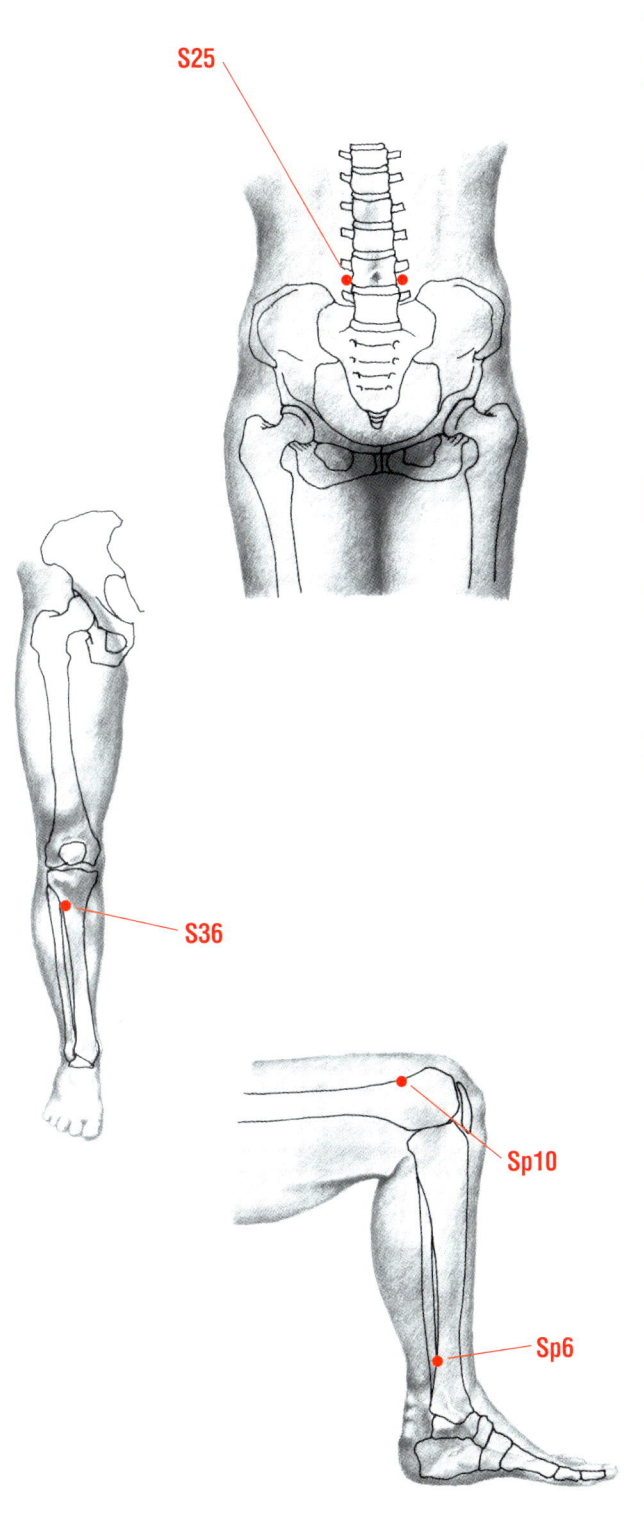

Abdominal distension

Recurring abdominal distension is a common problem, particularly in women. It is most commonly due to dysfunction of the colon. Some cases can be helped enormously by Electro-Acupuncture but often a dietary approach should also be considered. Most effective is to avoid foods such as sugar and yeast as distension is often due to candida (a Yeast-like organism) in the gut. Candida growth is stimulated by yeast and sugar. A balanced diet including appropriate vitamin and mineral supplements can be of great value - see page 0.1.

POINTS

S25 This is situated two thumb's width to each side of the navel.

S36 This lies three thumb's width below the joint under the kneecap lying on the outer side of the knee. One finger's width back from the sharp edge of the shin bone.

Sp6 This lies one hand's width (four fingers) up from the inner ankle joint. It lies just behind the tibia bone at this point.

Ear Ear point

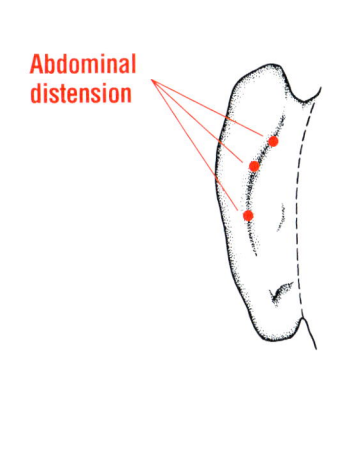

Abdominal distension

4. ABDOMINAL PROBLEMS

Colitis

Colitis is inflammation of the colon. The symptom is often loose bowels, with mucous and sometimes blood passed. Conventional approaches to colitis can sometimes be alarming, involving steroids. In the worst possible cases removal of the affected part of the colon is necessary. Simple first aid approaches such as Electro-Acupuncture are therefore welcome at the early stages. Attention to diet is also beneficial. Colitis can in most cases be due to food sensitivity. The most common foods involved are milk and dairy products. Temporary avoidance of these foods is well worth experimenting with. A balanced diet including appropriate vitamin and mineral supplements can also be of great value - see page 0.1.

POINTS

S36 This lies three thumb's width below the joint under the kneecap lying on the outer side of the knee. One finger's width back from the sharp edge of the shin bone.

S40 This lies on a mid-point from the knee to the ankle, three fingers width back towards the fibula (ie., the outside of the lower leg), from the ridge on the front of the shin.

Sp6 This lies one hand's width (four fingers) up from the inner ankle joint. It lies just behind the tibia bone at this point.

Ear Ear point

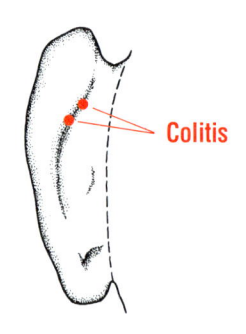

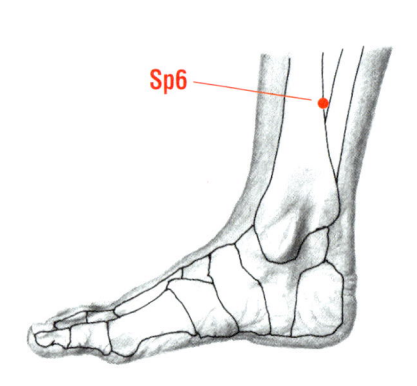

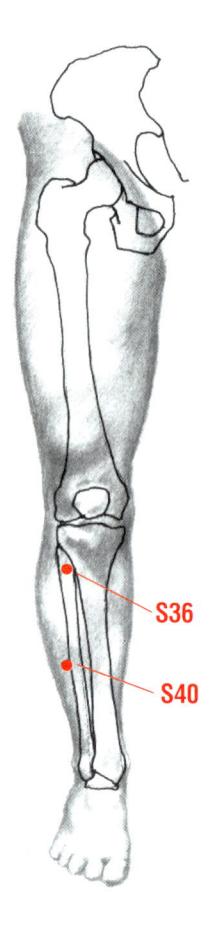

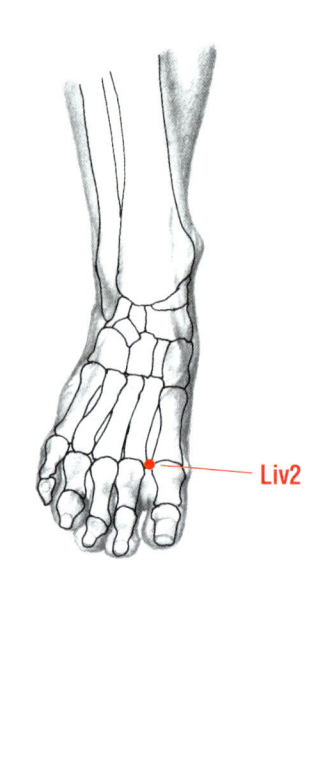

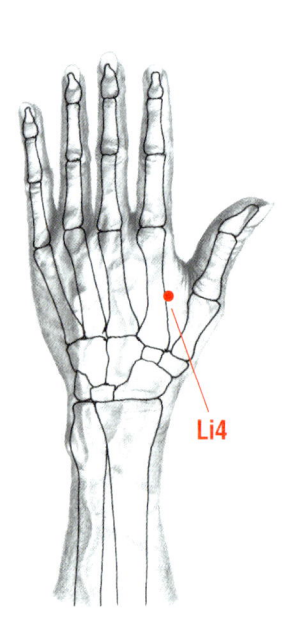

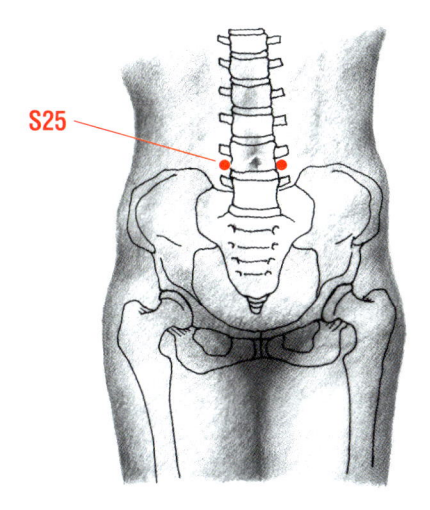

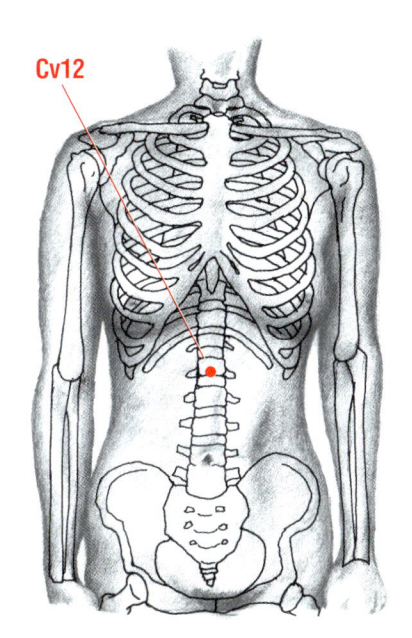

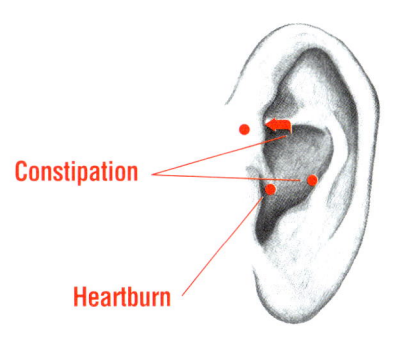

4. ABDOMINAL PROBLEMS

Constipation

All people with constipation should pay particular attention to diet - see page 0.1. A high roughage routine eating wholemeal bread (never white), lots of vegetables, particularly raw carrots, cauliflower and cabbage is recommended. Processed foods should be reduced as much as possible. It is also advisable to eat plenty of fresh fruit. Consider treating anxiety and stress points.

POINTS

Li4 — This lies on the side of the bone which runs from the forefinger knuckle down towards the wrist. See page 8 for a detailed description of this point.

Liv2 — This is one finger's width up from the web between the big toe and the second toe tendons.

S25 — This is situated two thumb's width to each side of the navel.

Ear — Ear point

Heartburn

This is due to regurgitation of stomach acids up the oesophagus. It is sometimes an accompaniment of hiatus hernia. This is often associated with overweight patients and therefore weight loss can be very helpful. A balanced diet including appropriate vitamin and mineral supplements can also be of great value - see page 0.1.

POINTS

Cv12 — This lies halfway between the lower end of the breastbone and the navel, exactly in the mid-line.

S36 — This lies three thumb's width below the joint under the kneecap lying on the outer side of the knee. One finger's width back from the sharp edge of the shin bone.

Ear — Ear point

4. ABDOMINAL PROBLEMS

Haemorrhoids

Haemorrhoids are varicosities of the veins around the lower end of the rectum. A balanced diet including appropriate vitamin and mineral supplements can be of great value - see page 0.1 for a general health plan. Diet is particularly important in controlling Haemorrhoids - call the HelpLine for a treatment protocol.

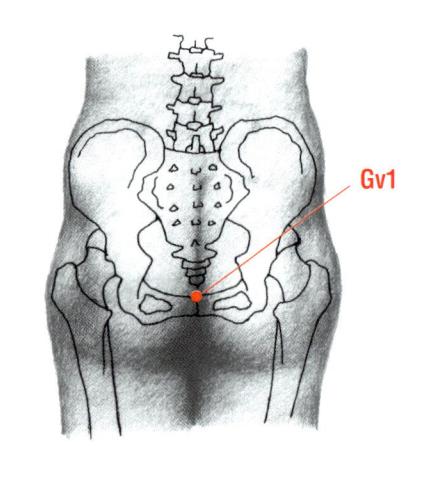

POINTS

B40 This lies directly behind the knee joint in the centre of the crease.

Gv1 This lies right at the base of the spine below the tip of the coccyx, midway towards the anus.

Gv20 This point lies right at the top of the head where two imaginary lines cross, one drawn from the top of one ear to the top of the other ear, the other line drawn from the top of the nose right over the top of the skull to the back of the skull. Where these lines cross is Gv20.

Ear Ear point

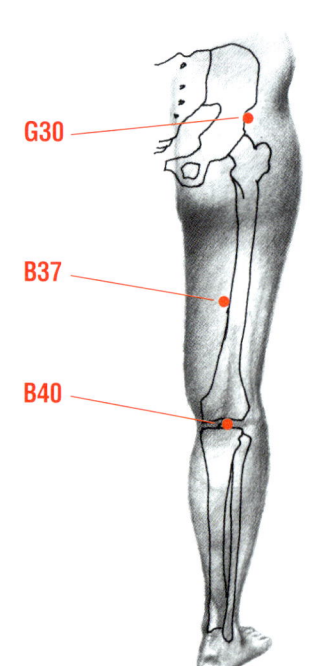

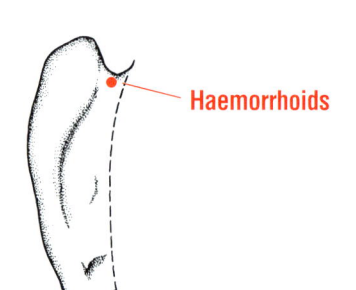

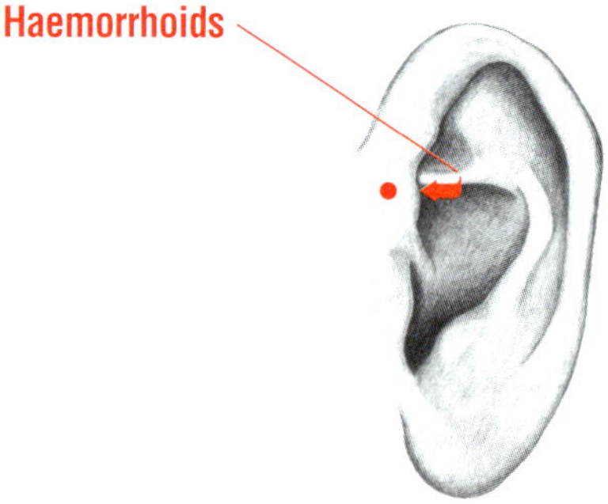

4. ABDOMINAL PROBLEMS

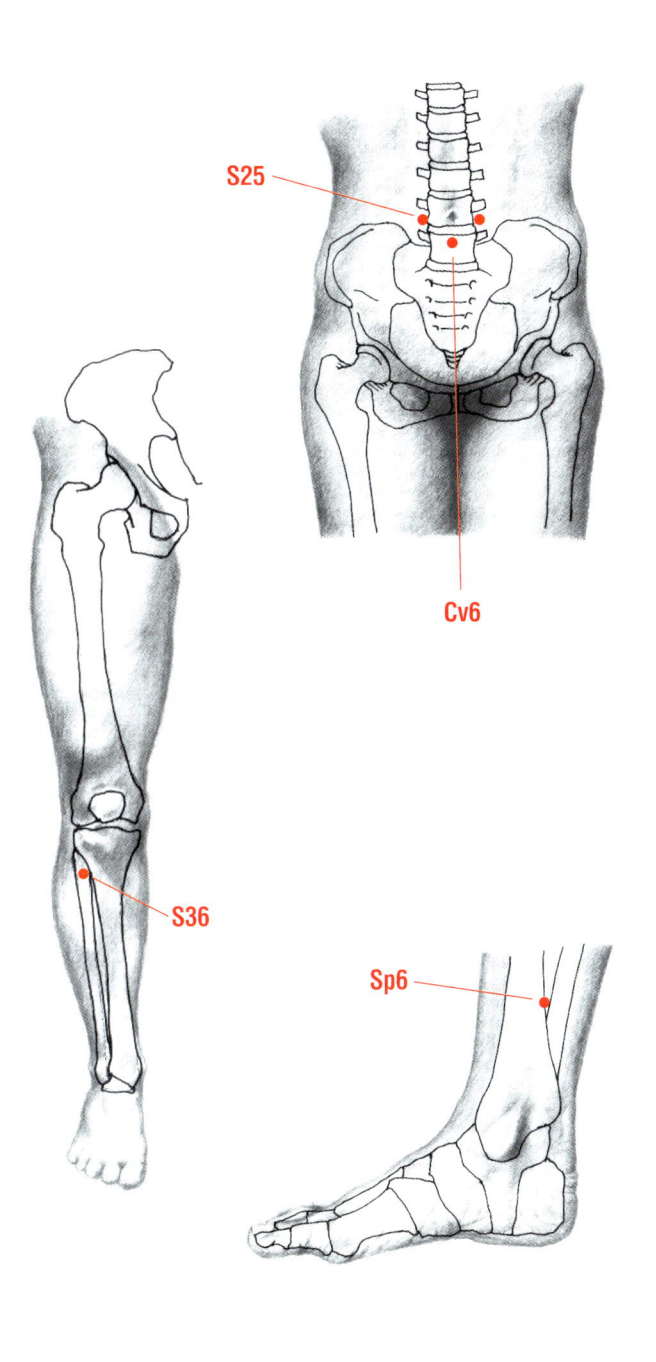

Diarrhoea

Diarrhoea, if it is chronic, is commonly due to colitis. If acute it may be infective. Acute infective diarrhoea is most often due to a virus but in some cases can be due to a more serious infection such as salmonella. In these cases appropriate medical advice should be sought with a view to treatment and its containment. If diarrhoea is accompanied by blood, a doctor should be consulted prior to treatment.

POINTS

Cv6   This lies one and a half thumb's width below the navel.

S25   This is situated two thumb's width to each side of the navel.

S36   This lies three thumb's width below the joint under the kneecap lying on the outer side of the knee. One finger's width back from the sharp edge of the shin bone.

Sp6   This lies one hand's width (four fingers) up from the inner ankle joint. It lies just behind the tibia bone at this point.

Ear   Ear point

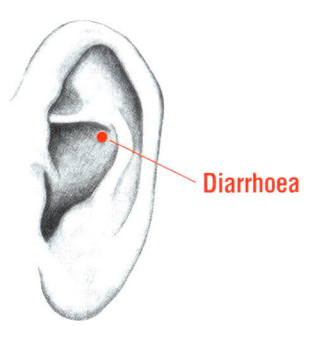

4. ABDOMINAL PROBLEMS

Liver trouble

Liver trouble is often accompanied by general biliousness and intolerance to fatty foods. Intake of dietary fats should be reduced as it is the liver that has to cope, in the main, with these fats.

POINTS

Cv12 This lies halfway between the lower end of the breastbone and the navel, exactly in the mid-line.

Liv3 This lies in between the tendons of the big toe and the first toe, two thumb's width towards the top of the foot from the web.

Liv14 This lies at the tip of the ninth rib, approximately halfway along the lower end of the ribcage on the front of the body from the mid-line to the side.

Ear Ear point

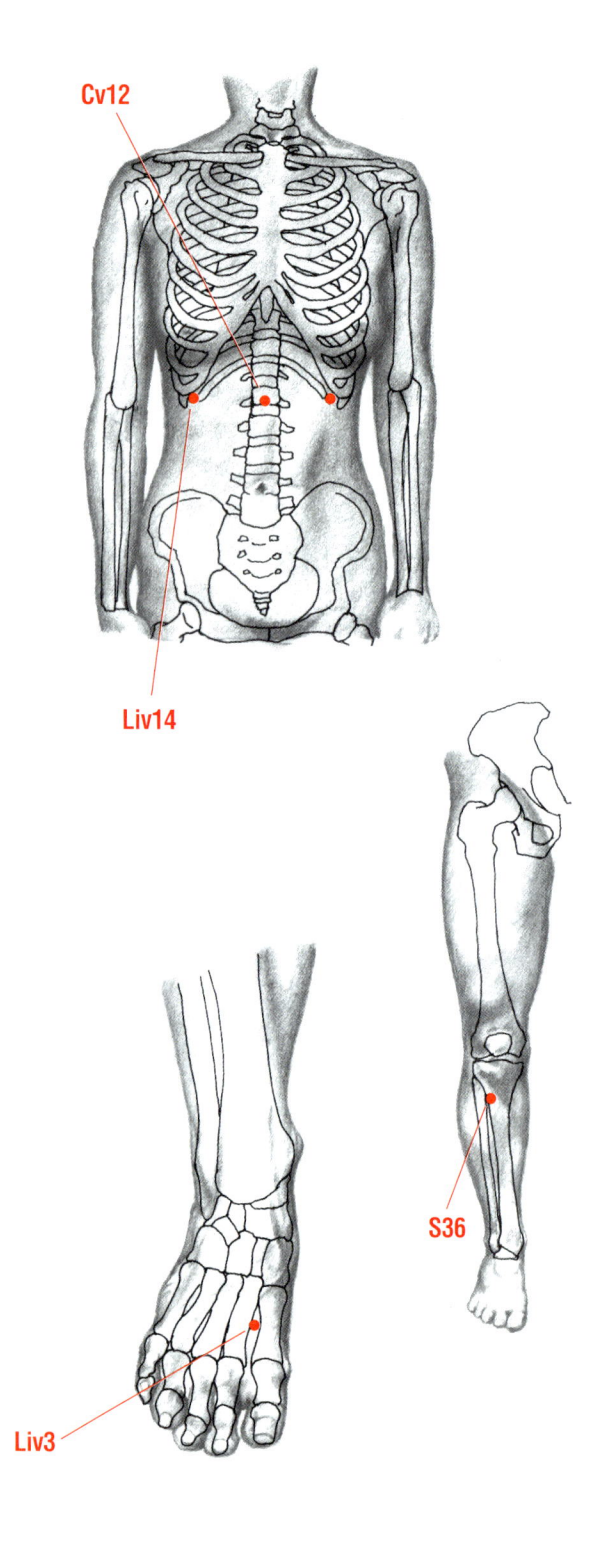

Nausea - Sea Sickness - Motion Sickness

Nausea can occur for many reasons, but Electro-Acupuncture offers a useful aid.

POINTS

P6 This lies two thumb's width up from the palm wrist crease towards the elbow, directly in the centre between the two tendons.

S36 This lies three thumb's width below the joint under the kneecap lying on the outer side of the knee. One finger's width back from the sharp edge of the shin bone.

Ear Ear point

4. ABDOMINAL PROBLEMS

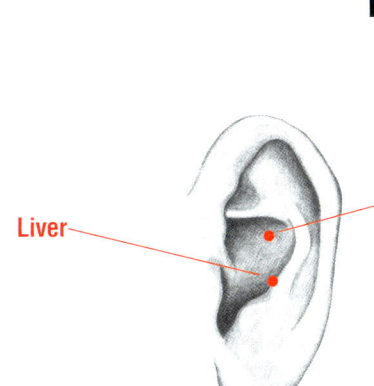

Upper Abdominal Pain - Stomach Ache

Upper abdominal pain is a very common problem and diagnosis is essential. The problem sometimes arises in the stomach, (for example, due to a peptic ulcer), or in some cases the gall bladder.

POINTS

Cv12 This lies halfway between the lower end of the breastbone and the navel, exactly in the mid-line.

Liv14 This lies at the tip of the ninth rib, approximately halfway along the lower end of the ribcage on the front of the body from the mid-line to the side.

Sp6 This lies one hand's width (four fingers) up from the inner ankle joint. It lies just behind the tibia bone at this point.

Sp9 This lies just below the inside of the kneecap and below the top of the tibia. This point is usually tender when pressed with a finger tip.

T6 This lies on the back of the wrist, three thumbs width towards the elbow from the wrist crease.

Ear Ear point

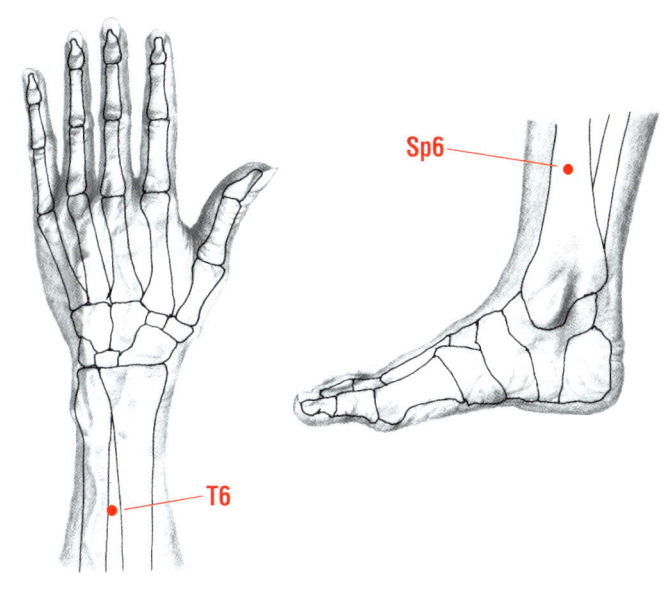

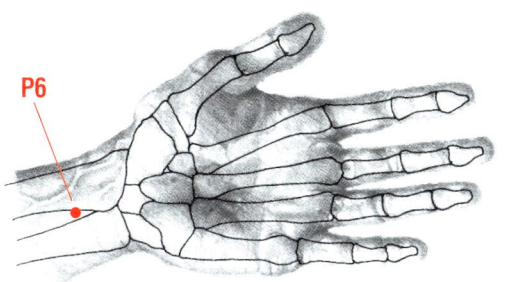

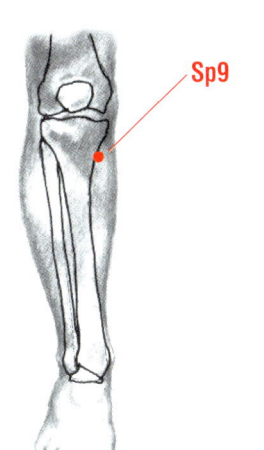

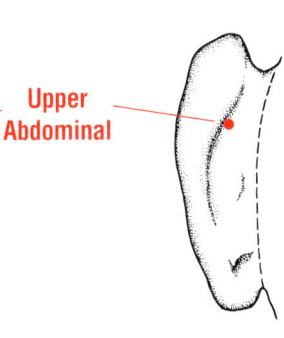

4. ABDOMINAL PROBLEMS

Gallbladder Disease

Inflammation of the gallbladder is relatively common. Correct diagnosis is essential as many other conditions mimic gallbladder disease. Dietary approach is important, and avoidance of fatty foods is essential. It is entirely acceptable to treat gallbladder disease with Electro-Acupuncture, even if small stones are present. Large gall stones are usually removed surgically. Treat the points indicated as and when the pain occurs.

POINTS

B18 This is situated one and a half thumb's width on each side of the centre of the spine at the level of the ninth thoracic vertebra. It is at the lower end of the rib cage at the back.

B19 This lies one thumb's width below B18. Again it is situated on both sides of the mid-line.

G34 This is just below and in front of the knobbly head of the fibula, which is the bone just below the outer side of knee. This point is in a slight depression and is sometimes tender when pressed with a finger tip.

Liv14 This lies at the tip of the ninth rib, approximately halfway along the lower end of the ribcage on the front of the body from the mid-line to the side.

P6 This lies two thumb's width up from the palm wrist crease towards the elbow, directly in the centre between the two tendons.

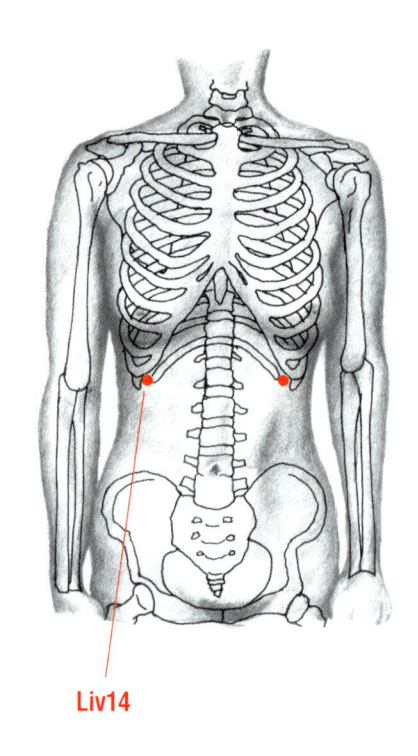

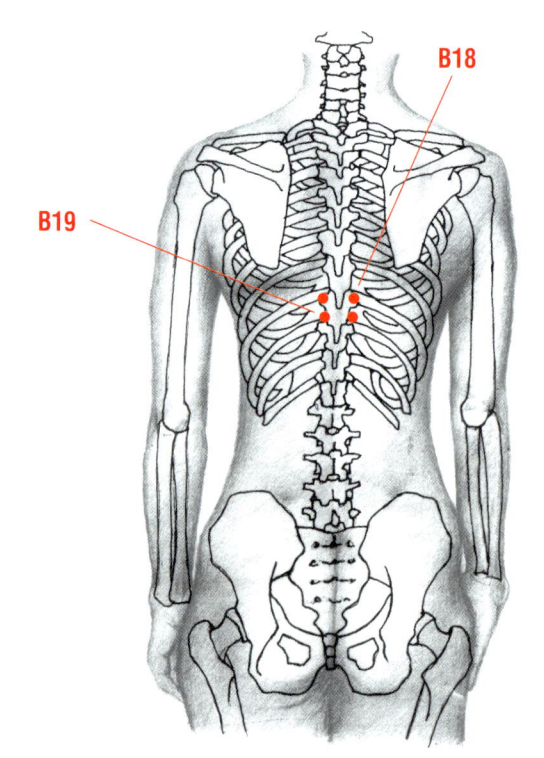

4. ABDOMINAL PROBLEMS

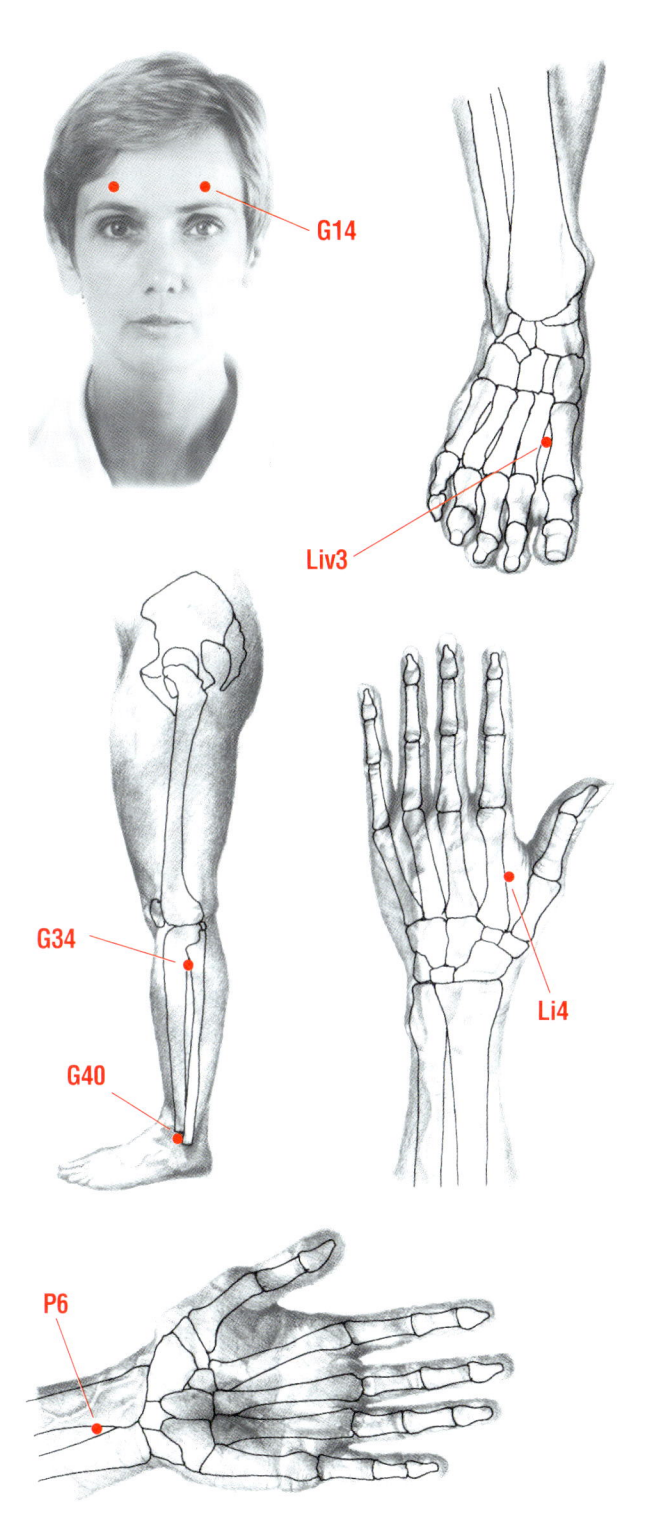

Gallbladder Colic (Biliary Colic)

This is pain caused by a stone in the bile duct that passes from the gallbladder into the duodenum. This is colicky pain, which comes in spasms. While medical advice should be sought, treatment with Electro-Acupuncture is often successful.

POINTS

G14 — This lies one thumb's width above the mid point of the eyebrow.

G34 — This is just below and in front of the knobbly head of the fibula, which is the bone just below the outer side of knee. This point is in a slight depression and is sometimes tender when pressed with a finger tip.

G40 — This lies just in front of the knob of bone on the outside ankle bone.

Li4 — This lies on the side of the bone which runs from the forefinger knuckle down towards the wrist. See page 8 for a detailed description of this point.

Liv3 — This lies in between the tendons of the big toe and the first toe, two thumb's width towards the top of the foot from the web.

4. ABDOMINAL PROBLEMS

Hiatus Hernia

This is a bulging of the stomach through the diaphragm at the weakest point where the oesophagus (food pipe) passes through. The hernia is not visible and often symptomless. Symptoms when present are those of indigestion. A balanced diet including appropriate vitamin and mineral supplements can also be of great value - see page 0.1.

POINTS

Cv6 This lies one and a half thumb's width below the navel.

Cv12 This lies halfway between the lower end of the breastbone and the navel, exactly in the mid-line.

Liv3 This lies in between the tendons of the big toe and the first toe, two thumb's width towards the top of the foot from the web.

S25 This is situated two thumb's width to each side of the navel.

S36 This lies three thumb's width below the joint under the kneecap lying on the outer side of the knee. One finger's width back from the sharp edge of the shin bone.

S41 This lies directly over the middle point of the front of the foot joint.

Ear Ear point

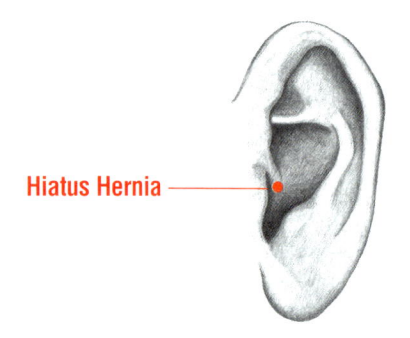

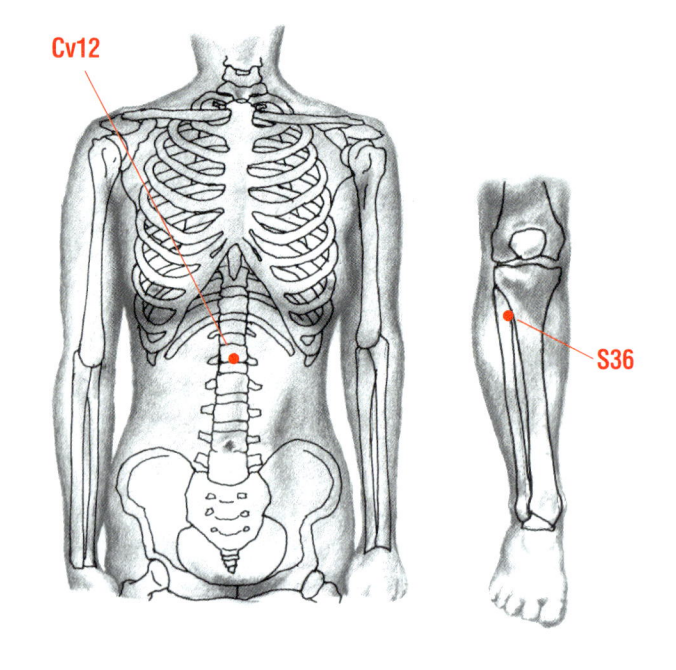

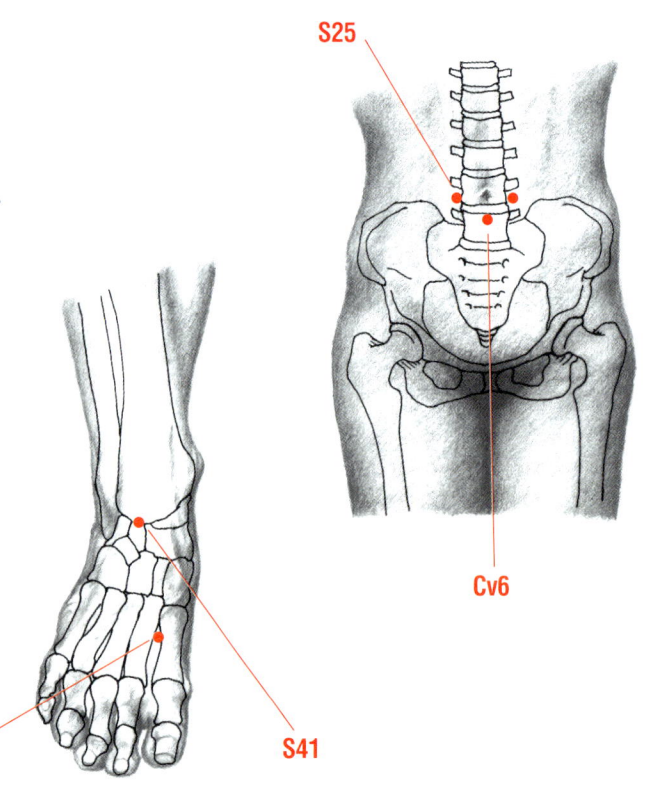

4.10

4. ABDOMINAL PROBLEMS

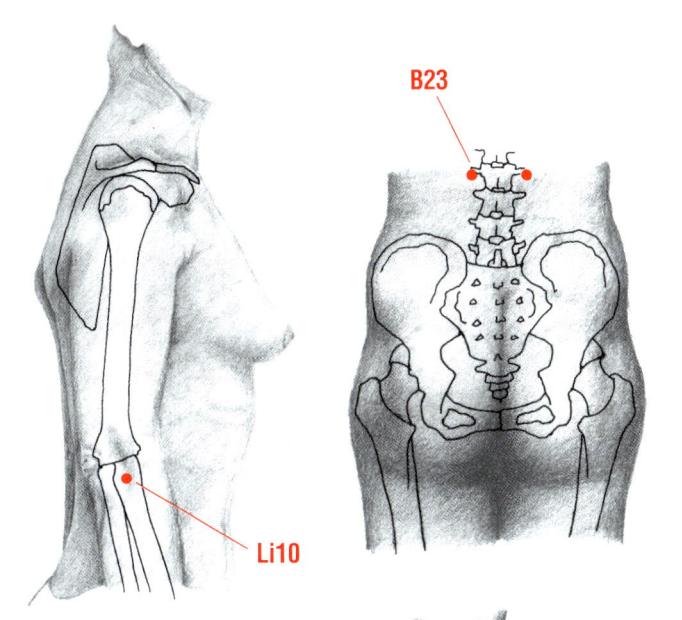

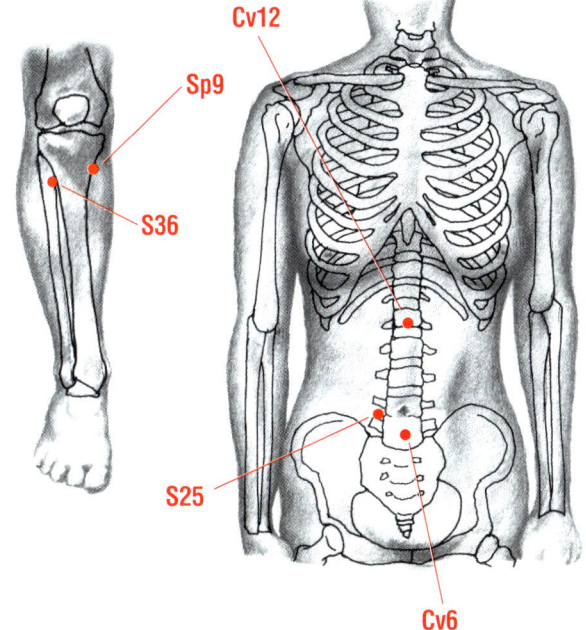

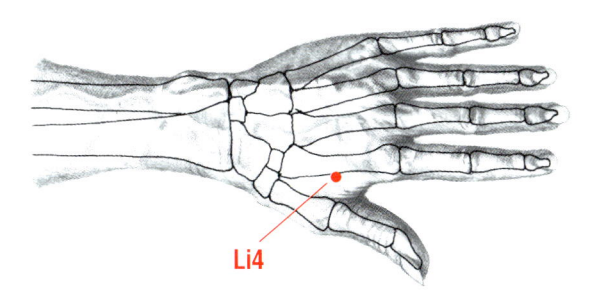

Irritable Bowel Syndrome

This is a disorder of the bowel. It is brought on by stress, anxiety or mild depression which cause the muscles of the lower colon to become overactive. A balanced diet including appropriate vitamin and mineral supplements can also be of great value - see page 0.1.

POINTS

B23 This lies one and a half thumb's width to each side of the second lumbar vertebra.

Cv6 This lies one and a half thumb's width below the navel.

Cv12 This lies halfway between the lower end of the breastbone and the navel, exactly in the mid-line.

Li4 This lies on the side of the bone which runs from the forefinger knuckle down towards the wrist. See page 8 for a detailed description of this point.

Li10 This lies two finger's width below Li11 on a line towards the thumb.

S25 This is situated two thumb's width to each side of the navel.

S36 This lies three thumb's width below the joint under the kneecap lying on the outer side of the knee. One finger's width back from the sharp edge of the shin bone.

Sp9 This lies just below the inside of the kneecap and below the top of the tibia. This point is usually tender when pressed with a finger tip.

Ear Ear point

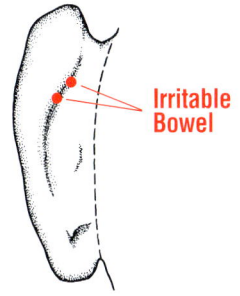

Irritable Bowel

4. ABDOMINAL PROBLEMS

Liver Problems including Hepatitis

Hepatitis is inflammation of the liver which can be caused by three different viruses. The progress of the disease follows a similar pattern in all three viruses. It is essential that you consult your doctor if liver problems are suspected. A balanced diet including appropriate vitamin and mineral supplements can also be of great value - see page 0.1.

POINTS

B20 This lies in the loin area, and is often tender in kidney problems. It lies one and a half thumb's width from the mid-line on each side.

Cv12 This lies halfway between the lower end of the breastbone and the navel, exactly in the mid-line.

G34 This is just below and in front of the knobbly head of the fibula, which is the bone just below the outer side of knee. This point is in a slight depression and is sometimes tender when pressed with a finger tip.

Liv3 This lies in between the tendons of the big toe and the first toe, two thumb's width towards the top of the foot from the web.

Liv14 This lies at the tip of the ninth rib, approximately halfway along the lower end of the ribcage on the front of the body from the mid-line to the side.

S36 This lies three thumb's width below the joint under the kneecap lying on the outer side of the knee. One finger's width back from the sharp edge of the shin bone.

Sp6 This lies one hand's width (four fingers) up from the inner ankle joint. It lies just behind the tibia bone at this point.

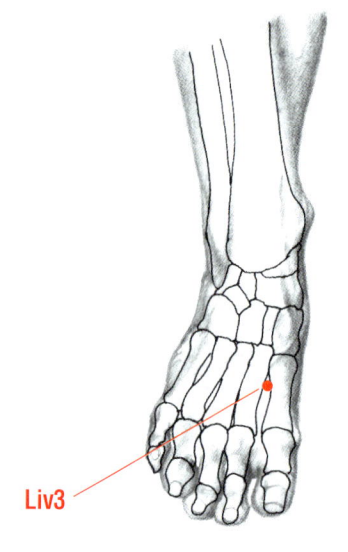

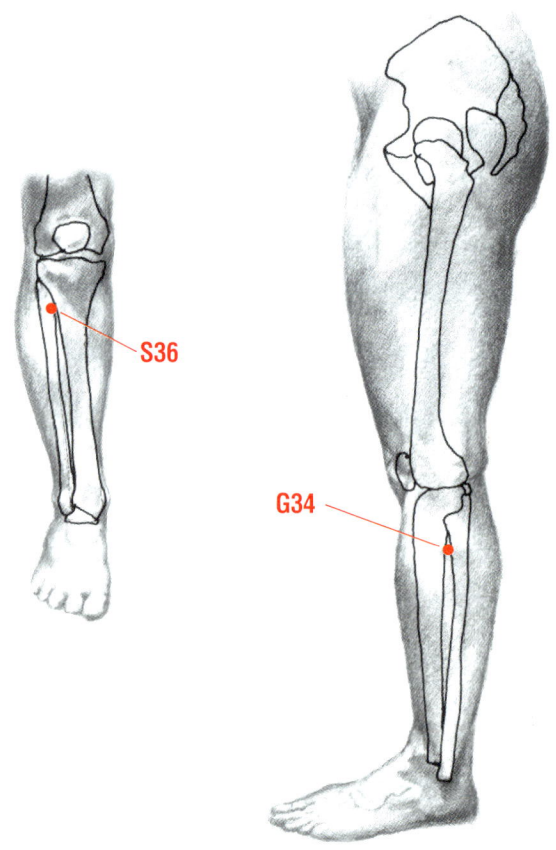

4. ABDOMINAL PROBLEMS

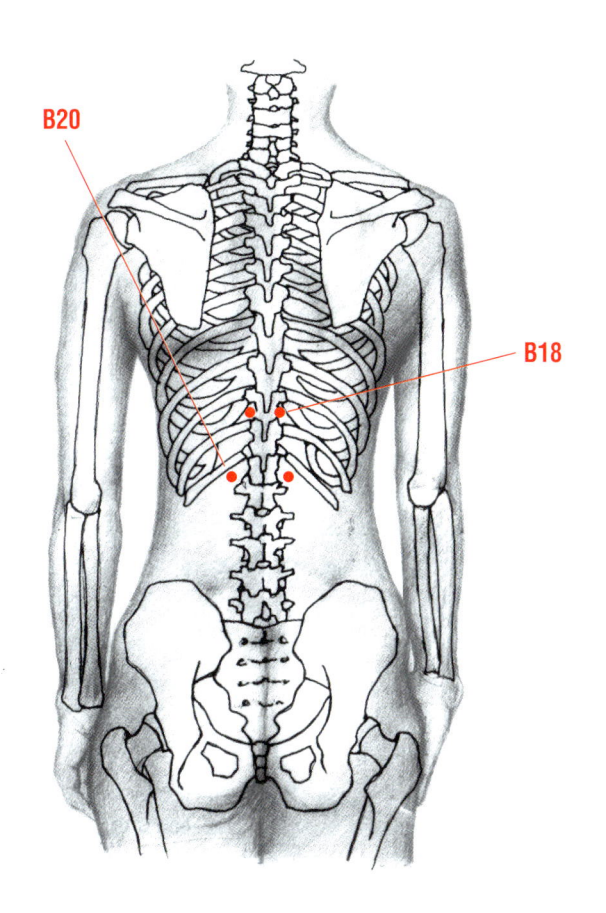

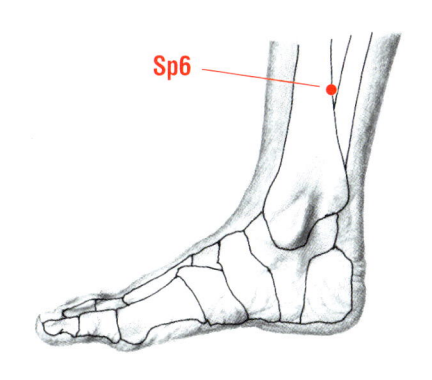

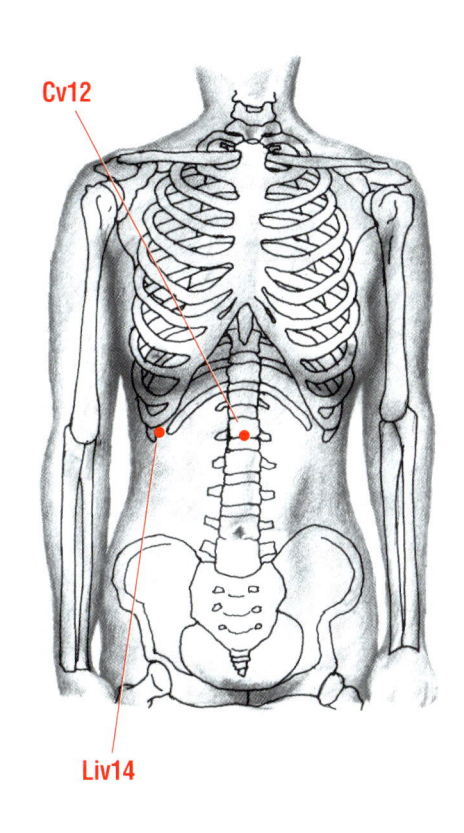

4.13

4. ABDOMINAL PROBLEMS

Duodenal Ulcer

This is an ulcer occurring the outlet where the stomach joins the duodenum (the first few inches of the small intestine) and the duodenum itself. It is three to four times more common in men than women. A balanced diet including appropriate vitamin and mineral supplements can also be of great value - see page 0.1.

POINTS

Cv12 — This lies halfway between the lower end of the breastbone and the navel, exactly in the mid-line.

Liv3 — This lies in between the tendons of the big toe and the first toe, two thumb's width towards the top of the foot from the web.

S36 — This lies three thumb's width below the joint under the kneecap lying on the outer side of the knee. One finger's width back from the sharp edge of the shin bone.

Sp6 — This lies one hand's width (four fingers) up from the inner ankle joint. It lies just behind the tibia bone at this point.

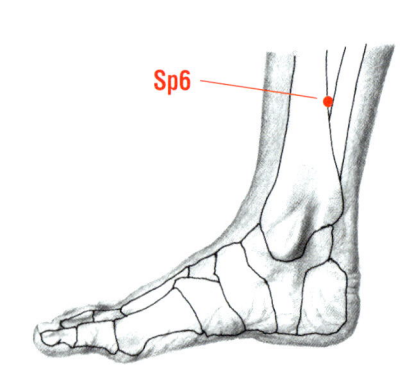

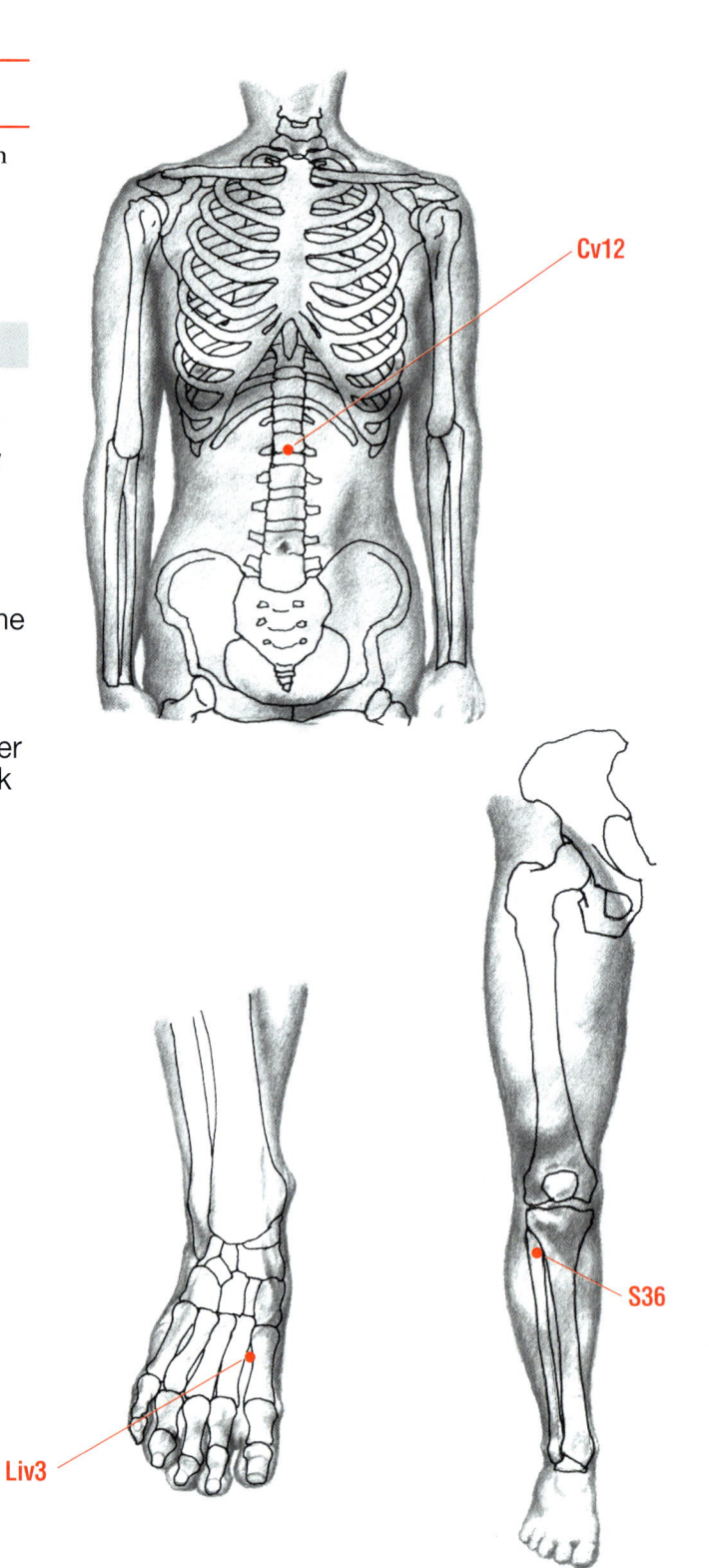

4.14

4. ABDOMINAL PROBLEMS

Crohn's Disease - Regional Ileitis

This is an inflammation that usually affects the ileum (the lower part of the small bowel) and occasionally other parts of the digestive tract. This is most common in people in their twenties. A balanced diet including appropriate vitamin and mineral supplements can be of great value - see page 0.1.

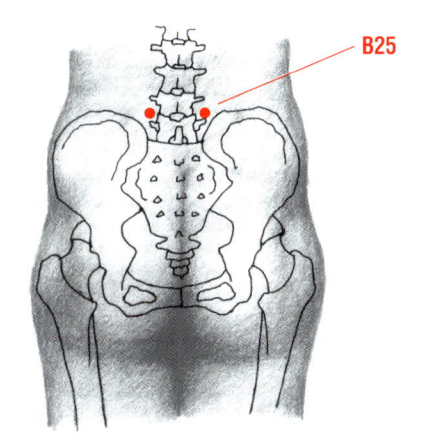

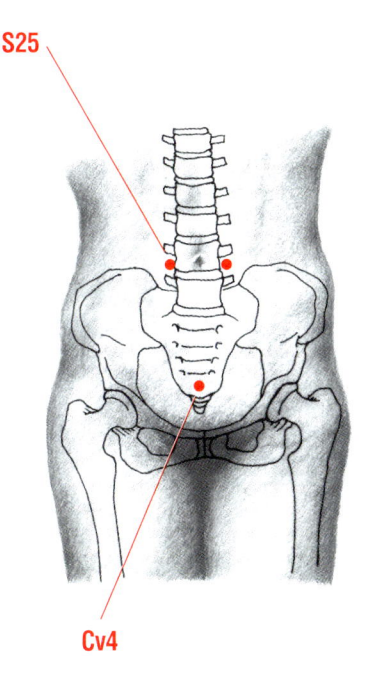

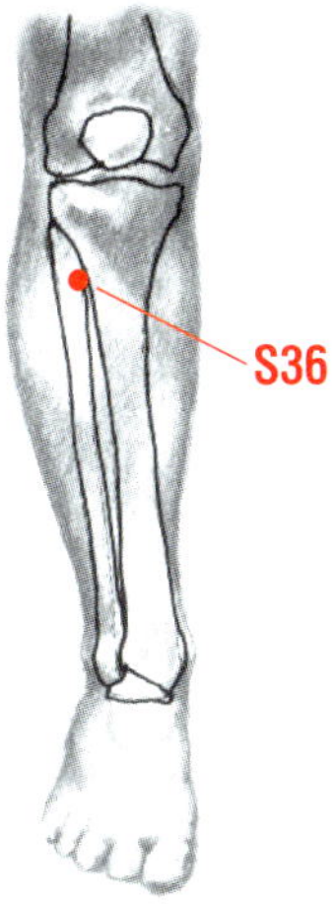

POINTS

B25 This lies one thumb's width above the sacral bone, one and a half thumb's width away from the midline.

Cv4 This lies two thumb's width above the pubic bone.

Cv12 This lies halfway between the lower end of the breastbone and the navel, exactly in the mid-line.

S25 This is situated two thumb's width to each side of the navel.

S36 This lies three thumb's width below the joint under the kneecap lying on the outer side of the knee. One finger's width back from the sharp edge of the shin bone.

4. ABDOMINAL PROBLEMS

Diverticulitis

Inflammation of one of the pouches formed in the intestine by Diverticular Disease of the Colon. A high roughage diet, with plenty of fresh vegetables, cleansing of the colon and appropriate vitamin and mineral supplements is strongly recommended - see page 0.1.

POINTS

B23 — This lies one and a half thumb's width to each side of the second lumbar vertebra.

Li4 — This lies on the side of the bone which runs from the forefinger knuckle down towards the wrist. See page 8 for a detailed description of this point.

Li10 — This lies two finger's width below Li11 on a line towards the thumb.

Cv12 — This lies halfway between the lower end of the breastbone and the navel, exactly in the mid-line.

S25 — This is situated two thumb's width to each side of the navel.

S36 — This lies three thumb's width below the joint under the kneecap lying on the outer side of the knee. One finger's width back from the sharp edge of the shin bone.

Sp9 — This lies just below the inside of the kneecap and below the top of the tibia. This point is usually tender when pressed with a finger tip.

Sp6 — This lies one hand's width (four fingers) up from the inner ankle joint. It lies just behind the tibia bone at this point.

Ear — Ear points

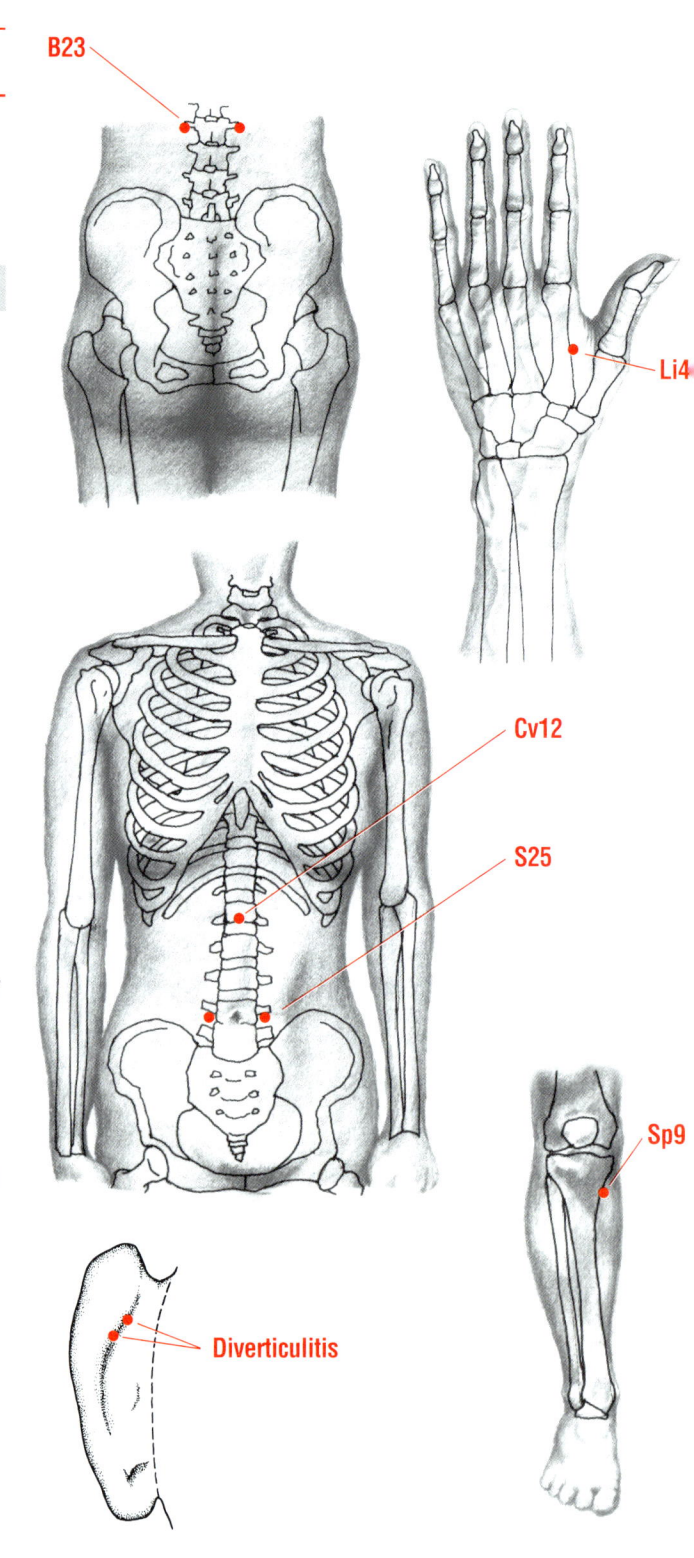

4.16

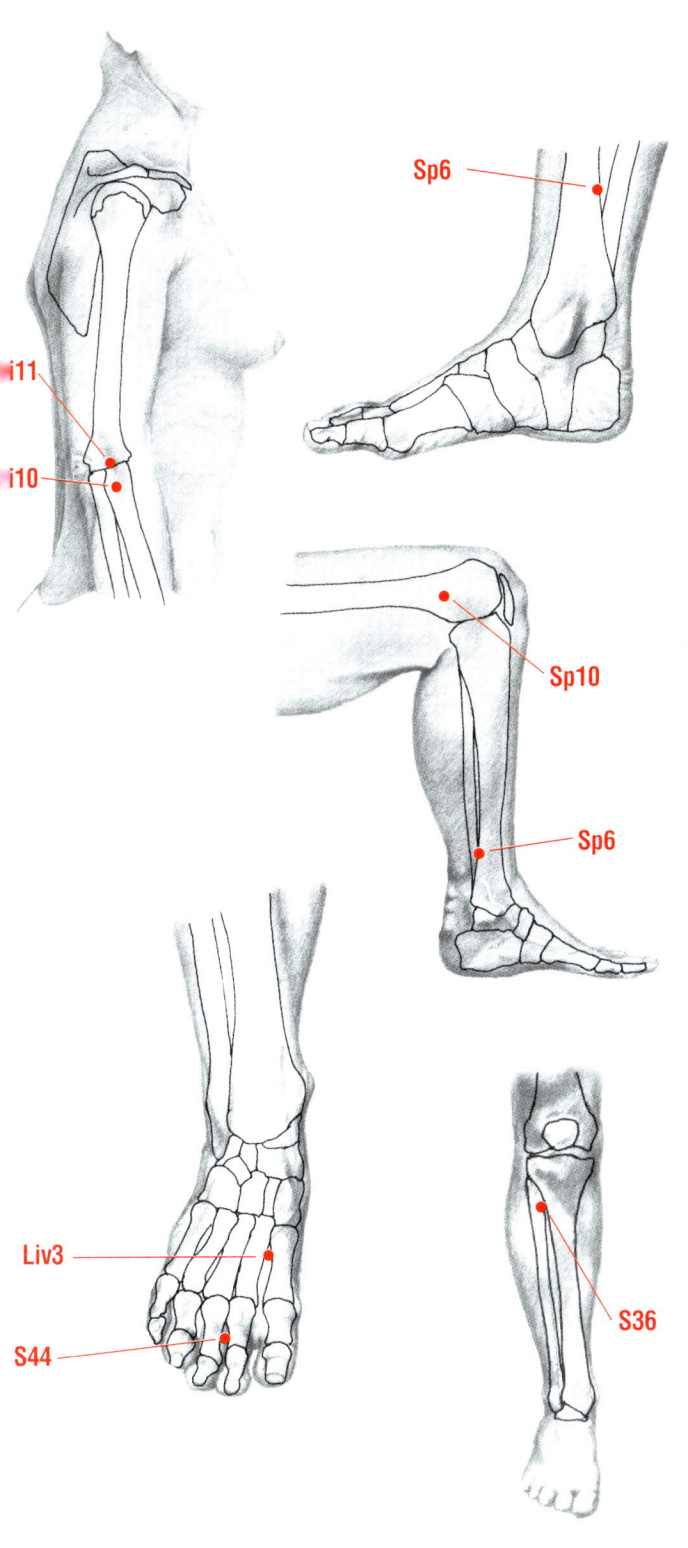

5. SKIN DISORDERS

General Allergies

Some points are useful as part of a treatment regime, which should include dietary controls. A balanced diet including appropriate vitamin and mineral supplements can also be of great value - see page 0.1.

POINTS

Liv3 — This lies in between the tendons of the big toe and the first toe, two thumb's width towards the top of the foot from the web.

Li4 — This lies on the side of the bone which runs from the forefinger knuckle down towards the wrist. See page 8 for a detailed description of this point.

Li11 — This lies 2cm beyond the end of the outer elbow crease with the arm bent.

S36 — This lies three thumb's width below the joint under the kneecap lying on the outer side of the knee. One finger's width back from the sharp edge of the shin bone.

S44 — This lies in the web between the second and third toes.

Sp6 — This lies one hand's width (four fingers) up from the inner ankle joint. It lies just behind the tibia bone at this point.

Sp10 — This lies at the lower end of the muscular bulge, two fingers above the inside of the knee cap.

Ear — Ear point

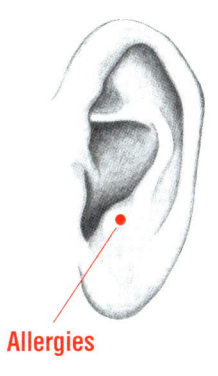

Allergies

5. SKIN DISORDERS

Acne

Acne is common in teenagers and many topically applied creams are recommended. Unfortunately the results from these creams are generally disappointing. While using Electro-Acupuncture one should pay attention to, amongst other things, bowel function. A change to a high roughage, low mucous diet (wholemeal bread, lots of raw vegetables and avoidance of red meat, milk and dairy products, eggs and particularly chocolate) is usually beneficial. Including an appropriate combination of vitamin and mineral supplements can also be of great value - see page 0.1. Use 3% Hydrogen Peroxide from drug stores to heal spots.

POINTS

Li4 — This lies on the side of the bone which runs from the forefinger knuckle down towards the wrist. See page 7 for a detailed description of this point.

S7 — This lies just below the mid point of the cheek bone, over the front part of the top end of the jaw bone.

S36 — This lies three thumb's width below the joint under the kneecap lying on the outer side of the knee. One finger's width back from the sharp edge of the shin bone.

Ear — Ear point

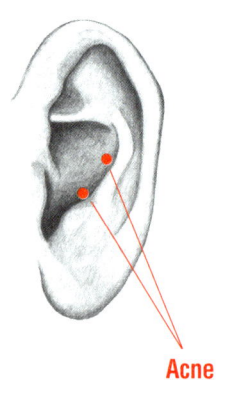

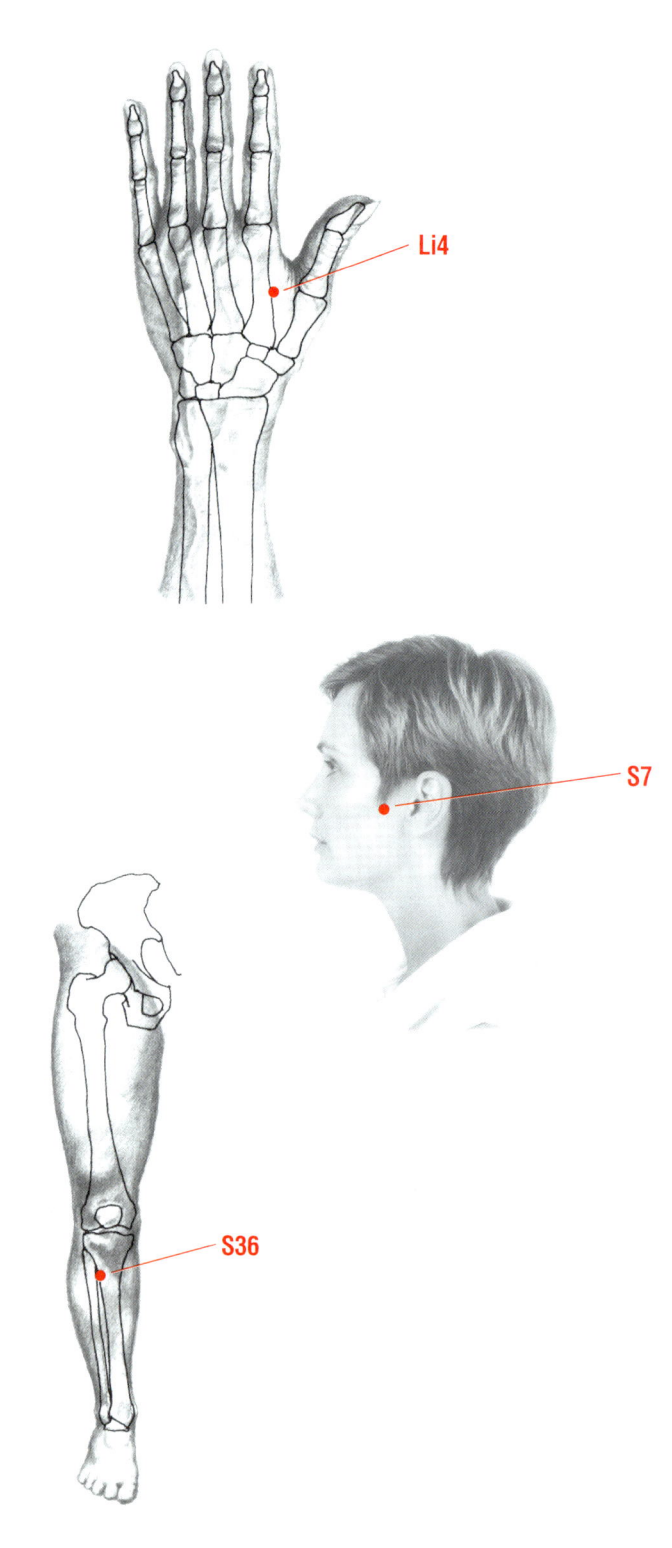

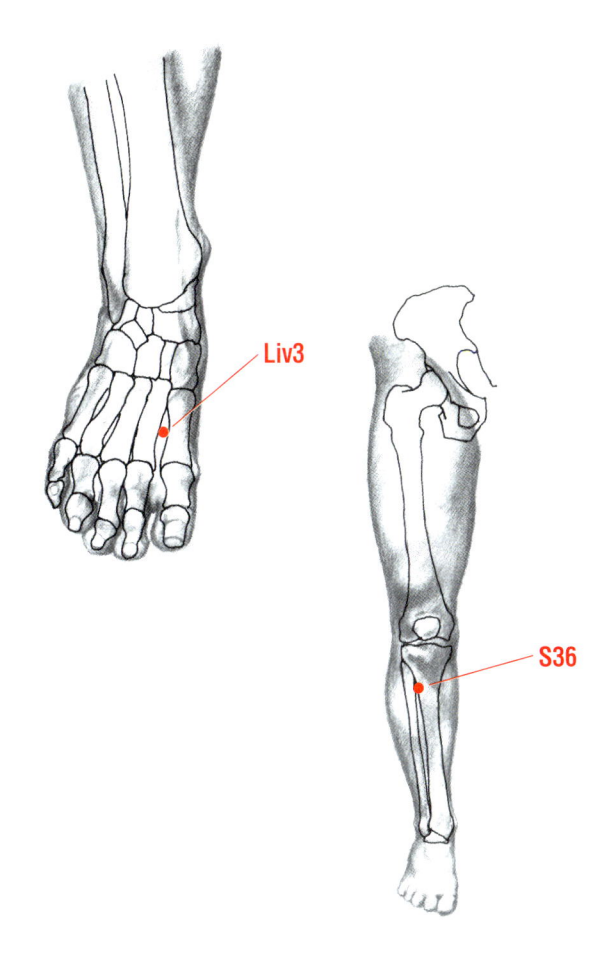

5. SKIN DISORDERS

Eczema

Eczema is an allergic inflammation of the skin. It commonly occurs in skin folds such as the elbows and knees. Conventional controls of eczema centre on the use of steroid creams. These are often problematical, as long-term use causes skin thinning. Therefore any alternative approach without side effects is most welcome. Eczema can in some cases be due to food sensitivity. The most common foods implicated are milk, wheat, dairy products and eggs. Experimenting in avoidance of these foods can be useful. Including an appropriate combination of vitamin and mineral supplements can also be of great value - see page 0.1.

POINTS

Liv3 This lies in between the tendons of the big toe and the first toe, two thumb's width towards the top of the foot from the web.

S36 This lies three thumb's width below the joint under the kneecap lying on the outer side of the knee. One finger's width back from the sharp edge of the shin bone.

Ear Ear point

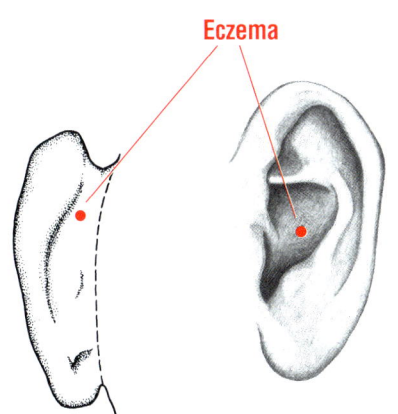

Warts & Verrucas (Warts underneath the Foot)

These are small solid growths on the skin, also known as verrucas. There are five types, usually occurring on different parts of the body. All are caused by viruses and are slightly contagious. Treatment by Electro-Acupuncture has shown to be effective in many cases.

POINTS

Treat the area immediately surrounding the Wart or Verruca - you can treat as many points as you wish, but ensure that you treat a sufficient number to encircle the wart.

Treat with colloidal silver (see page 0.1) - apply to the affected area and take 1/2 teaspoon under the tongue. You can also treat the wart with a 6% Hydrogen Peroxide solution - it will sting, but this is to be expected.

5. SKIN DISORDERS

Psoriasis

A recurring scaly eruption of the skin. Psoriasis usually begins between the ages of five and 25. It is not infectious. Treat with colloidal silver - apply to the affected area and take ½ teaspoon under the tongue. A balanced diet including appropriate vitamin and mineral supplements can be of great value - see page 0.1.

POINTS

L5 — This lies on the thumb side of the elbow joint at the edge of the elbow crease.

L7 — This lies one and a half thumb's width up from the inside wrist crease on the thumb side close to the radial pulse.

Liv3 — This lies in between the tendons of the big toe and the first toe, two thumb's width towards the top of the foot from the web.

Sp6 — This lies one hand's width (four fingers) up from the inner ankle joint. It lies just behind the tibia bone at this point.

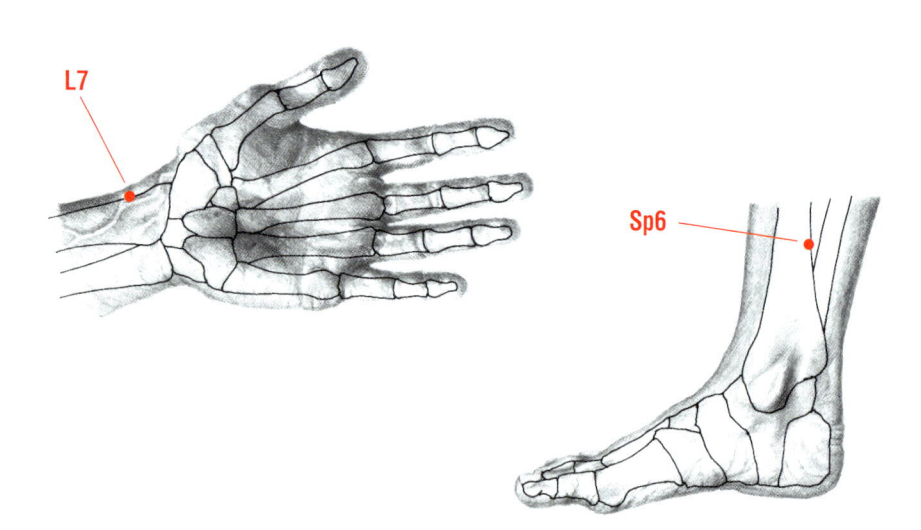

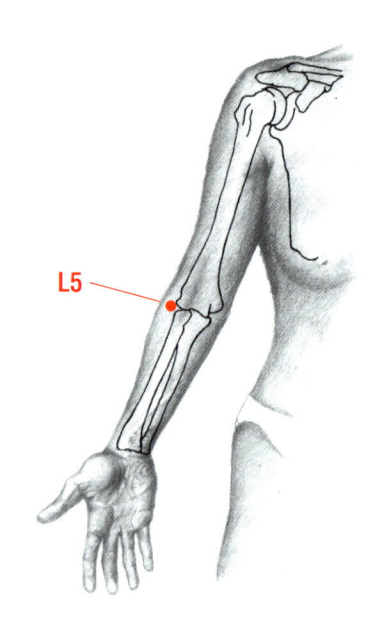

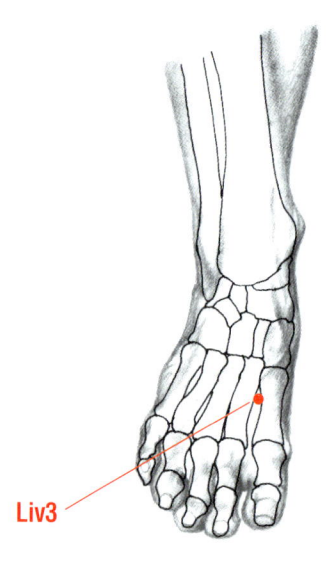

6. CHEST DISEASES

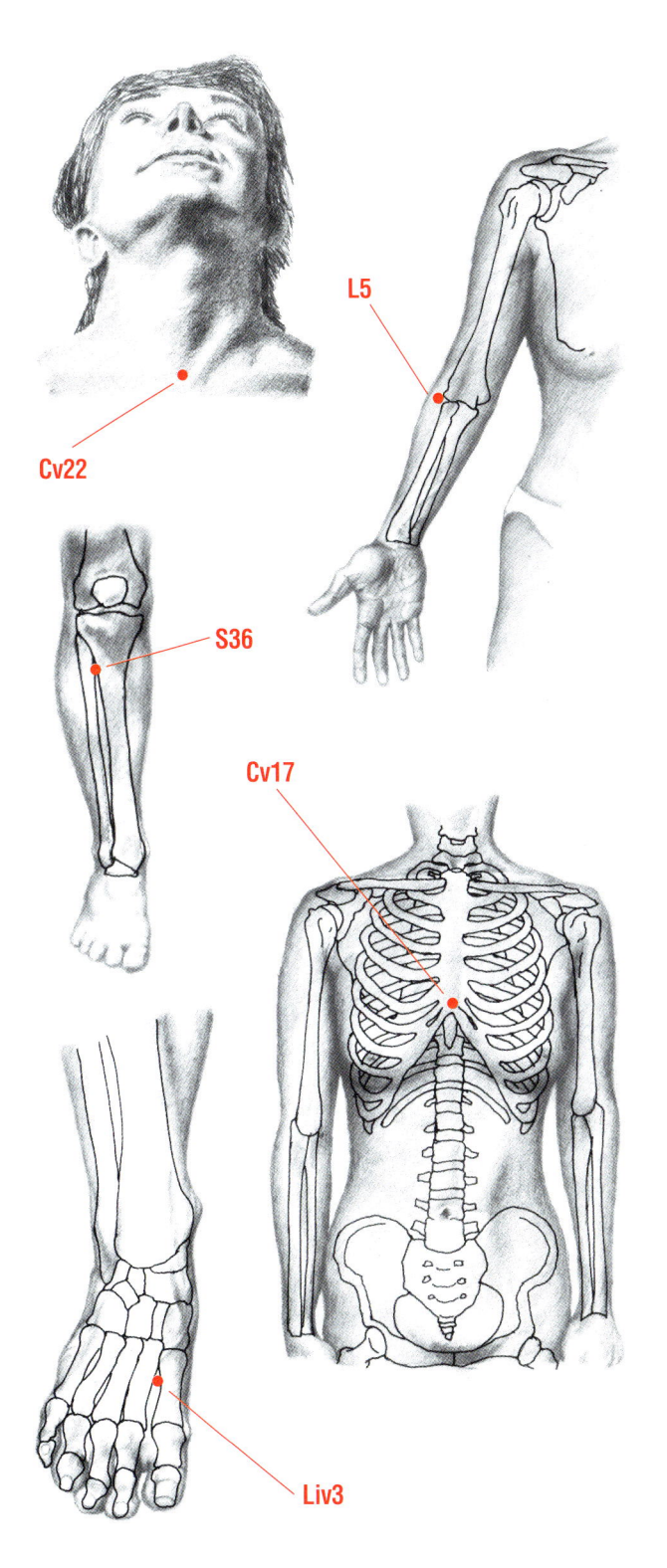

Cough

If you have a persistent cough you should seek medical advice.

If there is no serious cause then treatment using Electro-Acupuncture is a good method of control. You should also treat with colloidal silver - take ½ teaspoon under the tongue.

POINTS

Cv17 This lies in a depression at the centre of the front of the chest on a line joining both nipples.

Cv22 This lies in the hollow directly over the front of the larynx in the centre of the lower part of the neck.

L5 This lies on the thumb side of the elbow joint at the edge of the elbow crease.

L7 This lies one and a half thumb's width up from the inside wrist crease on the thumb side close to the radial pulse.

Liv3 This lies in between the tendons of the big toe and the first toe, two thumb's width towards the top of the foot from the web.

S36 This lies three thumb's width below the joint under the kneecap lying on the outer side of the knee. One finger's width back from the sharp edge of the shin bone.

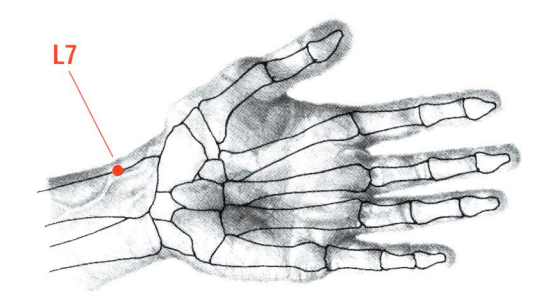

6. CHEST DISEASES

Asthma

Electro-Acupuncture can offer a successful approach to asthma and although many people have successfully replaced all drugs with electro-acupuncture it should not be taken as a complete substitute for drugs until definite progress is being made, and then only after consultation with your physician. This applies particularly to severe attacks and if no immediate result is obtained with Electro-Acupuncture, the bronchodilator drugs should be taken. If steroids/antibiotics have been taken for some time, advice is needed for actions to boost your own auto-immune system. Avoid the same foods as per eczema as well as avoiding other irritants. A balanced diet including appropriate vitamin and mineral supplements can also be of great value - see page 0.1.

POINTS

For acute attacks:

B13 — This lies one and a half thumb's width to each side of the centre of the spine at the level of the third thoracic vertebra.

Cv17 — This lies in a depression at the centre of the front of the chest on a line joining both nipples.

Cv22 — This lies in the hollow directly over the front of the larynx in the centre of the lower part of the neck.

For long term replacement of drugs:

Treat the above three points plus -

K7 — This lies two thumb's width above the bone forming the inner ankle joint.

S36 — This lies three thumb's width below the joint under the kneecap lying on the outer side of the knee. One finger's width back from the sharp edge of the shin bone.

Sp6 — This lies one hand's width (four fingers) up from the inner ankle joint. It lies just behind the tibia bone at this point.

Ear — Ear point

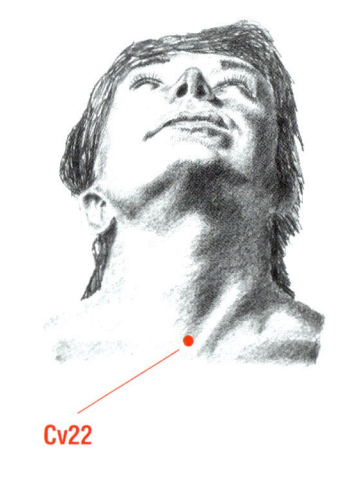

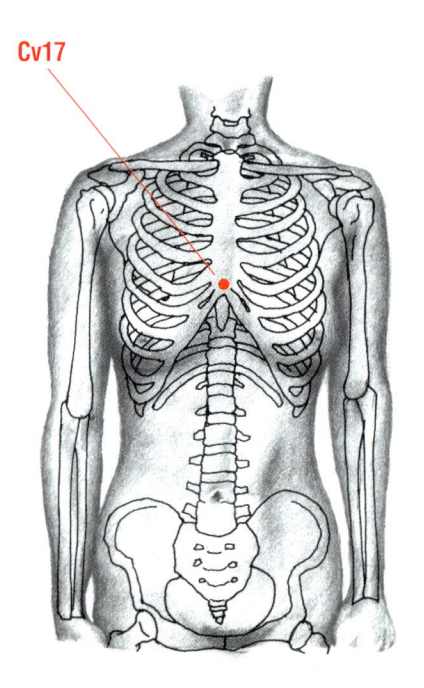

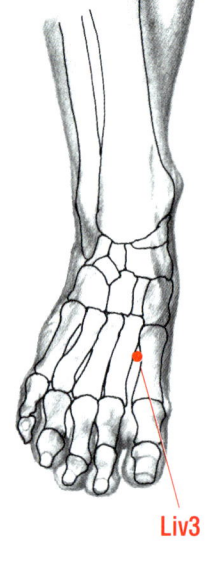

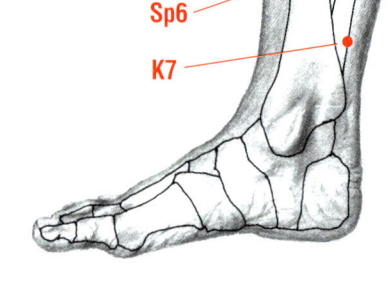

6.2

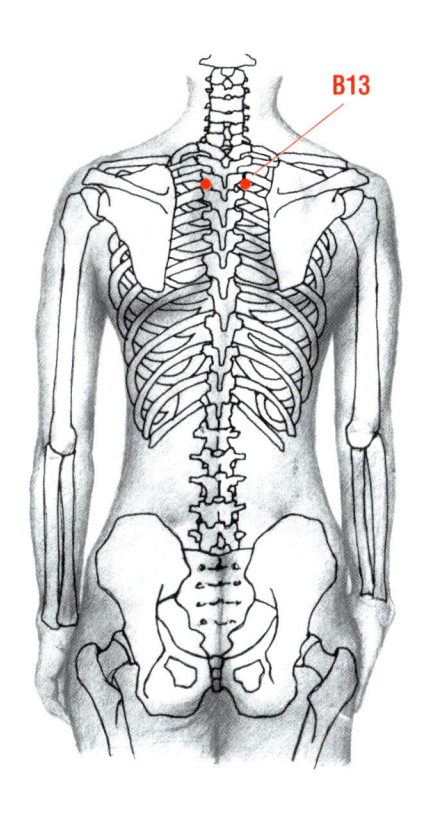

6. CHEST DISEASES

Bronchitis

Bronchitis can occur during the winter months or in more chronic cases, all the year round. It is important that patients with bronchitis stop smoking and avoid polluted places as much as possible such as city centres or factories. If steroids/antibiotics have been taken for some time, advice is needed for actions to boost your own auto-immune system. A balanced diet including appropriate vitamin and mineral supplements can also be of great value - see page 0.1. Avoid foods as eczema.

POINTS

B13 This lies one and a half thumb's width to each side of the centre of the spine at the level of the third thoracic vertebra.

Cv17 This lies in a depression at the centre of the front of the chest on a line joining both nipples.

S40 This lies on a mid-point from the knee to the ankle, three fingers width back towards the fibula (ie., the outside of the lower leg), from the ridge on the front of the shin.

Sp6 This lies one hand's width (four fingers) up from the inner ankle joint. It lies just behind the tibia bone at this point.

Ear Ear point

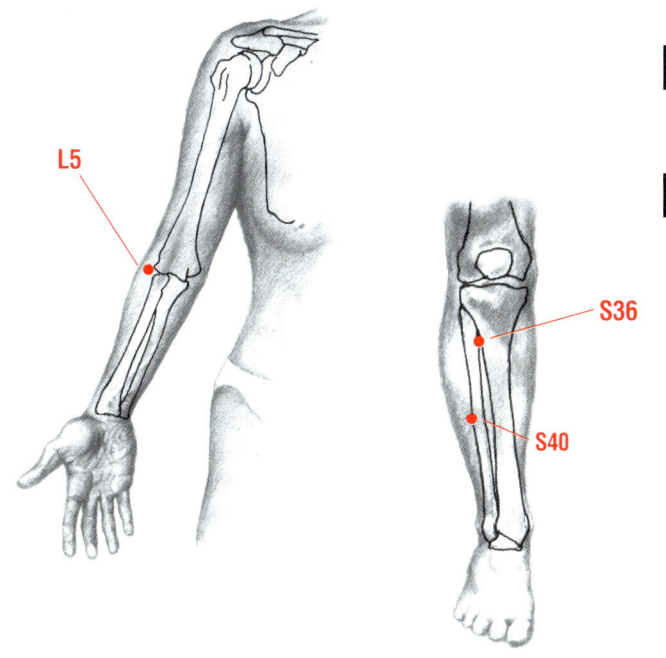

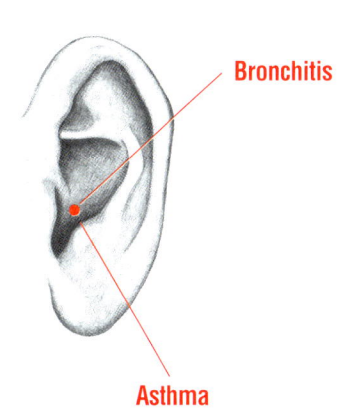

6. CHEST DISEASES

Croup - Laryngeal Tracheitis

Croup is characterised by severe laryngeal spasm, causing great difficulty in breathing. It is often due to a virus, and can be greatly helped by humidifying the atmosphere (keeping a kettle boiling in the room). Electro-Acupuncture should be used on this condition, treatment often needs to be given half hourly until the acute situation settles. A balanced diet including appropriate vitamin and mineral supplements can also be of great value - see page 0.1.

POINTS

Cv17 This lies in a depression at the centre of the front of the chest on a line joining both nipples.

Cv22 This lies in the hollow directly over the front of the larynx in the centre of the lower part of the neck.

L5 This lies on the thumb side of the elbow joint at the edge of the elbow crease.

L11 This is situated on the outer side of the nail bed of the thumb.

Li4 This lies on the side of the bone which runs from the forefinger knuckle down towards the wrist. See page 8 for a detailed description of this point.

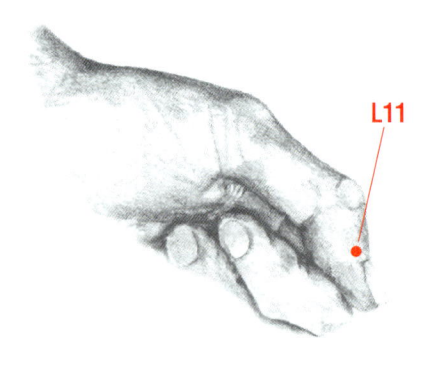

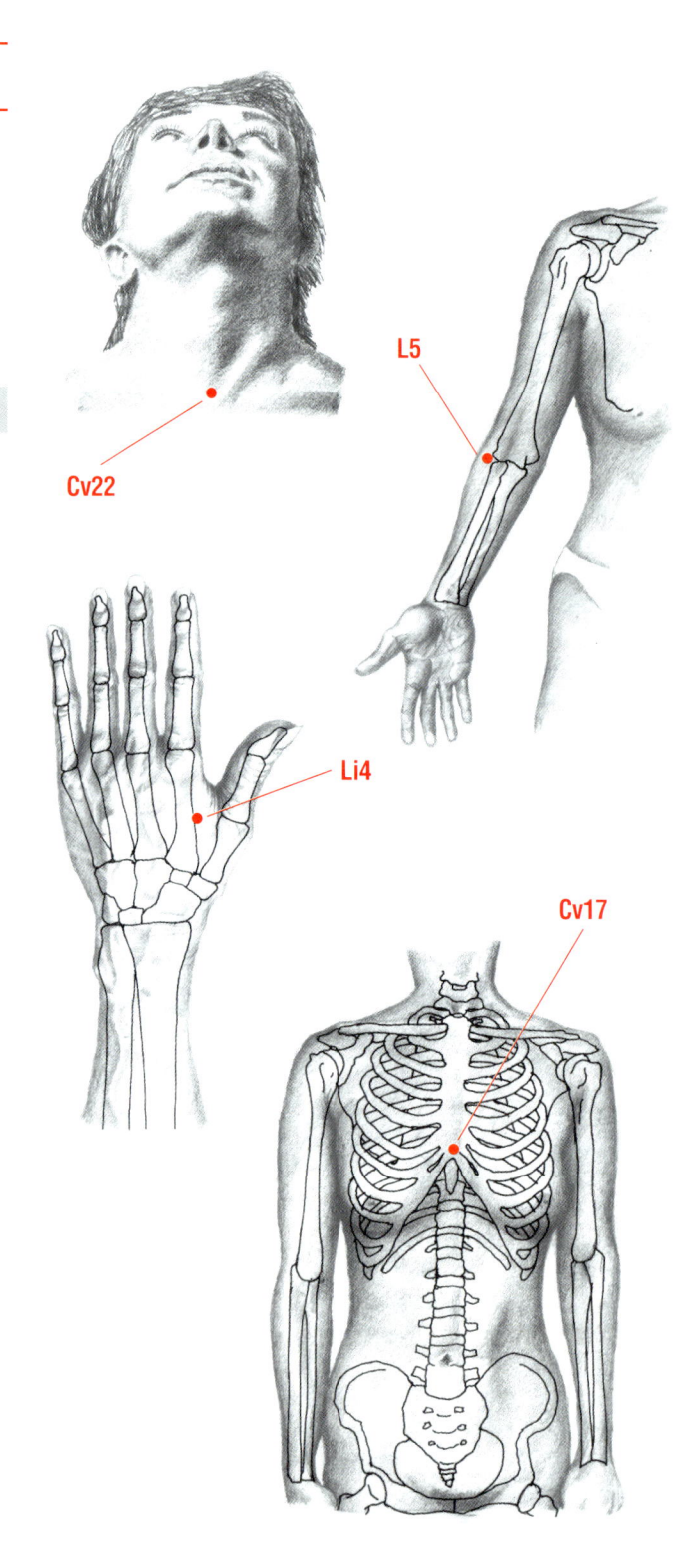

7. GENITO-URINARY PROBLEMS

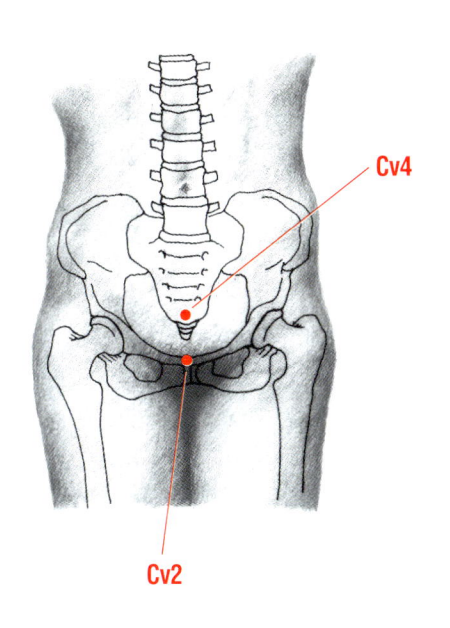

Bed-wetting (enuresis)

Electro-Acupuncture offers useful assistance to enuresis and is particularly worth trying in children.

POINTS

Cv4 This lies two thumb's width above the pubic bone.

K3 This lies midway between the tip of the inner ankle bone and the achilles tendon (in the hollow)

Sp6 This lies one hand's width (four fingers) up from the inner ankle joint. It lies just behind the tibia bone at this point.

Ear Ear point

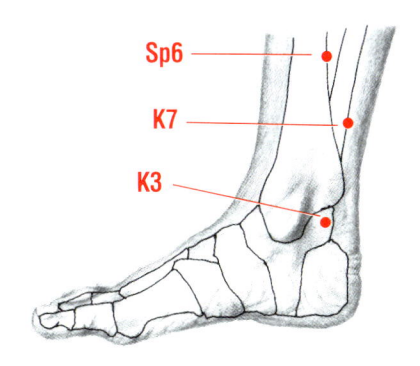

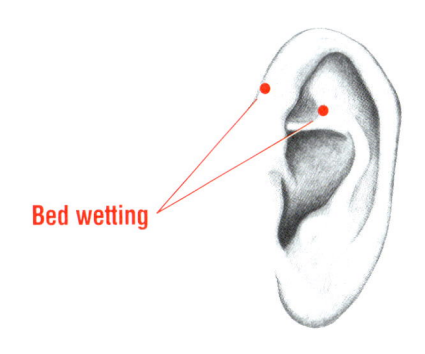

7. GENITO-URINARY PROBLEMS

Prostate problems and Irritable bladder

Difficulty in passing urine due to prostate obstruction, can be treated with Electro-Acupuncture if obstruction is not severe. Irritable bladder can also be treated in this way. If no benefit is observed it is important to seek proper medical advice. A herbal preparation has proved to be helpful in treating this condition.

POINTS

B23 This lies one and a half thumb's width to each side of the second lumbar vertebra.

B28 This lies one and half thumb's width to each side of the centre of the top the sacrum.

B40 This lies directly behind the knee joint in the centre of the crease.

Cv2 This lies just on the upper edge of the pubic bone in the mid-line.

Cv4 This lies two thumb's width above the pubic bone.

K3 This lies midway between the tip of the inner ankle bone and the achilles tendon (in the hollow).

K7 This lies two thumb's width above the bone forming the inner ankle joint.

Sp6 This lies one hand's width (four fingers) up from the inner ankle joint. It lies just behind the tibia bone at this point.

Ear Ear point

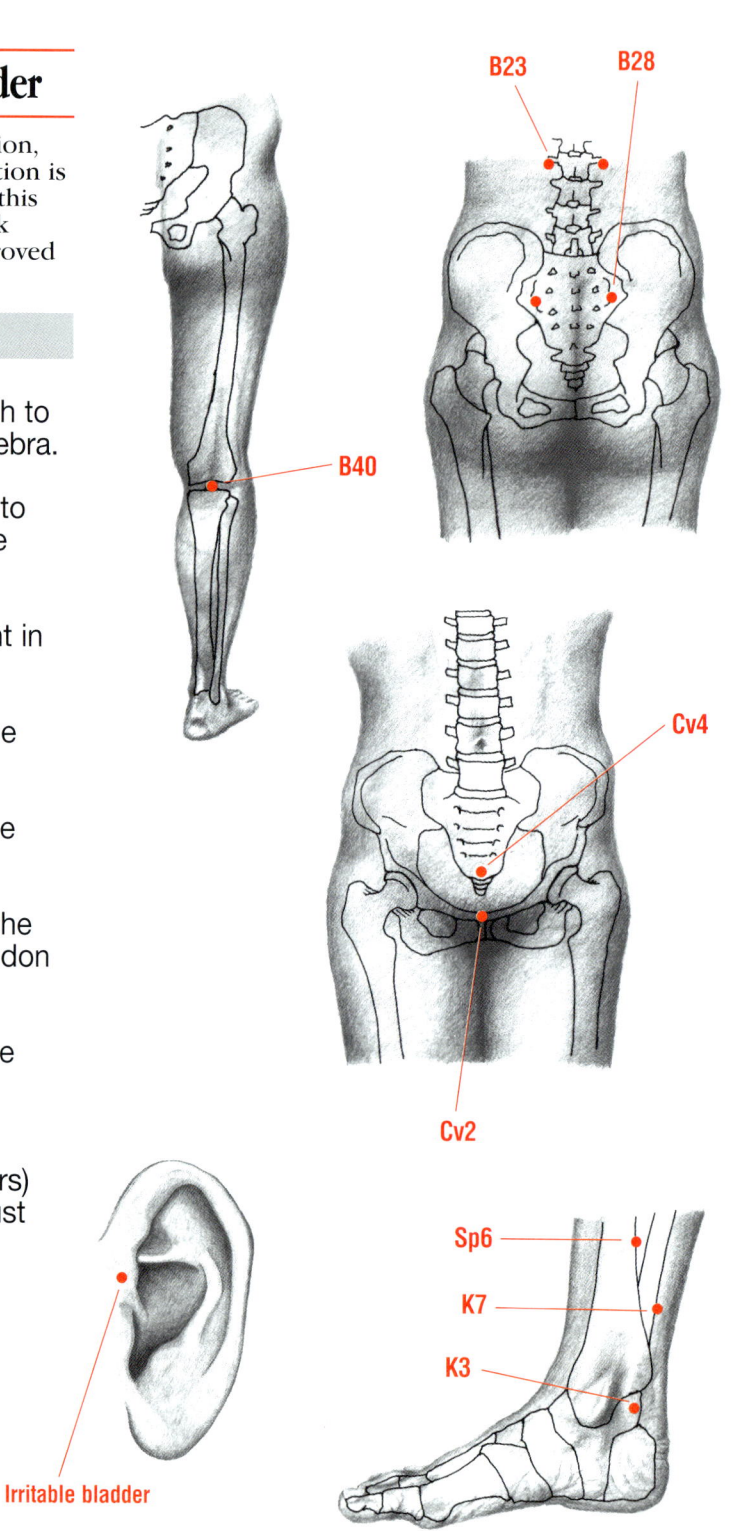

Irritable bladder

7. GENITO-URINARY PROBLEMS

Urinary incontinence

In older people urinary incontinence is common. Also in women who have had many children, there is sometimes difficulty in holding the urine especially when coughing or straining.

POINTS

B23 This lies one and a half thumb's width to each side of the second lumbar vertebra.

B28 This lies one and half thumb's width to each side of the centre of the top the sacrum.

B40 This lies directly behind the knee joint in the centre of the crease.

Cv2 This lies just on the upper edge of the pubic bone in the mid-line.

K7 This lies two thumb's width above the bone forming the inner ankle joint.

Liv3 This lies in between the tendons of the big toe and the first toe, two thumb's width towards the top of the foot from the web.

Sp6 This lies one hand's width (four fingers) up from the inner ankle joint. It lies just behind the tibia bone at this point.

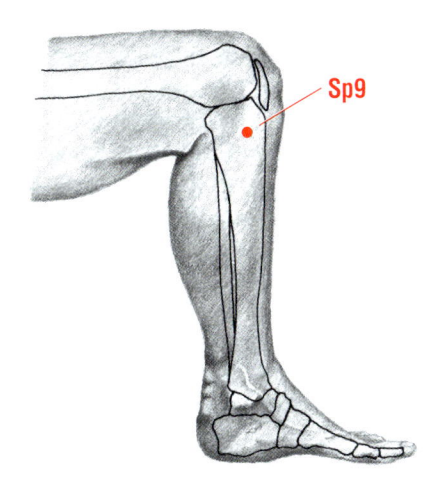

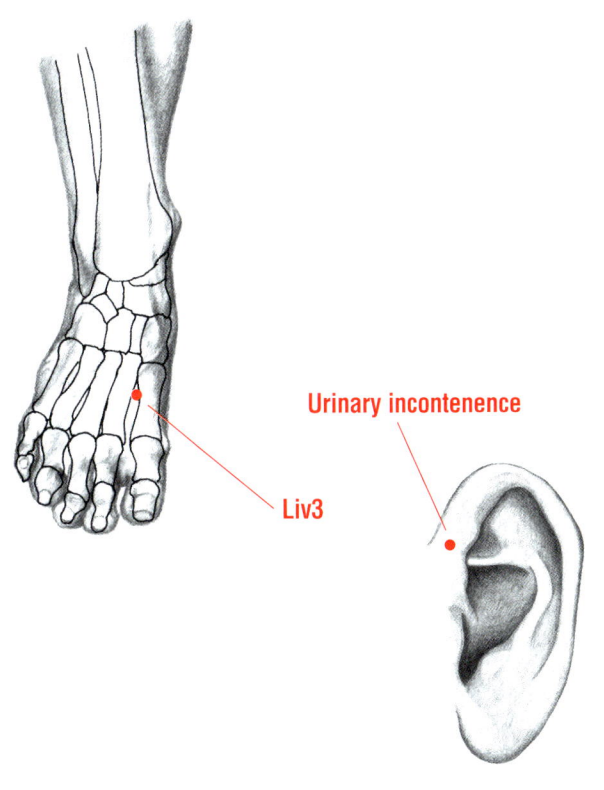

Sp9 This lies just below the inside of the kneecap and below the top of the tibia. This point is usually tender when pressed with a finger tip.

Ear Ear point

7. GENITO-URINARY PROBLEMS

Urinary retention

This occurs most often in elderly men and is most commonly due to enlargement of the prostate gland situated at the base of the bladder. If it is recurrent, it is important that the opinion of a urological surgeon is sought. The approach with Electro-Acupuncture can be very useful if the retention is caught early.

POINTS

B28 This lies one and half thumb's width to each side of the centre of the top the sacrum.

Sp6 This lies one hand's width (four fingers) up from the inner ankle joint. It lies just behind the tibia bone at this point.

Sp9 This lies just below the inside of the kneecap and below the top of the tibia. This point is usually tender when pressed with a finger tip.

Ear Ear point

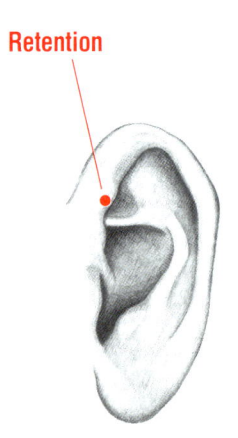

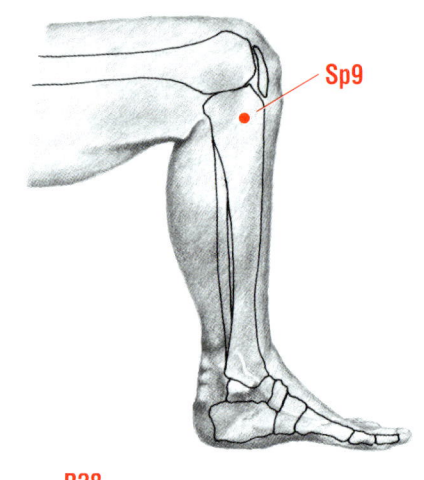

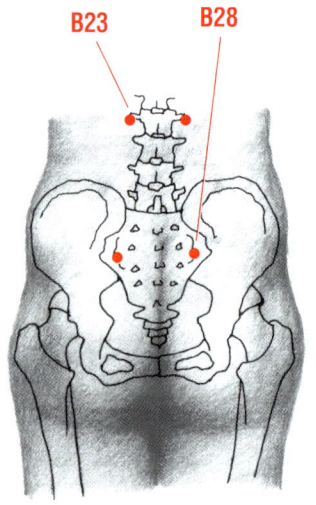

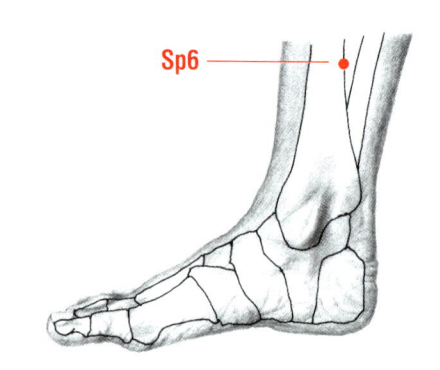

Retention

7.4

7. GENITO-URINARY PROBLEMS

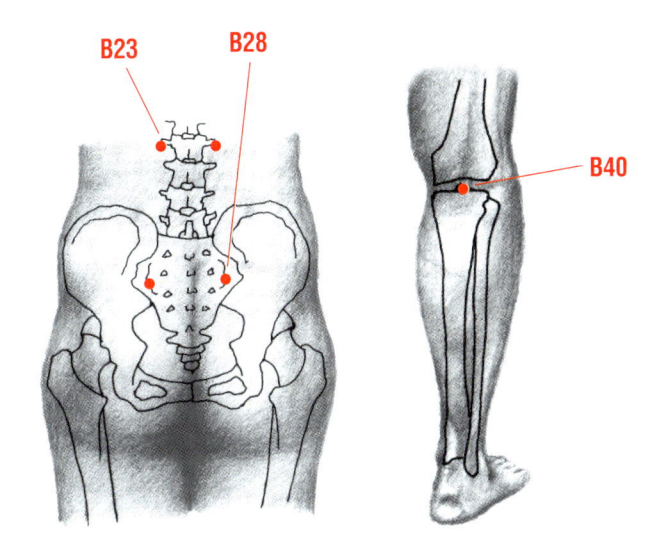

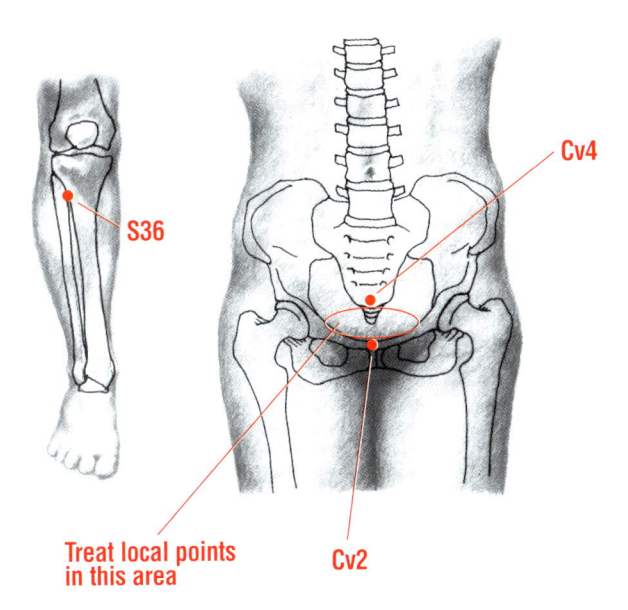

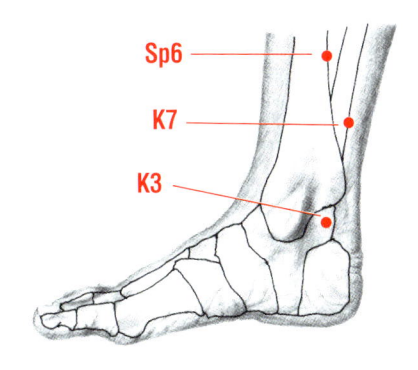

Cystitis

Inflammation of the lining of the bladder, can be treated with Electro-Acupuncture. This is most common in newly married or pregnant women. If no benefit is observed it is important to seek proper medical advice.

POINTS

B23 This lies one and a half thumb's width to each side of the second lumbar vertebra.

B28 This lies one and half thumb's width to each side of the centre of the top the sacrum.

B40 This lies directly behind the knee joint in the centre of the crease.

Cv2 This lies just on the upper edge of the pubic bone in the mid-line.

Cv4 This lies two thumb's width above the pubic bone.

K3 This lies midway between the tip of the inner ankle bone and the achilles tendon (in the hollow)

K7 This lies two thumb's width above the bone forming the inner ankle joint.

Sp6 This lies one hand's width (four fingers) up from the inner ankle joint. It lies just behind the tibia bone at this point.

Ah Shi Any local tender acupuncture points to be found in the area shown opposite that give a reaction when stimulated

8. MISCELLANEOUS DISORDERS

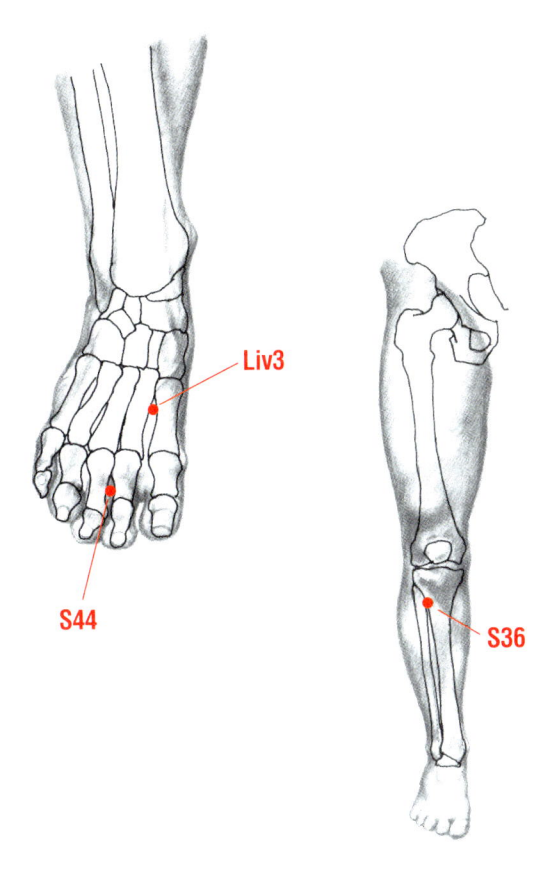

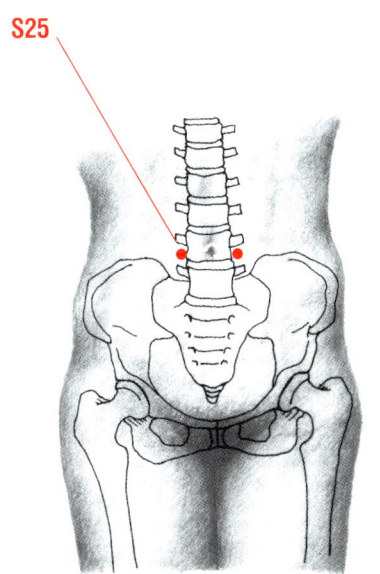

Appetite Reduction

Electro-Acupuncture may prove useful when used in conjunction with a balanced, healthy diet. A combination of chromium picolinate and herbs has proven to be highly effective in reducing food and sugar cravings - see page 0.1.

POINTS

Liv3 — This lies in between the tendons of the big toe and the first toe, two thumb's width towards the top of the foot from the web.

S25 — This is situated two thumb's width to each side of the navel.

S36 — This lies three thumb's width below the joint under the kneecap lying on the outer side of the knee. One finger's width back from the sharp edge of the shin bone.

S44 — This lies in the web between the second and third toes.

Ear — Ear point

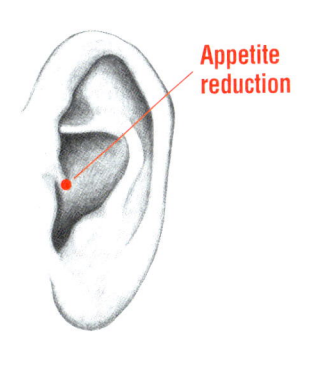

8. MISCELLANEOUS DISORDERS

Conjunctivitis

Conjunctivitis is inflammation of the outer coating of the eyeball. If this is recurrent then an ophthalmologic opinion should be sought. Treat with colloidal silver (see page 0.1) - apply drops to the eye.

POINTS

Liv3 — This lies between the tendons of the big toe and the first toe, two thumb's width towards the top of the foot from the web.

S36 — This lies three thumb's width below the joint under the kneecap lying on the outer side of the knee. One finger's width back from the sharp edge of the shin bone.

Taiyang — This lies one thumb's width behind the outer edge of the eye. It lies in the centre of the temples.

Ear — Ear point

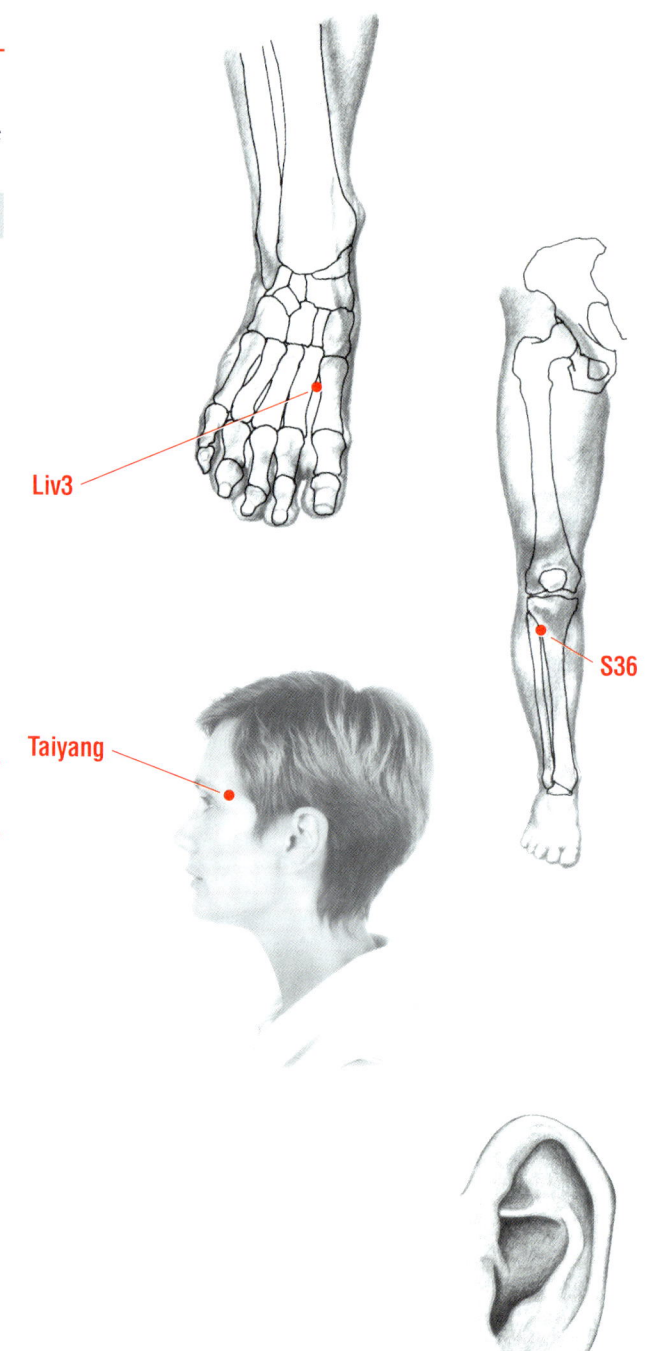

Immune Deficiency

Treat these daily, when suffering from anything that affects the immune system such as a viral infection (i.e. colds, laryngitis, etc.) These points can be useful in some mild cases of post viral syndrome or M.E., in these cases treatment needs to be given twice a day. A balanced diet including appropriate vitamin and mineral supplements can also be of great value - see page 0.1.

POINTS

Cv6 — This lies one and a half thumb's width below the navel.

S36 — This lies three thumb's width below the joint under the kneecap lying on the outer side of the knee. One finger's width back from the sharp edge of the shin bone.

Sp6 — This lies one hand's width (four fingers) up from the inner ankle joint. It lies just behind the tibia bone at this point.

8. MISCELLANEOUS DISORDERS

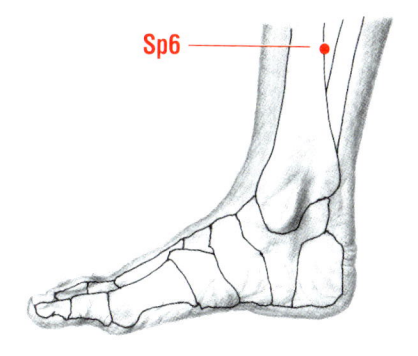

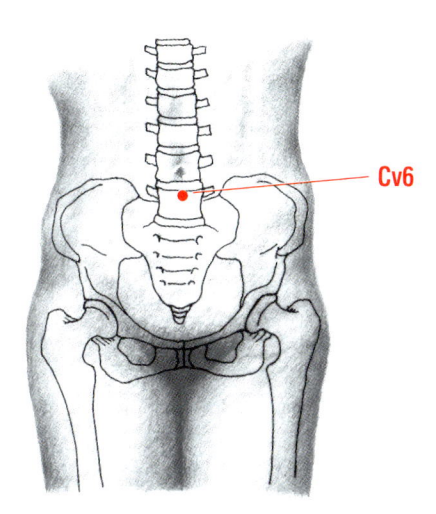

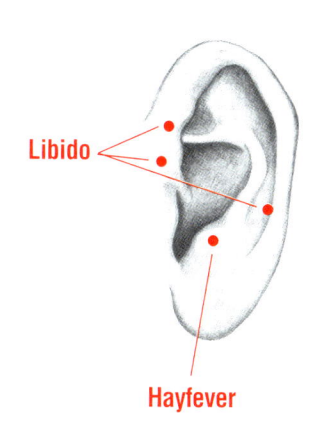

Hay Fever

Hay fever is an allergic reaction to grass and flower pollens and is therefore a seasonal affliction. Electro-Acupuncture can be useful in treating this problem and will sometimes suffice. A homeopathic approach using homeopathic grass and flower pollens is a worthwhile adjunct. If an attack has started, treat Sinusitis (and/or asthma) points as well for relief. A balanced diet including appropriate vitamin and mineral supplements can also be of great value - see page 0.1.

POINTS

Liv3 — This lies in between the tendons of the big toe and the first toe, two thumb's width towards the top of the foot from the web.

S36 — This lies three thumb's width below the joint under the kneecap lying on the outer side of the knee. One finger's width back from the sharp edge of the shin bone.

Ear — Ear point.

Decreased libido

Electro-Acupuncture can be a useful approach to decreased libido and will work in some cases. This treatment cannot be regarded as aphrodisiac. Also consider anxiety and stress points. A balanced diet including appropriate vitamin and mineral supplements, particularly zinc, can also help - see page 0.1.

POINTS

Cv6 — This lies one and a half thumb's width below the navel.

S36 — This lies three thumb's width below the joint under the kneecap lying on the outer side of the knee. One finger's width back from the sharp edge of the shin bone.

Sp6 — This lies one hand's width (four fingers) up from the inner ankle joint. It lies just behind the tibia bone at this point.

Ear — Ear points.

8. MISCELLANEOUS DISORDERS

Stroke Recovery

Electro-Acupuncture can be useful to hasten recovery from a stroke. Possibly, due to lack of early attention, some people never fully recover from a stroke, therefore treatment at an early stage is important. Do not however, under any circumstances start treating in this way until one week after the stroke. A stroke will affect either the arm, leg or both.

Treat twice daily in the first instance and combine this with exercises attempting to use the arm or leg (or both if both are affected), as much as possible. It is advisable to consult a physiotherapist as to the best exercises for your particular case.

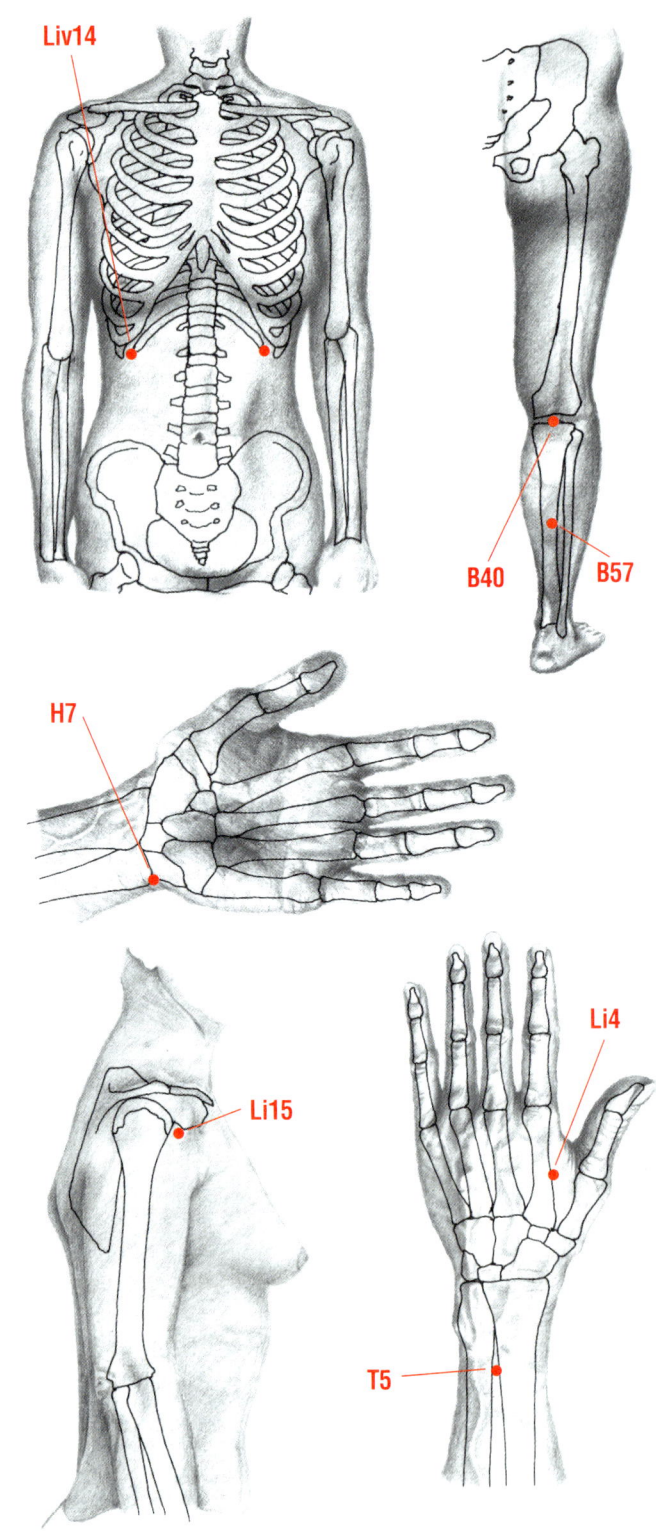

POINTS : ARM

H7 — This lies on the little finger side of the palm wrist crease just inside the small prominent bone.

Li4 — This lies on the side of the bone which runs from the forefinger knuckle down towards the wrist. See page 8 for a detailed description of this point.

Li15 — This lies just in front of the shoulder joint, in a depression which is produced when the arm is lifted above the head, it can be tender with finger tip pressure.

Liv14 — This lies at the tip of the ninth rib, approximately halfway along the lower end of the ribcage on the front of the body from the mid-line to the side.

Ear — Ear points.

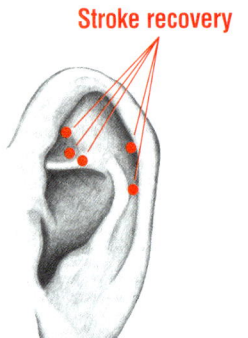

Continued on next page...

8. MISCELLANEOUS DISORDERS

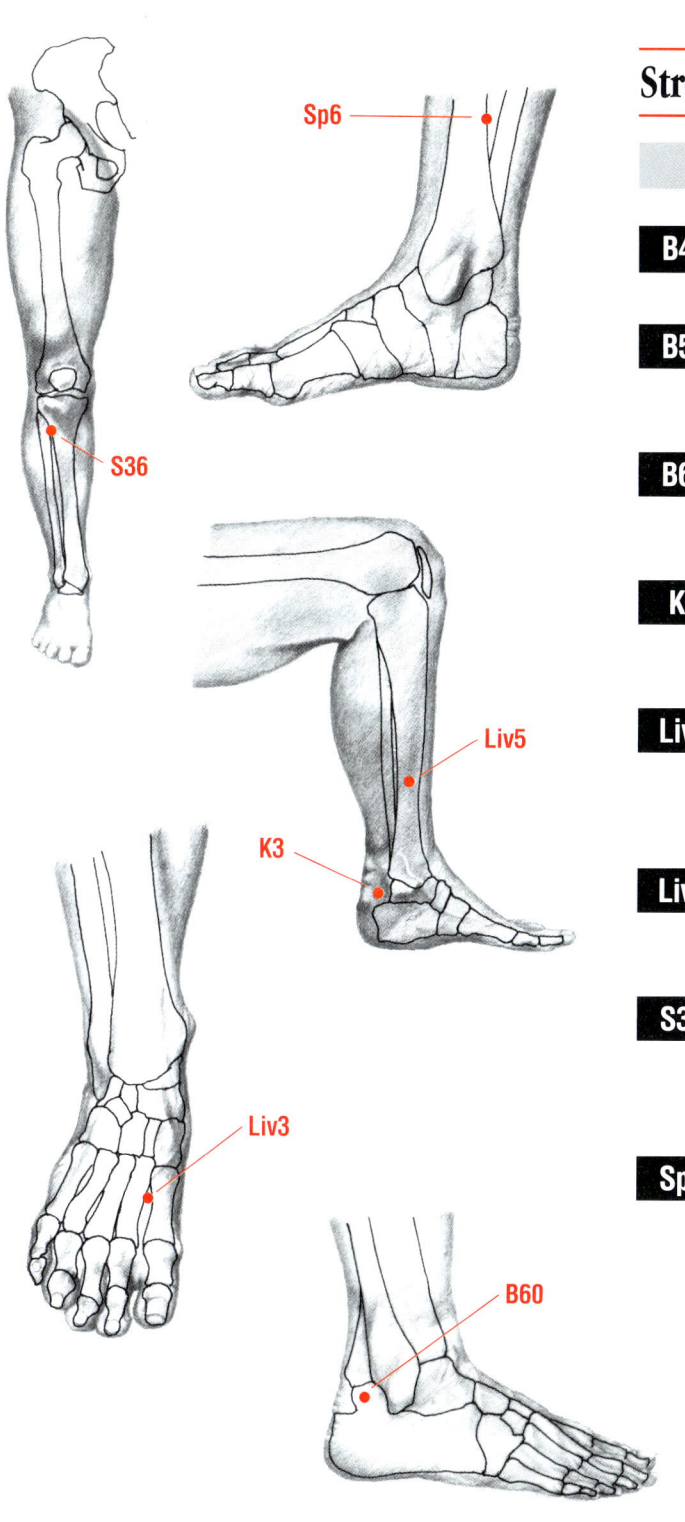

Stroke Recovery - *continued*

POINTS : LEG

B40 This lies directly behind the knee joint in the centre of the crease.

B57 This lies in the centre of the back of the calf, just where the fleshy mass of muscle narrows down into tendon.

B60 This lies midway between the tip of the outer ankle bone and the achilles tendon (in the hollow).

K3 This lies midway between the tip of the inner ankle bone and the achilles tendon (in the hollow)

Liv3 This lies in between the tendons of the big toe and the first toe, two thumb's width towards the top of the foot from the web.

Liv5 This is five fingers above the inner ankle bone, over the surface of the tibia, which is the main bone in the lower leg.

S36 This lies three thumb's width below the joint under the kneecap lying on the outer side of the knee. One finger's width back from the sharp edge of the shin bone.

Sp6 This lies one hand's width (four fingers) up from the inner ankle joint. It lies just behind the tibia bone at this point.

Treatment continued ▶

8. MISCELLANEOUS DISORDERS

Stroke Recovery - *Scalp Treatment*

Scalp acupuncture is an important way of treating strokes. There is an increasing body of very good clinical-trial evidence to indicate that stroke sufferers, if treated in this way, can recover much more rapidly and completely than sufferers treated in the conventional manner.

Because the nerves from the body cross over when they reach the brain, the side of the head opposite the side of the body which is affected should be treated. You are effectively treating the area of the scalp directly overlying the particular part of the brain which is sending messages out to the affected part.

The areas to treat are based on the Motor Area Line (see upper diagram). The upper one fifth of this line relates to paralysis of the lower limb of the *opposite side*. The middle two fifths relate to paralysis of the upper limb of the *opposite side*. The lower two fifths relate to facial paralysis on the *opposite side*, loss of ability to speak, dribbling saliva and difficulty in swallowing.

The most common strokes involve loss of use in one or a number of these areas, so treatment ought to be given on these areas - intensively in the first instance - as soon as the stroke has happened if possible. Initially as much as 10 times a day, in other words hourly. The number of treatments given can be reduced considerably as and when the stroke starts and continues to improve.

If you have a stroke which involves sensory loss then you need to treat the Sensory Area Line which is just behind the motor area line (see lower diagram).

The upper one fifth of the sensory area line is used when there is loss of sensation and/or tingling in the lower back and leg of the *opposite side.* The middle two fifths of the sensory area line are to be used when there is loss of sensation or tingling of the upper limb of the *opposite side.* The lower two fifths of the sensory area line are for loss of sensation and tingling in the head and facial region of the *opposite side*.

There is also a specific area which is the Speech Area (see lower diagram). This should be treated on **both sides** of the head if there is any speech problem as well as the other areas indicated.

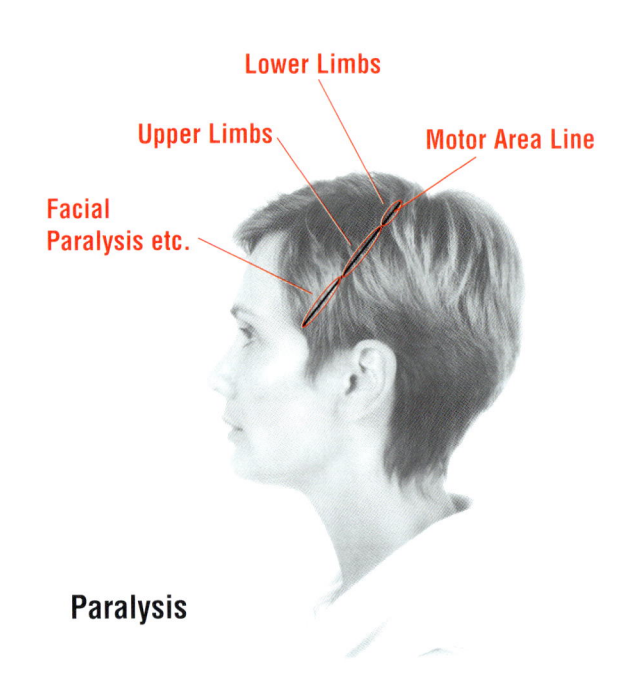

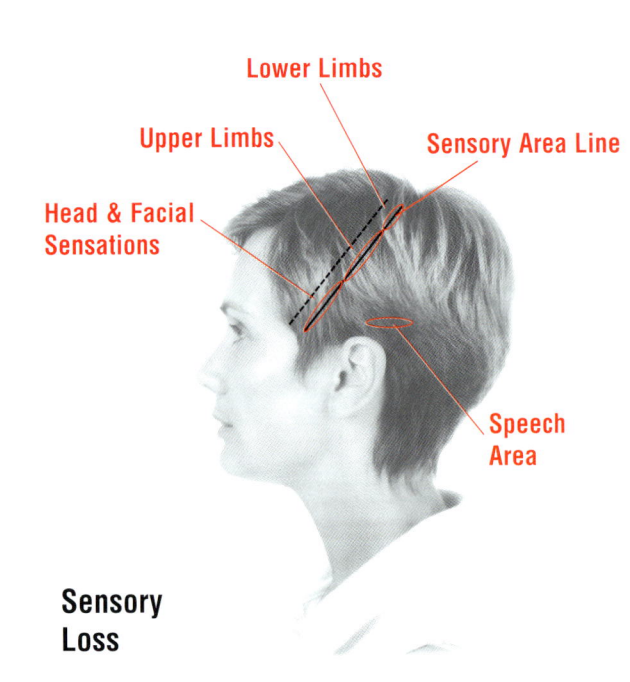

Paralysis

- Lower Limbs
- Upper Limbs
- Motor Area Line
- Facial Paralysis etc.

Sensory Loss

- Lower Limbs
- Upper Limbs
- Sensory Area Line
- Head & Facial Sensations
- Speech Area

8. MISCELLANEOUS DISORDERS

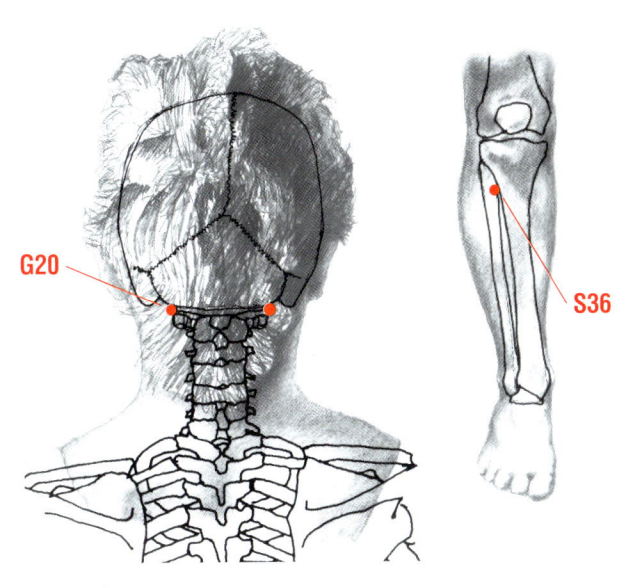

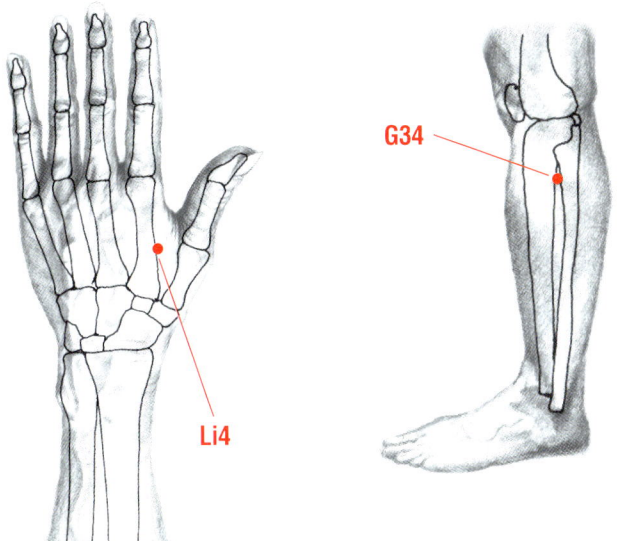

Restless Legs

Electro-Acupuncture can be a useful approach and has proven to be effective in some cases.

POINTS

G20   Just below the skull bone and outside the muscle bulge.

G34   This is just below and in front of the knobbly head of the fibula, which is the bone just below the outer side of knee. This point is in a slight depression and is sometimes tender when pressed with a finger tip.

H7   This lies on the little finger side of the palm wrist crease just inside the small prominent bone.

Li4   This lies on the side of the bone which runs from the forefinger knuckle down towards the wrist. See page 8 for a detailed description of this point.

S36   This lies three thumb's width below the joint under the kneecap lying on the outer side of the knee. One finger's width back from the sharp edge of the shin bone.

Sp6   This lies one hand's width (four fingers) up from the inner ankle joint. It lies just behind the tibia bone at this point.

Ear   Ear point - Shenmen

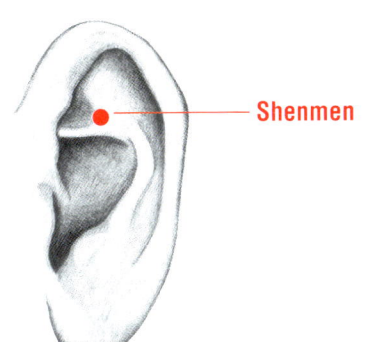

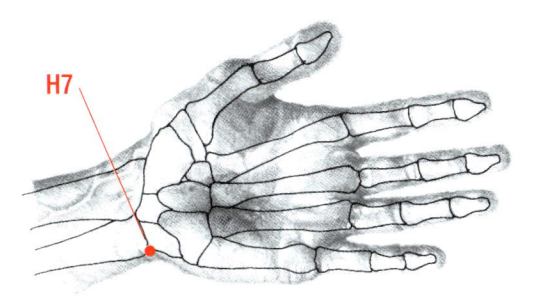

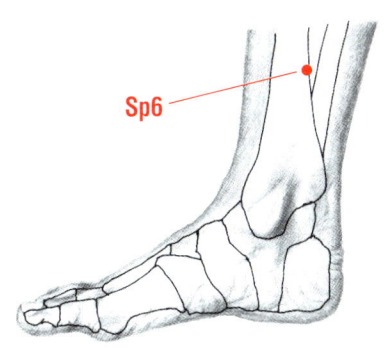

8. MISCELLANEOUS DISORDERS

Insomnia, Snoring and Sleep Apnoea

This is lack of sleep, which most commonly occurs for no apparent reason. Purely symptomatic approaches (sleeping tablets) therefore tend to be have been the rule. Electro-Acupuncture can help reduce dependence on these sleep inducing drugs. Consider anxiety and stress points. You should also abstain from food after 7pm.

POINTS

Gv20 This point lies right at the top of the head where two imaginary lines cross, one drawn from the top of one ear to the top of the other ear, the other line drawn from the top of the nose right over the top of the skull to the back of the skull. Where these lines cross is Gv20.

H7 This lies on the little finger side of the palm wrist crease just inside the small prominent bone.

K3 This lies midway between the tip of the inner ankle bone and the achilles tendon (in the hollow)

L7 This lies one and a half thumb's width up from the inside wrist crease on the thumb side close to the radial pulse.

Li4 This lies on the side of the bone which runs from the forefinger knuckle down towards the wrist. See page 8 for a detailed description of this point.

Sp6 This lies one hand's width (four fingers) up from the inner ankle joint. It lies just behind the tibia bone at this point.

Yintang This lies directly between the eyebrows, just above the bridge of the nose.

Ear Ear point for Snoring - Shenmen

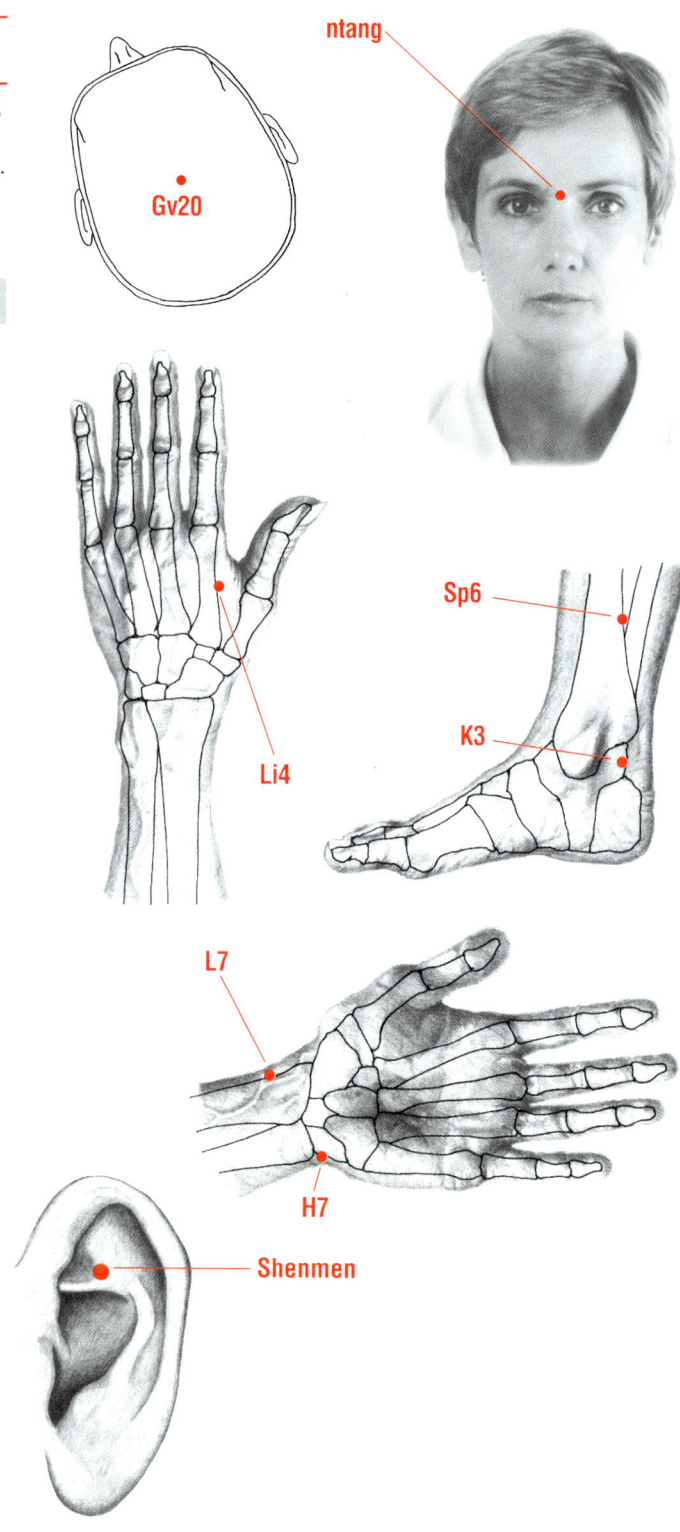

8. MISCELLANEOUS DISORDERS

Fainting Attacks

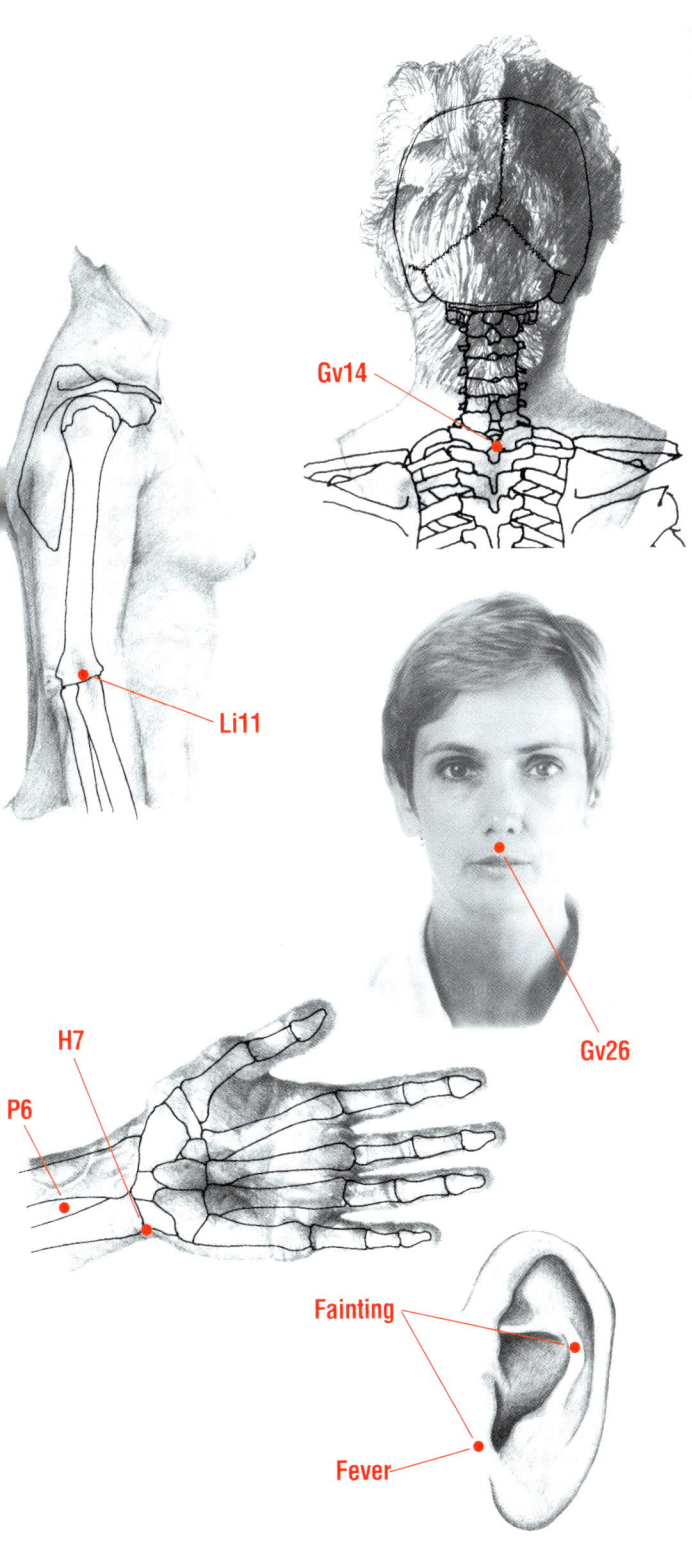

If fainting attacks occur regularly then a medical opinion should be sought. It is perfectly reasonable to use Electro-Acupuncture as detailed here.

POINTS

Gv26 — This is at the junction of the upper third and lower two thirds of a line joining the nose and the middle of the upper lip.

H7 — This lies on the little finger side of the palm wrist crease just inside the small prominent bone.

P6 — This lies two thumb's width up from the palm wrist crease towards the elbow, directly in the centre between the two tendons.

Ear — Ear point

Fever

Electro-Acupuncture offers a symptomatic approach to fever but the cause must also be treated. Treat with colloidal silver - take ½ teaspoon under the tongue (see page 0.1).

POINTS

Gv14 — This lies just below the most prominent knob of bone at the base of the neck in the mid-line.

Li4 — This lies on the side of the bone which runs from the forefinger knuckle down towards the wrist. See page 8 for a detailed description of this point.

Li11 — This lies 2cm beyond the end of the outer elbow crease with the arm bent.

Ear — Ear point

8. MISCELLANEOUS DISORDERS

Fluid Retention

This may arise for many reasons. In women it is often due too hormonal imbalance. In some cases it can be due to heart failure, particularly in elderly people. In these cases a proper diagnosis is necessary. Electro-Acupuncture can be useful in treating some cases of fluid retention. A balanced diet including appropriate vitamin and mineral supplements can be of great value - see page 0.1.

POINTS

B23 This lies one and a half thumb's width to each side of the second lumbar vertebra.

K3 This lies midway between the tip of the inner ankle bone and the achilles tendon (in the hollow)

Liv2 This is one finger's width up from the web between the big toe and the second toe tendons.

Liv3 This lies between the tendons of the big toe and the first toe, two thumb's width towards the top of the foot from the web.

S36 This lies three thumb's width below the joint under the kneecap lying on the outer side of the knee. One finger's width back from the sharp edge of the shin bone.

Sp6 This lies one hand's width (four fingers) up from the inner ankle joint. It lies just behind the tibia bone at this point.

Sp9 This lies just below the inside of the kneecap and below the top of the tibia. This point is usually tender when pressed with a finger tip.

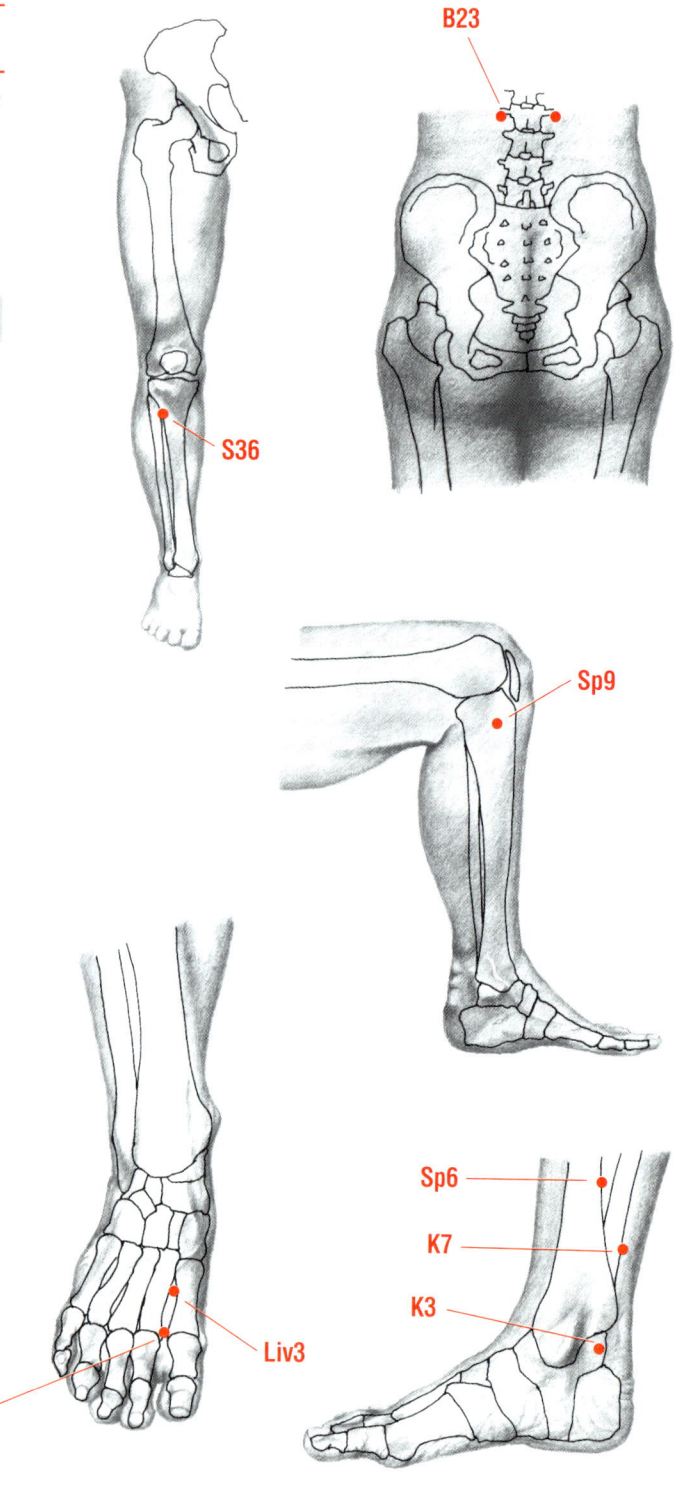

8.10

8. MISCELLANEOUS DISORDERS

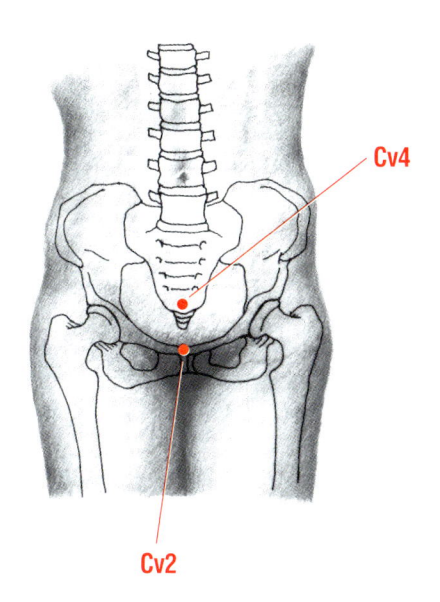

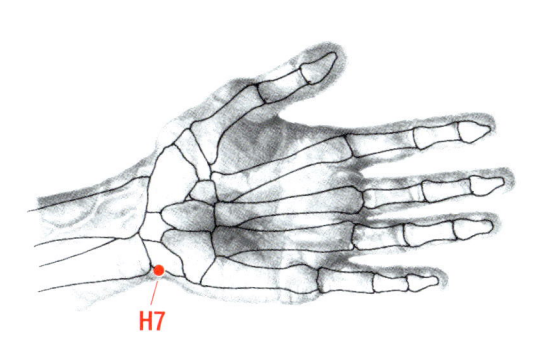

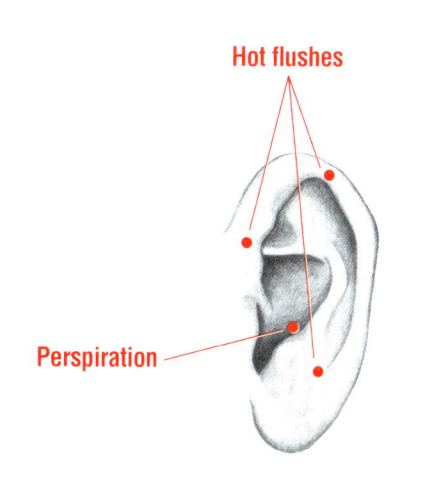

Excessive perspiration

Sweating can occur for many reasons such as fever, general debilitation, stress and tension. In some cases Electro-Acupuncture can be a useful treatment.

POINTS

H7 — This lies on the little finger side of the palm wrist crease just inside the small prominent bone.

K7 — This lies two thumb's width above the bone forming the inner ankle joint.

Ear — Ear point

Hot flushes - Menopause problems

Hot flushes most often occur during the menopause, and are due to a hormonal imbalance that occurs at this time. They are particularly troublesome to treat and Electro-Acupuncture offers a safe and often effective method of coping with them. Treatment should be carried out on a regular basis even though at the time of treatment no hot flush may be occurring. A balanced diet including appropriate vitamin and mineral supplements can be of great value - see page 0.1.

POINTS

S36 — This lies three thumb's width below the joint under the kneecap lying on the outer side of the knee. One finger's width back from the sharp edge of the shin bone.

Sp6 — This lies one hand's width (four fingers) up from the inner ankle joint. It lies just behind the tibia bone at this point.

Ear — Ear points

8. MISCELLANEOUS DISORDERS

Hyperactivity - Attention Deficiency Syndrome

This is common in young children, particularly little boys. There are often associated food allergies, commonly sugar, food additives and colourings, milk and dairy products. Avoiding these items in the diet is an important part of treatment. **Important:** a balanced diet including appropriate vitamin and mineral supplements is essential - see page 0.1.

POINTS

Gv20 This point lies right at the top of the head where two imaginary lines cross, one drawn from the top of one ear to the top of the other ear, the other line drawn from the top of the nose right over the top of the skull to the back of the skull. Where these lines cross is Gv20.

H3 This is at the end of the inner elbow crease.

H7 This lies on the little finger side of the palm wrist crease just inside the small prominent bone.

Li4 This lies on the side of the bone which runs from the forefinger knuckle down towards the wrist. See page 8 for a detailed description of this point.

P6 This lies two thumb's width up from the palm wrist crease towards the elbow, directly in the centre between the two tendons.

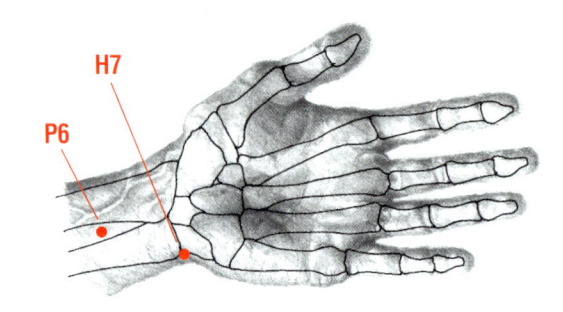

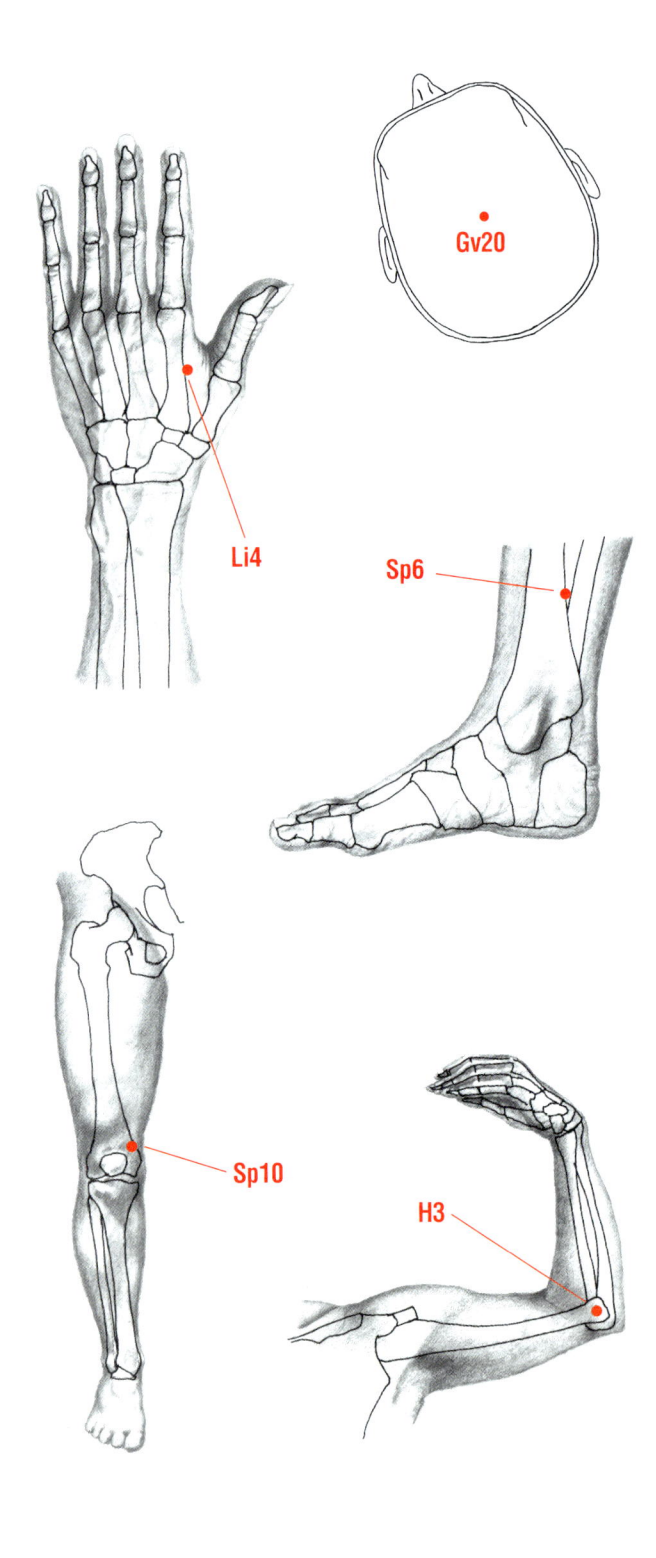

8. MISCELLANEOUS DISORDERS

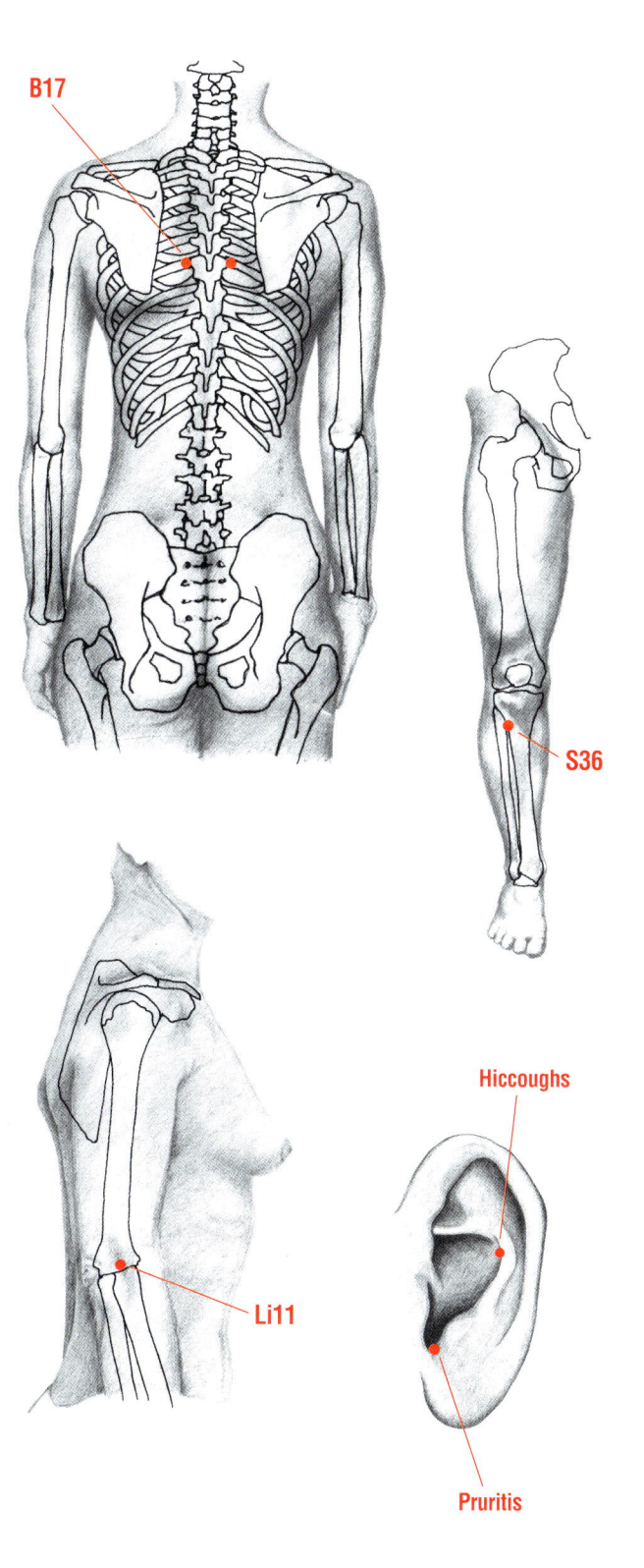

Hiccoughs (Hiccups)

Hiccoughs can be a particularly troublesome complaint. Electro-Acupuncture offers useful help. It is often worth combining this with drinking a glass of cold water whilst holding the nose and therefore holding the breath. This has the effect of splinting the diaphragm as Hiccoughs are a spasmodic contraction of the diaphragm.

POINTS

B17 — This point lies one and a half thumb's width each side of the mid-line at the level of the seventh thoracic vertebra.

S36 — This lies three thumb's width below the joint under the kneecap lying on the outer side of the knee. One finger's width back from the sharp edge of the shin bone.

Ear — Ear point

Pruritis (itching)

If Pruritis is accompanied by a rash medical advice should be sought. Electro-Acupuncture offers a useful approach in the treatment of itching in general, but if there is an underlying cause a doctor's advice should again be sought.

POINTS

Li11 — This lies 2cm beyond the end of the outer elbow crease with the arm bent.

Sp6 — This lies one hand's width (four fingers) up from the inner ankle joint. It lies just behind the tibia bone at this point.

Sp10 — This lies at the lower end of the muscular bulge, two fingers above the inside of the knee cap.

Ear — Ear point

8. MISCELLANEOUS DISORDERS

Chronic Fatigue Syndrome (M.E.)

This is also known as post viral syndrome or M.E. (Myalgic Encephalomyelitis). M.E. is characterised by extreme fatigue, aching muscles, depression, poor memory and in many cases abdominal symptoms (bloating and flatulence). Electro-Acupuncture can help in a majority of cases, but it should be combined with other measures such as the following

1. Avoid sugar, coffee, alcohol, milk and dairy products and processed foods (especially starchy foods). Eat as much fresh food, especially vegetables, as possible.
2. Take plenty of rest. Do NOT push yourself beyond reasonable limits.
3. Take a full spectrum of colloidal minerals, high doses of B group vitamins, zinc and magnesium (have a magnesium blood test).
4. Avoid polluted places (such as city centres or factories) as much as possible.
5. A cleanse and detox is essential, including an anti-fungal, antibacterial regime.

   Treat twice daily. Call the HelpLine for a protocol.

POINTS

Cv6 This lies one and a half thumb's width below the navel.

K3 This lies midway between the tip of the inner ankle bone and the achilles tendon (in the hollow)

Liv3 This lies in between the tendons of the big toe and the first toe, two thumb's width towards the top of the foot from the web.

S36 This lies three thumb's width below the joint under the kneecap lying on the outer side of the knee. One finger's width back from the sharp edge of the shin bone.

Sp6 This lies one hand's width (four fingers) up from the inner ankle joint. It lies just behind the tibia bone at this point.

Continued on next page...

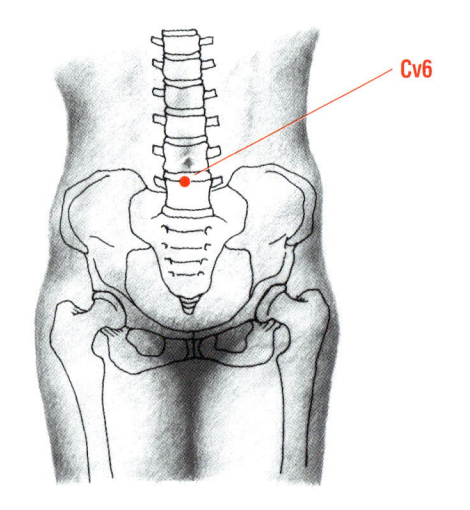

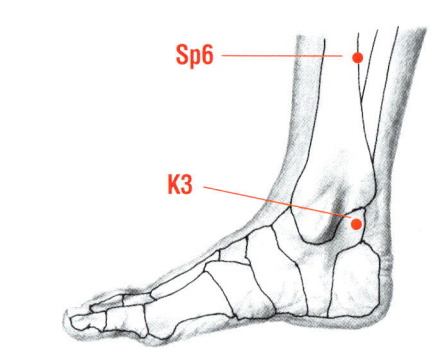

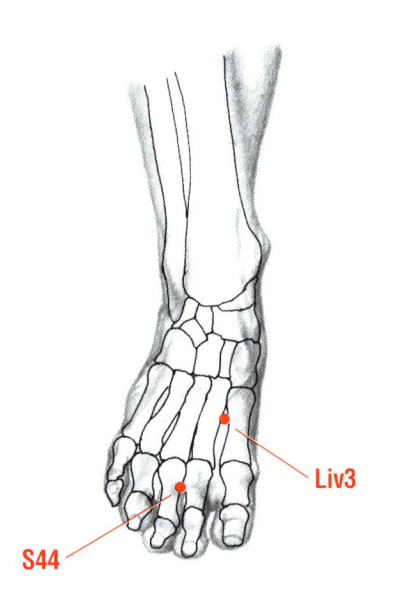

8. MISCELLANEOUS DISORDERS

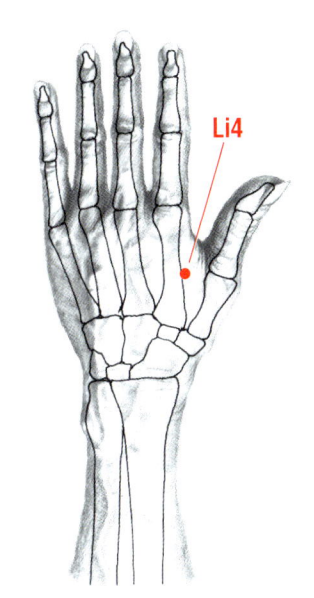

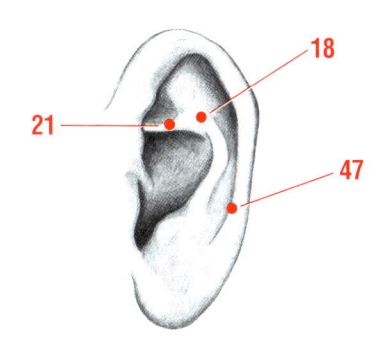

Chronic Fatigue Syndrome - *continued*

Gv20 This point lies right at the top of the head where two imaginary lines cross, one drawn from the top of one ear to the top of the other ear, the other line drawn from the top of the nose right over the top of the skull to the back of the skull. Where these lines cross is Gv20.

Li4 This lies on the side of the bone which runs from the forefinger knuckle down towards the wrist. See page 8 for a detailed description of this point.

M.E. - *an alternative Protocol*

This protocol has been developed by Dr. N. D. Parkin M.D. F.R.C.Path., D.C.P. at the Pilgrim Trust Hospital, Boston, Lincolnshire, UK. It has been used successfully as the primary treatment in a large number of M.E. cases.

The protocol uses a highly unusual method of treating the points and should be adhered to carefully.

Technique - set the intensity of the unit to its highest setting and, ideally, set the treatment frequency to 100Hz. Locate the treatment point with the unit as usual. Without pressing the treatment button, hold the probe on the point and you will feel a sensation. Maintain the probe's position on the point until the sensation has reached a maximum and then wait until the sensation diminishes slightly - then press the treatment button (keeping the intensity setting on high).

You should now feel a pulsing sensation. Continue treating the point until no further sensation is felt.

Repeat the treatment as above for each point.

POINTS

Gv20 As shown above

Ear Ear points 18, 21 and 47 (for exact locations, see ear chart on page 10.2)

8. MISCELLANEOUS DISORDERS

Lactation - Mastitis

Lactation, to start or increase the flow of breast milk. Mastitis, or nodular mastitis is a harmless condition of tender lumps in the breast and is experienced by many women at some time in their life.

POINTS

B31 This lies at the top of the sacral bone one and a half thumbs width away from the mid-line.

B32 This lies one finger's width below B31.

B33 This lies one finger's width below B32.

B34 This lies one finger's width below B33.

Cv17 This lies in a depression at the centre of the front of the chest on a line joining both nipples.

S18 This lies directly beneath the breast on each side.

S36 This lies three thumb's width below the joint under the kneecap lying on the outer side of the knee. One finger's width back from the sharp edge of the shin bone.

Ear Ear point

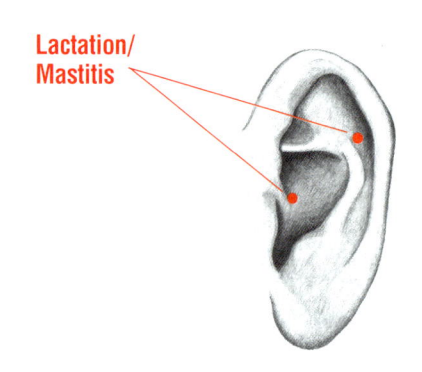

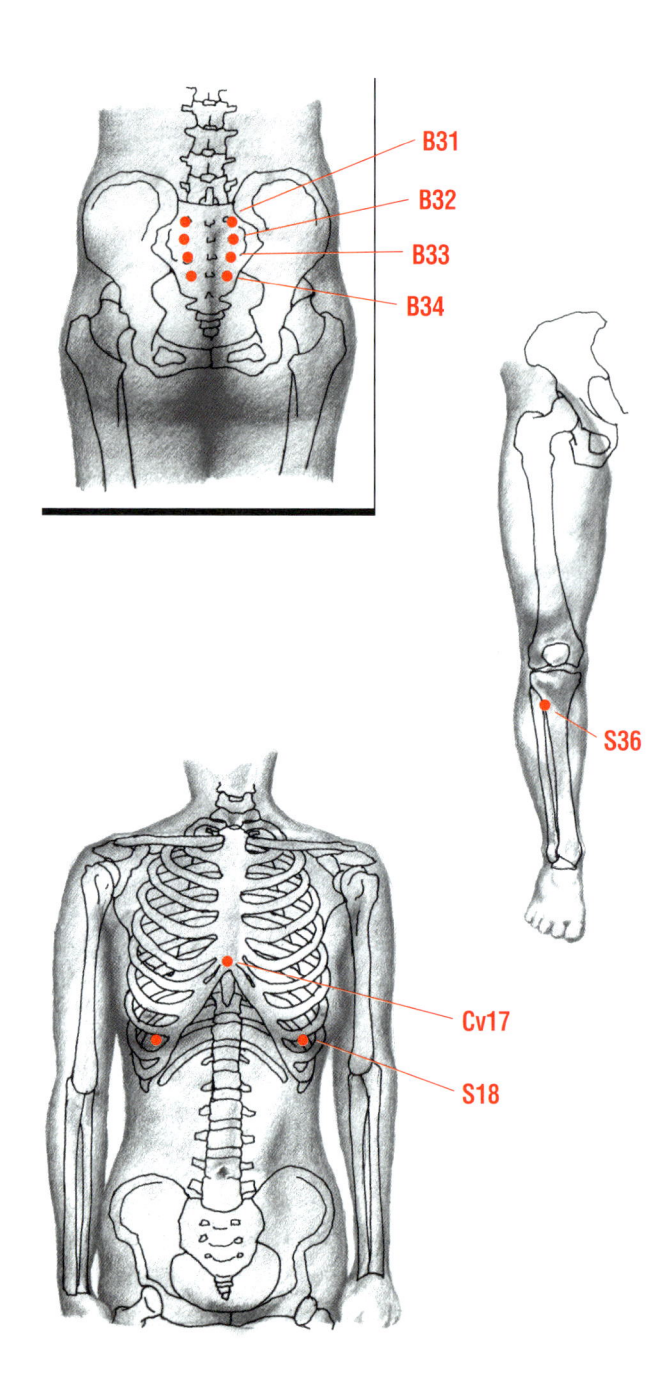

Lactation/Mastitis

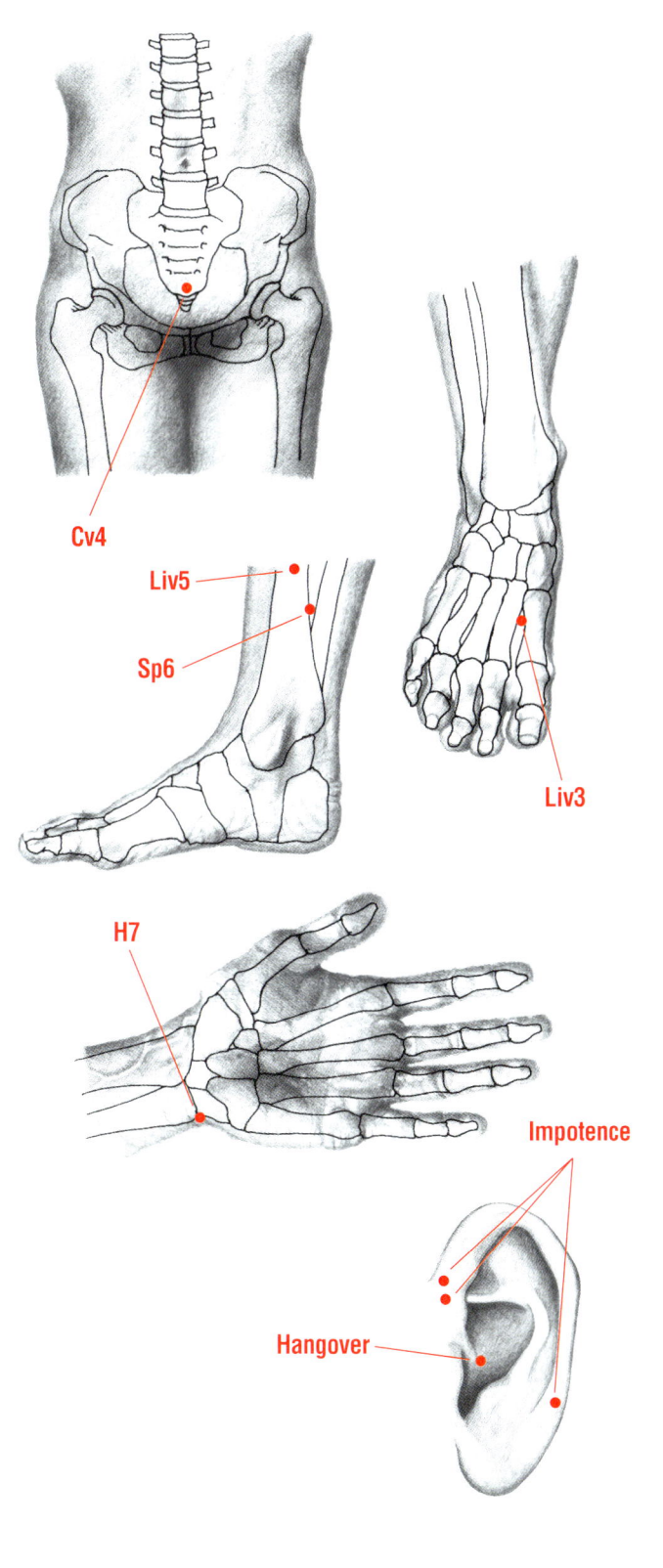

8. MISCELLANEOUS DISORDERS

Impotence

Impotence may be helped using Electro-Acupuncture. A balanced diet including appropriate vitamin and mineral supplements can be of great value - see page 0.1.

POINTS

Cv4 — This lies two thumb's width above the pubic bone.

H7 — This lies on the little finger side of the palm wrist crease just inside the small prominent bone.

Liv5 — This is five fingers above the inner ankle bone, over the surface of the tibia, which is the main bone in the lower leg.

Sp6 — This lies one hand's width (four fingers) up from the inner ankle joint. It lies just behind the tibia bone at this point.

Ear — Ear points.

Hangover

This is a useful list of points to use the morning after a heavy drinking session.

POINTS

Liv3 — This lies in between the tendons of the big toe and the first toe, two thumb's width towards the top of the foot from the web.

S36 — This lies three thumb's width below the joint under the kneecap lying on the outer side of the knee. One finger's width back from the sharp edge of the shin bone.

Sp6 — This lies one hand's width (four fingers) up from the inner ankle joint. It lies just behind the tibia bone at this point.

Ear — Ear point

8.17

8. MISCELLANEOUS DISORDERS

Anxiety and Stressful States

This can be treated effectively using Electro-Acupuncture.

POINTS

Gv20 This point lies right at the top of the head where two imaginary lines cross, one drawn from the top of one ear to the top of the other ear, the other line drawn from the top of the nose right over the top of the skull to the back of the skull. Where these lines cross is Gv20.

H3 This is at the end of the inner elbow crease.

H7 This lies on the little finger side of the palm wrist crease just inside the small prominent bone.

Li4 This lies on the side of the bone which runs from the forefinger knuckle down towards the wrist. See page 8 for a detailed description of this point.

P6 This lies two thumb's width up from the palm wrist crease towards the elbow, directly in the centre between the two tendons.

Yintang This lies directly between the eyebrows, just above the bridge of the nose.

Ear Ear points.

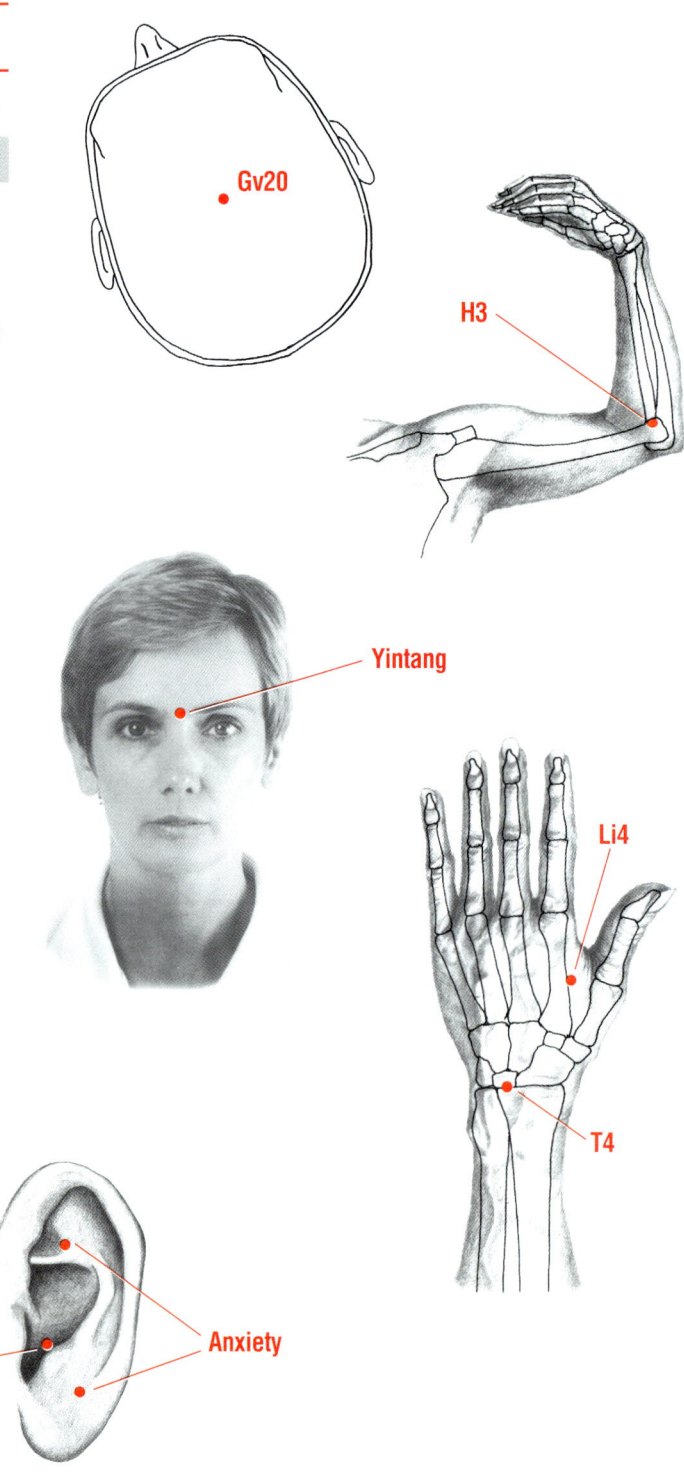

8.18

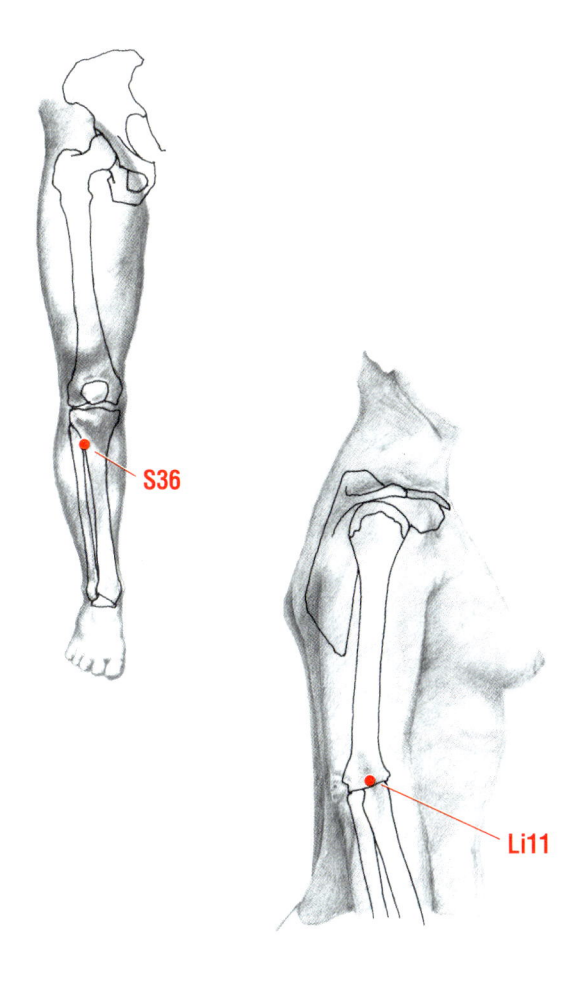

8. MISCELLANEOUS DISORDERS

Smoking

Electronic-stimulation is the most effective method of smoking withdrawal and has results 3-4 times better than most other methods.

Electro-Acupuncture can help you give up smoking. Acupuncture is very useful for addictions generally. It works largely by stimulating the production of natural opiate substances known as endorphins. This is how Electro-Acupuncture can help smokers 'kick the habit'. Treat the body points once a day, treat the ear points each time you want to have a cigarette, in other words as a substitute for the cigarette.

POINTS

Li4 — This lies on the side of the bone which runs from the forefinger knuckle down towards the wrist. See page 8 for a detailed description of this point.

S36 — This lies three thumb's width below the joint under the kneecap lying on the outer side of the knee. One finger's width back from the sharp edge of the shin bone.

Ear — Ear point

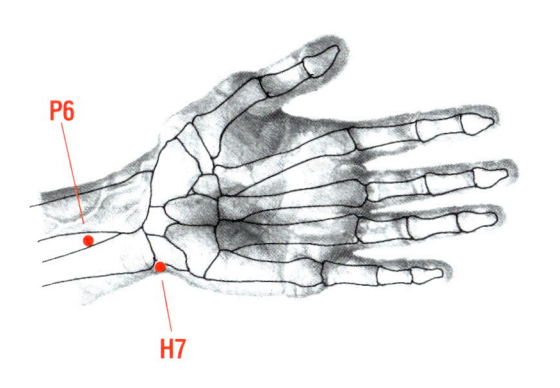

Jet lag

These points need to be treated several times during the flight as well as for a day or two afterwards.

POINTS

Li11 — This lies 2cm beyond the end of the outer elbow crease with the arm bent.

S36 — As shown above under 'Smoking'.

T4 — This lies on the back of the wrist, one finger's width towards the elbow from the wrist crease and next to the small prominent bone.

Gv20 — As described in 'Anxiety & Stressful States' on opposite page.

8. MISCELLANEOUS DISORDERS

Eye Problems - *See also Pages 11 - 13*

There are many different eye problems - see the list on the following page (page 8.21). If any problem becomes chronic, a qualified ophthalmologic opinion is essential.

POINTS

B2 — This lies just beneath the inner end of the eyebrow. **IT IS NOT LOCATED AT THE INNER END OF THE EYE**, and in no case stimulate this area.

G1 — This lies half a finger out from the outer corner of the eye.

G14 — This lies one thumb's width above the mid point of the eyebrow.

G20 — Just below the skull bone and outside the muscle bulge.

K3 — This lies midway between the tip of the inner ankle bone and the achilles tendon (in the hollow)

Li4 — This lies on the side of the bone which runs from the forefinger knuckle down towards the wrist. See page 8 for a detailed description of this point.

Liv2 — This is one finger's width up from the web between the big toe and the second toe tendons.

Liv3 — This lies in between the tendons of the big toe and the first toe, two thumb's width towards the top of the foot from the web.

S36 — This lies three thumb's width below the joint under the kneecap lying on the outer side of the knee. One finger's width back from the sharp edge of the shin bone.

Continued on next page...

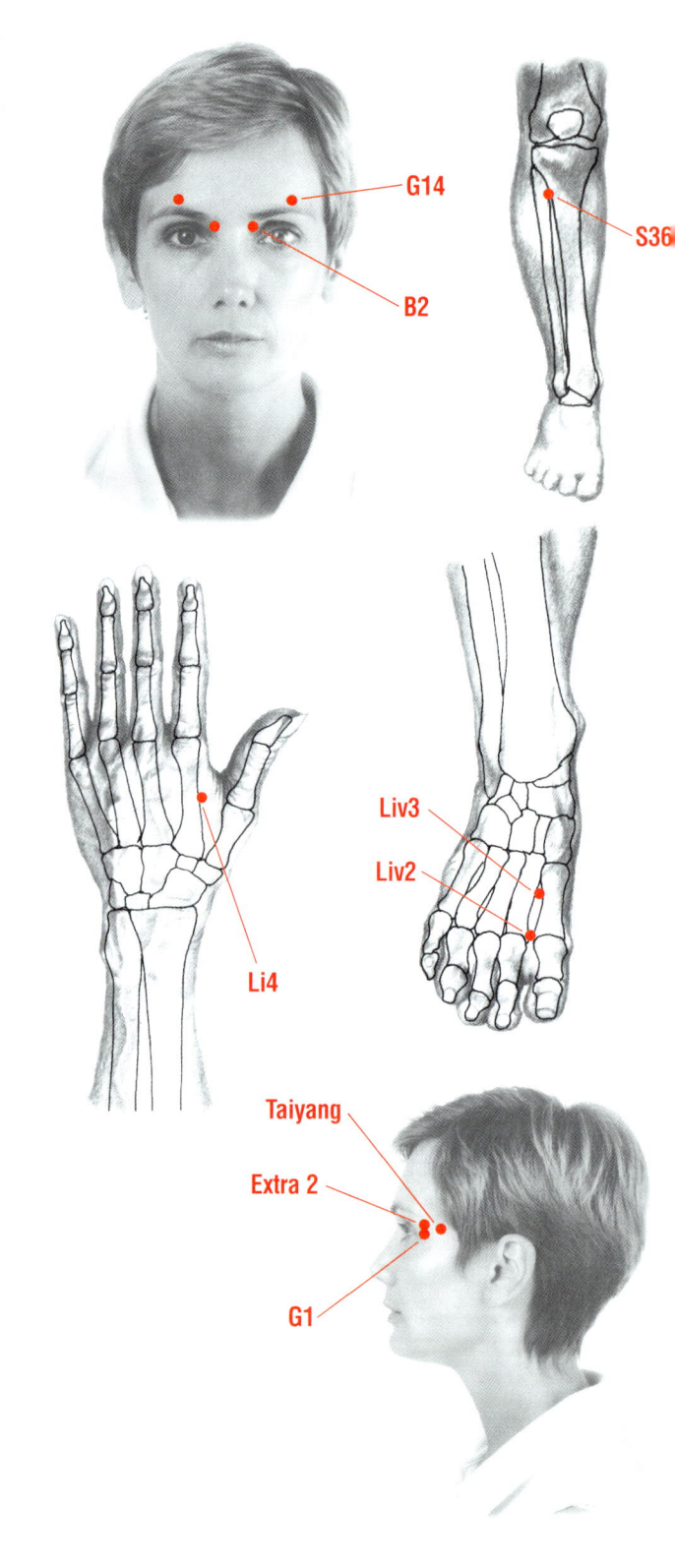

8. MISCELLANEOUS DISORDERS

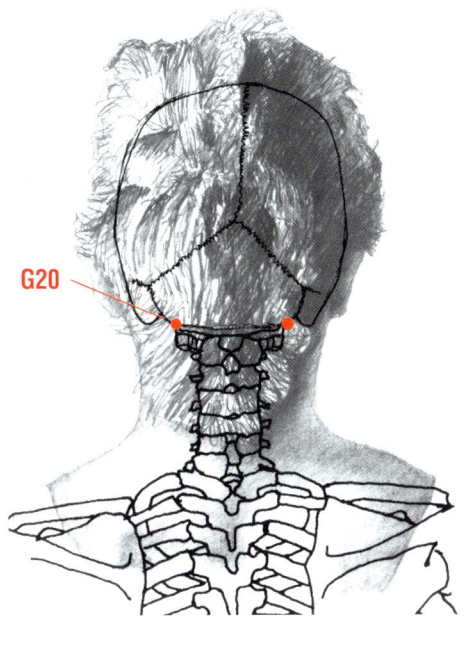

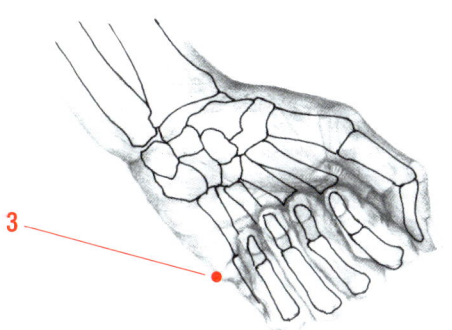

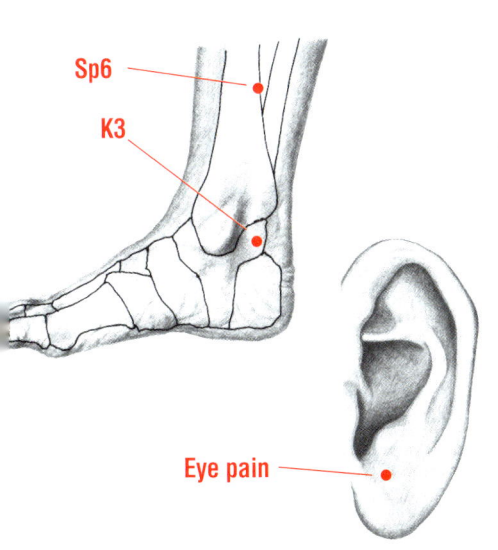

Eye Problems - *continued*

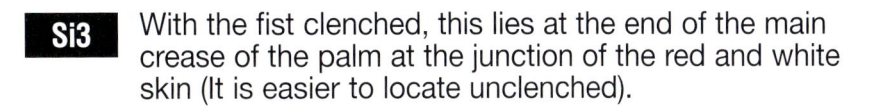

Si3 — With the fist clenched, this lies at the end of the main crease of the palm at the junction of the red and white skin (It is easier to locate unclenched).

Sp6 — This lies one hand's width (four fingers) up from the inner ankle joint. It lies just behind the tibia bone at this point.

Extra 2 — A finger behind a line drawn between the outer end of the eyebrow and the outer corner of the eye.

Taiyang — This lies one thumb's width behind the outer edge of the eye. It lies in the centre of the temples.

Ear — Ear point

Whilst there is no guarantee of success, in some cases the following specific disorders may respond to treatment. A balanced diet including Lutien and vitamin and mineral supplements can be also of value - see page 0.1 and the new book 'Turning a Blind Eye' By Robert Redfern.

In all cases, treat the basic points around the eye as shown on page 12

Also treat for:

Macular Degeneration (wet or dry, also Diabetic Retinopathy):
G14. G20, Li4, Liv2, Liv3, S36, Si3, T5, Taiyang, Yintang, Ear Point.

Cataracts:
G14, Li4, Liv 3, Si3, S36, Ear Point.

Squint:
G1, G20, Li4, B2.

Conjunctivitis:
G14, G20, Li4, Liv3, S36, Extra 2, Yintang, Ear.

Glaucoma:
B2, G20, K3, Li4, Liv2, Liv3, S36, Sp6.

Computer Eye Syndrome:
G14. G20, Li4, Liv3, S36, Yintang, Ear Point.

For Yintang location see page 8.18
For other conditions, call the helpline.

8. MISCELLANEOUS DISORDERS

M.S. (Multiple Sclerosis)

The condition results from damage to the sheaths surrounding individual nerve cells. the nerves are unable to function properly, causing problems of vision, sensation and muscular control. Electro-Acupuncture can be effective in providing relief from the symptoms of M.S. We would strongly advise you to seek the opinion a doctor who practices holistic medicine.

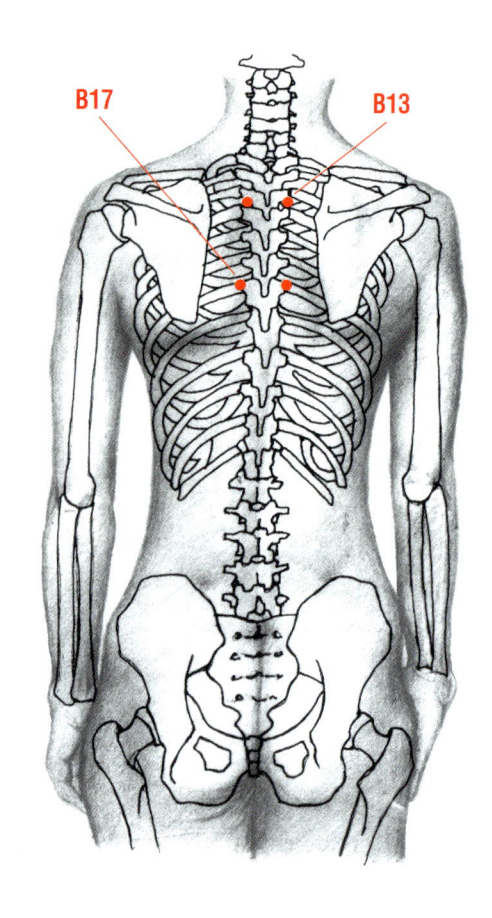

POINTS

B13 This lies one and a half thumb's width to each side of the centre of the spine at the level of the third thoracic vertebra.

B17 This point lies one and a half thumb's width each side of the mid-line at the level of the seventh thoracic vertebra.

G34 This is just below and in front of the knobbly head of the fibula, which is the bone just below the outer side of knee. This point is in a slight depression and is sometimes tender when pressed with a finger tip.

S36 This lies three thumb's width below the joint under the kneecap lying on the outer side of the knee. One finger's width back from the sharp edge of the shin bone.

Ah Shi Additional back points - treat all Ah-Shi points just below the vertebrae where there is a problem and half a finger out on each side.

Ear Ear points

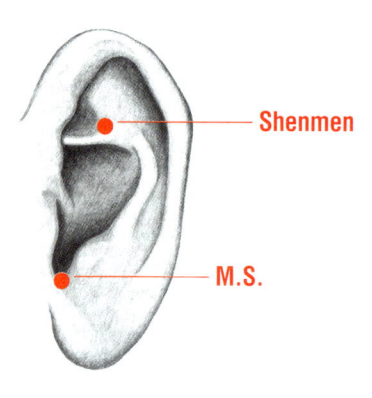

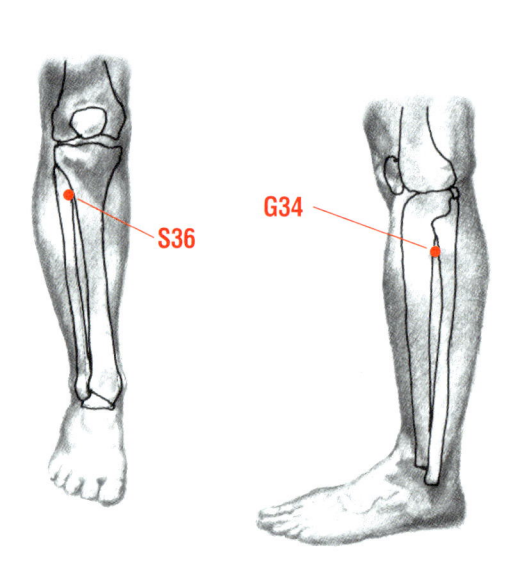

8.22

8. MISCELLANEOUS DISORDERS

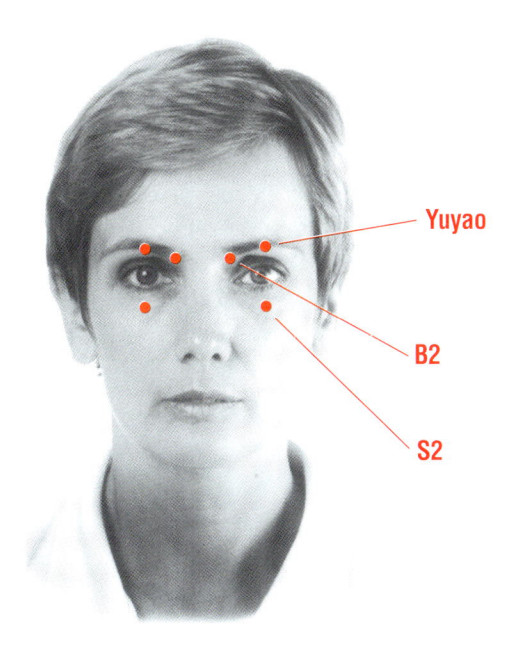

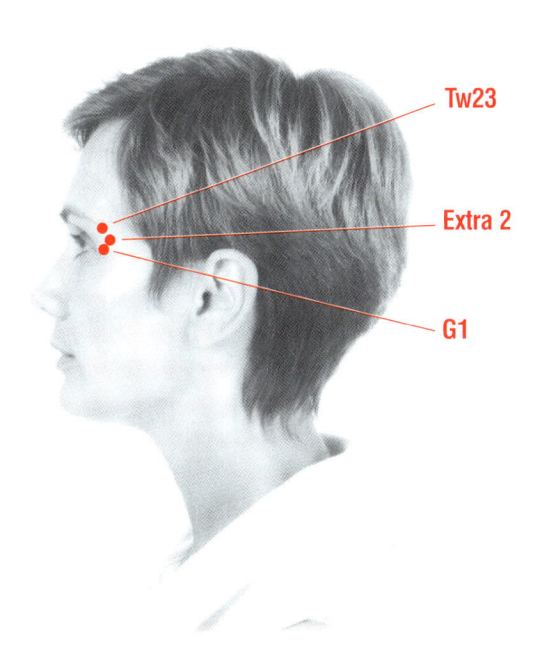

M.S. (Multiple Sclerosis) - Eye Problems

M.S. can often cause eye problems.

POINTS

B2 — This lies just beneath the inner end of the eyebrow. **IT IS NOT LOCATED AT THE INNER END OF THE EYE**, and in no case stimulate this area.

G1 — This lies half a finger out from the outer corner of the eye.

S2 — In the middle of the bony edge of the eye socket.

TW23 — This is located at the outer end of the eyebrow.

Extra 2 — A finger behind a line drawn between the outer end of the eyebrow and the outer corner of the eye.

Yuyao — This is located at the middle point of the eyebrow.

8. MISCELLANEOUS DISORDERS

Parkinson's Disease

A disease of the nervous system, in which muscular stiffness and tremors develop, becoming progressively worse with the passing of time. We would strongly advise you to seek the opinion a doctor who practices holistic medicine.

POINTS

G34 This is just below and in front of the knobbly head of the fibula, which is the bone just below the outer side of knee. This point is in a slight depression and is sometimes tender when pressed with a finger tip.

Gv20 This point lies right at the top of the head where two imaginary lines cross, one drawn from the top of one ear to the top of the other ear, the other line drawn from the top of the nose right over the top of the skull to the back of the skull. Where these lines cross is Gv20.

H7 This lies on the little finger side of the palm wrist crease just inside the small prominent bone.

Li4 This lies on the side of the bone which runs from the forefinger knuckle down towards the wrist. See page 8 for a detailed description of this point.

Li11 This lies 2cm beyond the end of the outer elbow crease with the arm bent.

Liv3 This lies in between the tendons of the big toe and the first toe, two thumb's width towards the top of the foot from the web.

P6 This lies two thumb's width up from the palm wrist crease towards the elbow, directly in the centre between the two tendons.

Continued on next page...

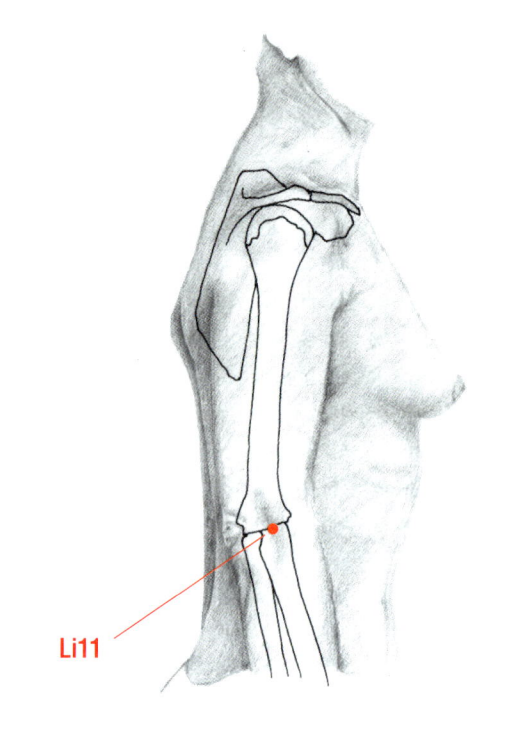

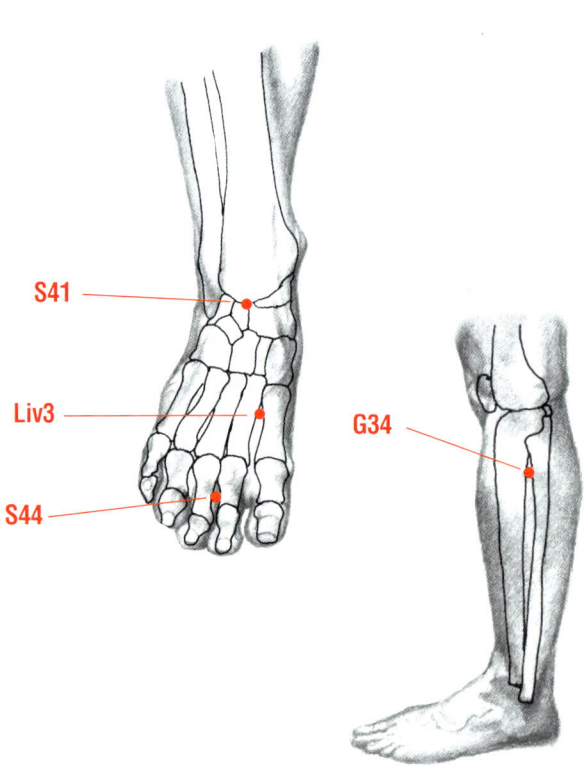

8. MISCELLANEOUS DISORDERS

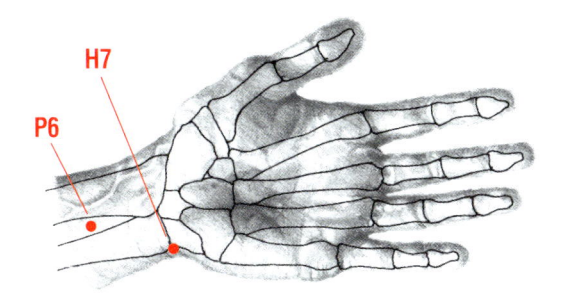

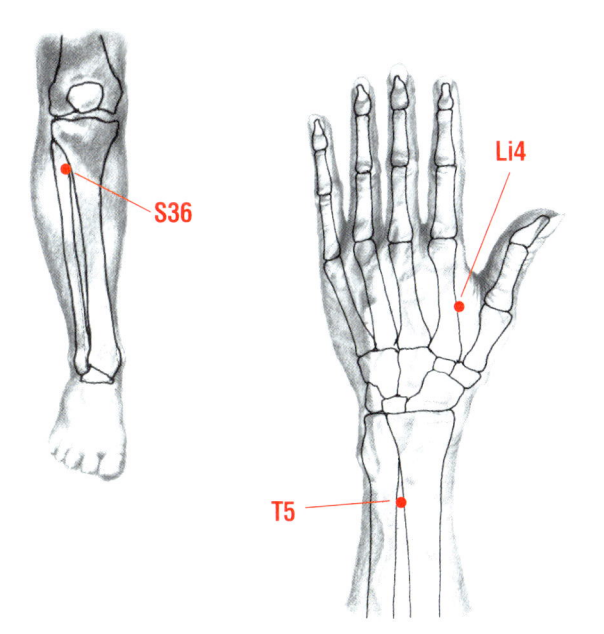

Parkinson's Disease - *continued*

POINTS

S36   This lies three thumb's width below the joint under the kneecap lying on the outer side of the knee. One finger's width back from the sharp edge of the shin bone.

S41   This lies directly over the middle point of the front of the foot joint.

S44   This lies in the web between the second and third toes.

T5   This lies on the back of the wrist, two thumb's width towards the elbow from the wrist crease.

Ear   Ear point

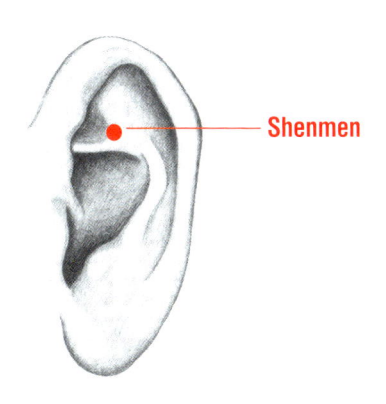

8. MISCELLANEOUS DISORDERS

Diabetes

A condition in which the body cannot properly use sugar and starches (carbohydrates) from the diet, because the pancreas is not producing enough of the hormone insulin. As a result, sugar accumulates in the blood and tissues and this causes defects in various parts of the body. All types of diabetes can be controlled with diet, or insulin replacement. Appropriate vitamin and mineral supplements can also be of great value - see page 0.1.

POINTS

Important - do not stop any treatments except on the advice of a medical practitioner.

Cv12 This lies halfway between the lower end of the breastbone and the navel, exactly in the mid-line.

G20 Just below the skull bone and outside the muscle bulge.

Gv14 This lies just below the most prominent knob of bone at the base of the neck in the midline.

K3 This lies midway between the tip of the inner ankle bone and the achilles tendon (in the hollow)

Li11 This lies 2cm beyond the end of the outer elbow crease with the arm bent.

Liv3 This lies between the tendons of the big toe and the first toe, two thumb's width towards the top of the foot from the web.

Sp6 This lies one hand's width (four fingers) up from the inner ankle joint. It lies just behind the tibia bone at this point.

S36 This lies three thumb's width below the joint under the kneecap lying on the outer side of the knee. One finger's width back from the sharp edge of the shin bone.

Cv4 This lies two thumb's width above the pubic bone.

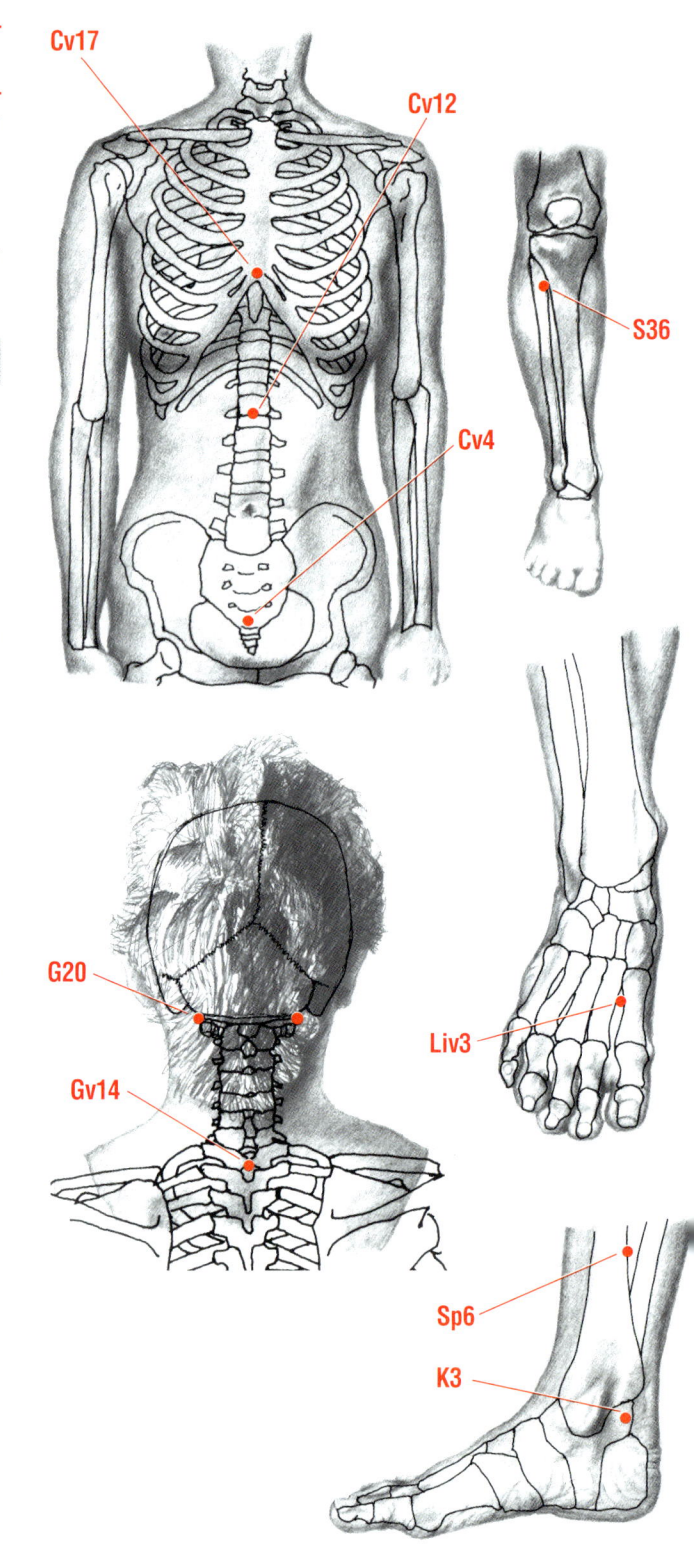

8. MISCELLANEOUS DISORDERS

Thyroid - Balancing

The thyroid gland can sometimes become either over-active or under-active. Electro-acupuncture can be useful in correcting the balance.

POINTS

Important - do not stop any treatments except on the advice of a medical practitioner.

Cv17 This lies in a depression at the centre of the front of the chest on a line joining both nipples.

Cv22 This lies in the hollow directly over the front of the larynx in the centre of the lower part of the neck.

Li4 This lies on the side of the bone which runs from the forefinger knuckle down towards the wrist. See page 8 for a detailed description of this point.

Li18 This lies three fingers lateral to the larynx (adam's apple).

Liv3 This lies between the tendons of the big toe and the first toe, two thumb's width towards the top of the foot from the web.

S36 This lies three thumb's width below the joint under the kneecap lying on the outer side of the knee. One finger's width back from the sharp edge of the shin bone.

Si17 This lies behind the jaw, just in front of the neck muscle.

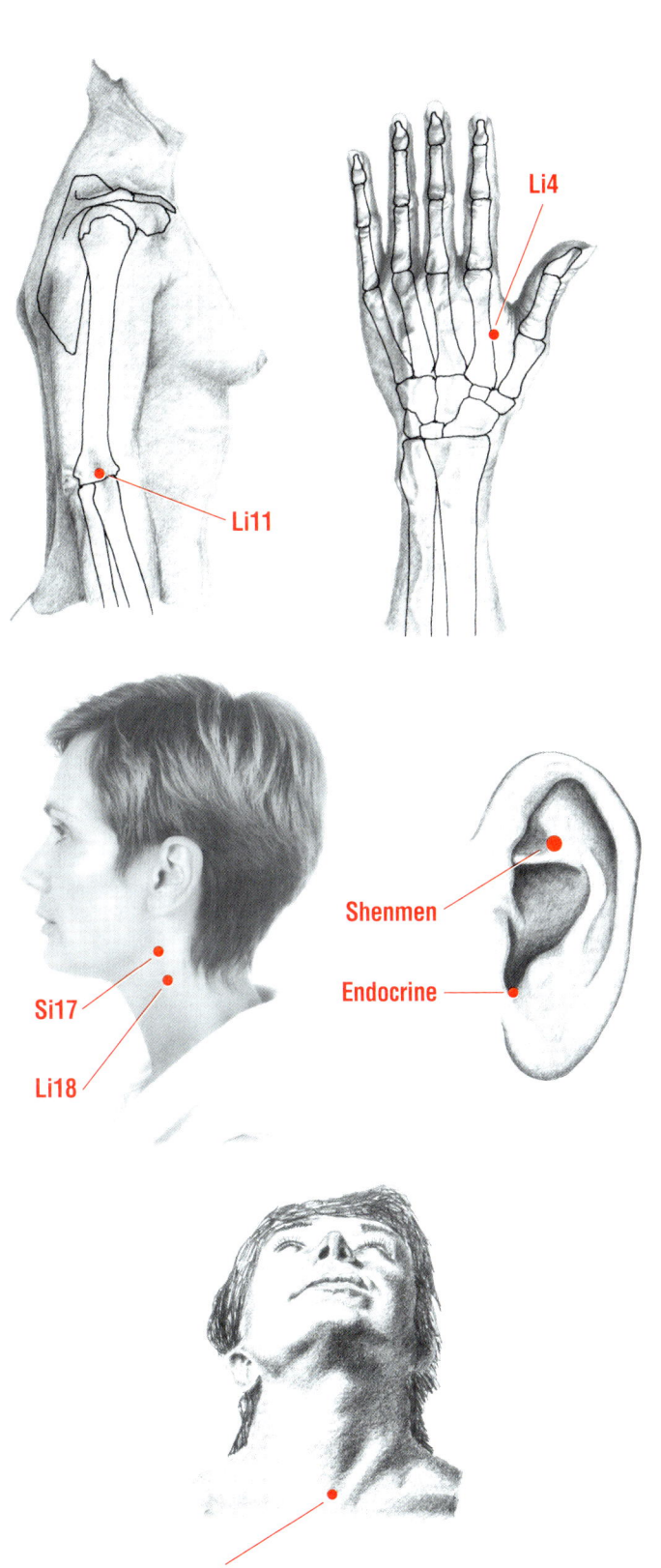

Ear Ear points - shenmen and endocrine

8.27

8. MISCELLANEOUS DISORDERS

Morning sickness

While this can be treated effectively by Electro-Acupuncture, treatment before the end of the third month of pregnancy should be given under medical supervision only.

POINTS

P6 — This lies two thumb's width up from the palm wrist crease towards the elbow, directly in the centre between the two tendons.

S36 — This lies three thumb's width below the joint under the kneecap lying on the outer side of the knee. One finger's width back from the sharp edge of the shin bone.

S44 — This lies in the web between the second and third toes.

Sp6 — This lies one hand's width (four fingers) up from the inner ankle joint. It lies just behind the tibia bone at this point.

Ear — Ear point

Depression

Electro-Acupuncture can be useful in the treatment of some cases of depression. A balanced diet including appropriate vitamin and mineral supplements can often help - see page 0.1.

POINTS

P6 — This lies two thumb's width up from the palm wrist crease towards the elbow, directly in the centre between the two tendons.

S36 — This lies three thumb's width below the joint under the kneecap lying on the outer side of the knee. One finger's width back from the sharp edge of the shin bone.

Liv3 — This lies in between the tendons of the big toe and the first toe, two thumb's width towards the top of the foot from the web.

Ear — Ear point

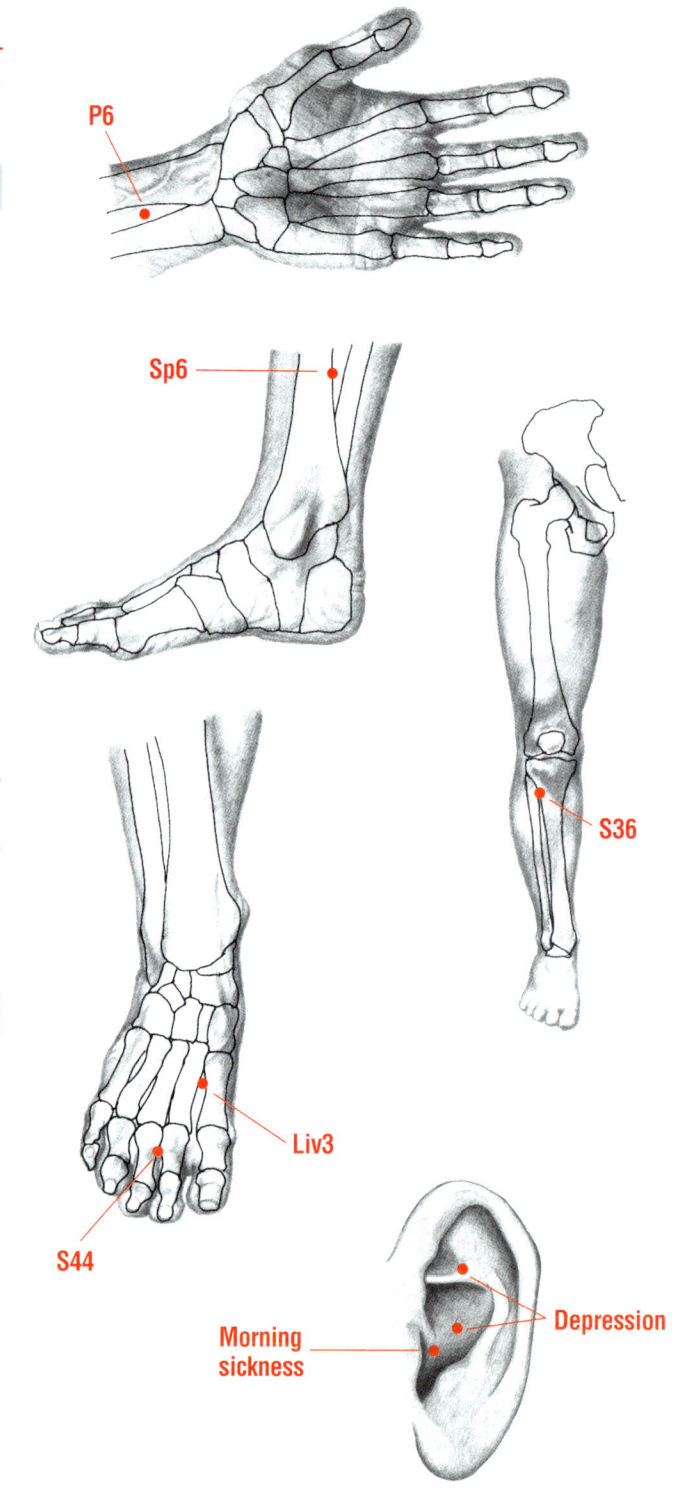

9. SPORTS & INDUSTRIAL INJURIES

Introduction

Many more people, of all ages, are participating in one sport or another, with the resultant increase in the number of associated injuries. From a treatment point of view the most important thing is the early treatment of an injury. Electro-Acupuncture offers a **"First Aid"**.

It is clearly impossible to have a doctor or physiotherapist available at every sporting event. The average sportsman will be able to read and understand this section of the book and use Electro-Acupuncture competently.

IF YOU ARE IN ANY DOUBT WHATSOEVER ABOUT THE SERIOUSNESS OF THE INJURY, APPROPRIATE MEDICAL ADVICE MUST BE SOUGHT.

> Remember that in any injury situation there is a possibility of fracture. Electro-Acupuncture is not a satisfactory or acceptable method of treating a fracture. Commonly sports injuries involve bruising of varying degree and severity, partial or complete muscle tears, tendon injuries and tendon inflammation (tenosynovitis). Electro-Acupuncture is an effective method of treating all of these conditions (except total tendon rupture, most commonly occurring at the Achilles tendon).

As well as using Electro-Acupuncture, other measures are important such as:

1. Resting the injured part, and the use of ice packs which cool the tissues and reduce bleeding.

2. When bleeding is present compression, produced by firmly bandaging the affected area, serves to limit further blood loss. Do not, however, bandage so tightly that blood flow stops altogether. In the event of the fingers or toes of the bandaged limb beginning to turn blue the bandage should be released a little.

3. Elevation of the affected part is also helpful in reducing tissue swelling around the injury.

4. Electro-Acupuncture can be used successfully when the initial injury period has passed and the bleeding stopped. If Electro-Acupuncture is used with skill the tissue swelling (known as oedema) will often disappear within minutes. In practice this means that the sports injury is dealt with more effectively, and therefore recovery time is shortened. The player may then be able to return to his sporting activities sooner than he otherwise would.

9. SPORTS & INDUSTRIAL INJURIES

ARM INJURIES

Shoulder Joint

This is a common injury and should be treated vigorously. Electro-Acupuncture is usually effective in treatment of the pain. If shoulder pain is left for more than a month then a frozen shoulder may ensue in which stiffness of the joint, as well as pain, occurs. In a chronically painful shoulder that is also stiff, then physiotherapy is an essential approach to treatment.

POINTS

B57 — This lies in the centre of the back of the calf, just where the fleshy mass of muscle narrows down into tendon.

G21 — This lies halfway between the knob of bone in the centre at the bottom of the neck and the tip of the shoulder, in the fleshy mass of muscle passing over the shoulder.

Li11 — This lies 2cm beyond the end of the outer elbow crease with the arm bent.

Li15 — This lies just in front of the shoulder joint, in a depression which is produced when the arm is lifted above the head, it can be tender with finger tip pressure.

S38 — This lies exactly halfway down the lower leg, two finger's width away from the midline measured from the ridge of bone running down the front of the shin.

T14 — This lies in a depression behind the shoulder joint, which is produced again by putting the arm above the head.

Ear — Ear point

Rehabilitation:

1. It is possible, even with a very painful shoulder, to keep it mobile. Stand facing the back of a chair leaning with the unaffected arm, and gently rotate the affected arm in ever increasing circles.
2. In a standing position close the hands together and use the good arm to help the other above the head.
3. Despite the pain try to continue performing everyday activities.

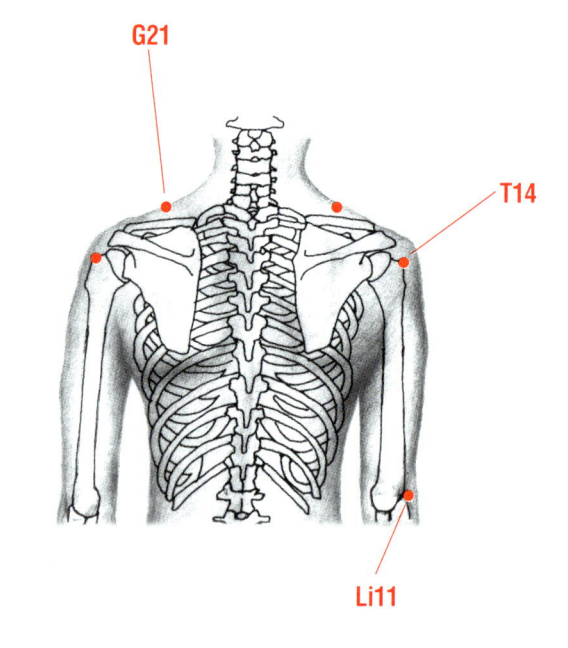

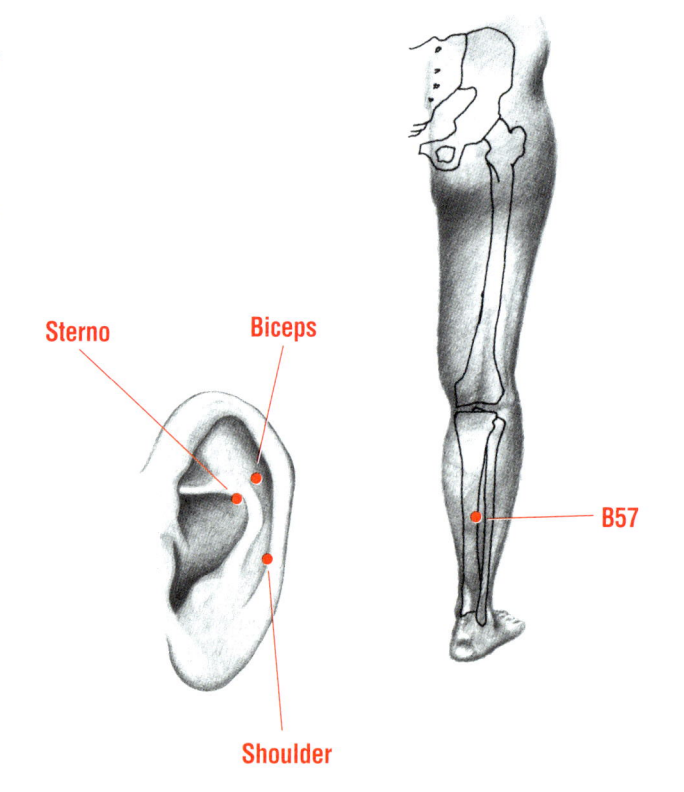

9. SPORTS & INDUSTRIAL INJURIES

Sterno - Clavicular Pain

The Sterno Clavicular joint is situated at the inner end of the collar bone, between the collar bone and the breast bone. Sterno-Clavicular pain is often aggravated by a fall onto the outstretched hand and Electro-Acupuncture is an effective way of treating this pain.

POINTS

Ah Shi — Any local tender acupuncture points to be found in the area of pain that give a reaction when stimulated

Ear — Ear point

Rehabilitation:

1. It is possible, even with a very painful shoulder, to keep it mobile. Stand facing the back of a chair leaning with the unaffected arm, and gently rotate the affected arm in ever increasing circles.

2. In a standing position close the hands together and use the good arm to help the other above the head.

3. Despite the pain try to continue performing everyday activities.

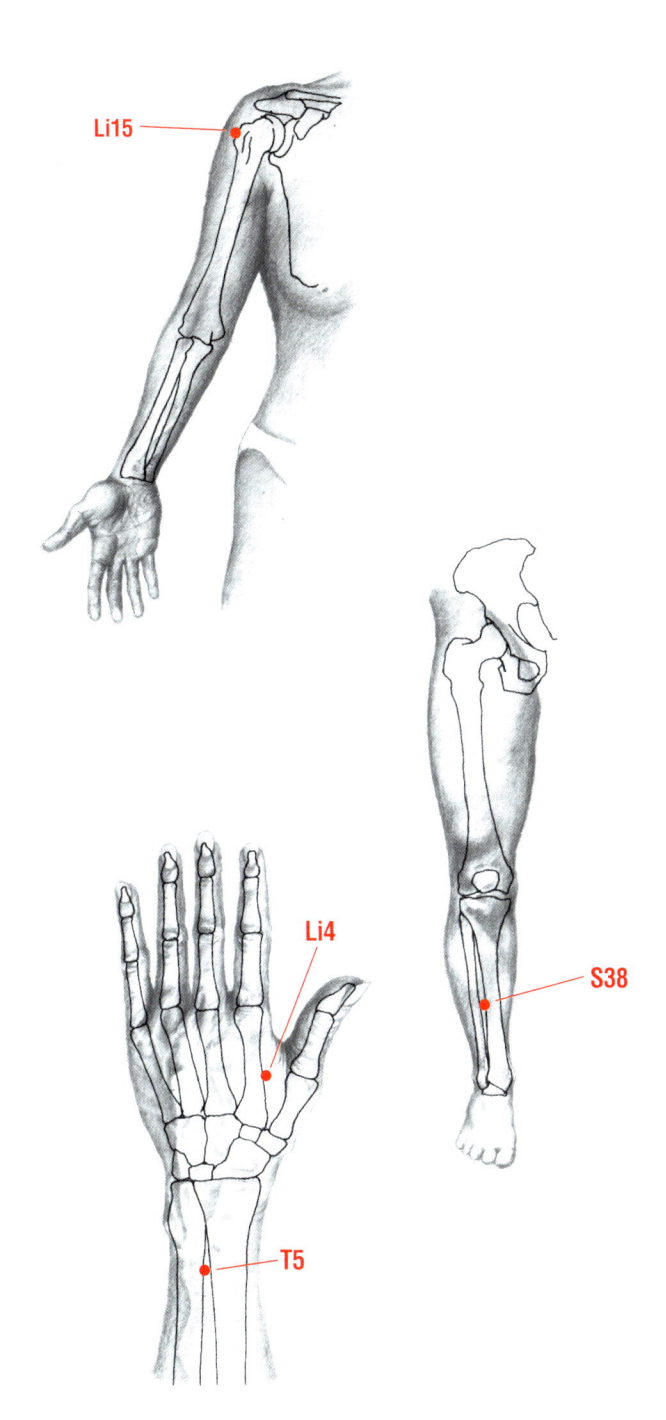

Biceps Tendonitis (Inflammation of the Biceps Tendon)

This gives pain along the front of the shoulder joint where the long head of the biceps lies. The injury is common in sports which require vigorous shoulder rotation such as throwing or swimming. Pain is most commonly felt when the arm is reaching in a backwards direction.

POINTS

Ah Shi — Any local tender acupuncture points to be found in the area of pain that give a reaction when stimulated

Li4 — This lies on the side of the bone which runs from the forefinger knuckle down towards the wrist. See page 8 for a detailed description of this point.

T5 — This lies on the back of the wrist, two thumb's width towards the elbow from the wrist crease.

Ear — Ear point

9. SPORTS & INDUSTRIAL INJURIES

Painful Arc (Specific Form of Shoulder Pain)

This is a condition that gives pain when the arm is brought up above the head. During the middle part of this movement pain is felt in the shoulder. It's due either to inflammation in one of the tendons around the head of the humerus, or inflammation in the bursa, (situated just beneath the acromion), lying between the acromion, and the head of the humerus.

POINTS

Li4 — This lies on the side of the bone which runs from the forefinger knuckle down towards the wrist. See page 8 for a detailed description of this point.

Ah Shi — Any local tender acupuncture points to be found in the area of pain that give a reaction when stimulated

Ear — Ear point

Rehabilitation:

Allow six weeks for recovery.
It is important to maintain shoulder mobility even though the pain may limit everyday activity.

1. Sit at a polished table with the arm resting on a dry cloth. Keep the arm straight and move the cloth from side to side.

2. Lie on your back with both hands closed together in your lap. Take both hands up and over your head and return.

3. Lie on your back with both arms at your side. Take the injured limb out to the side and then above the head.

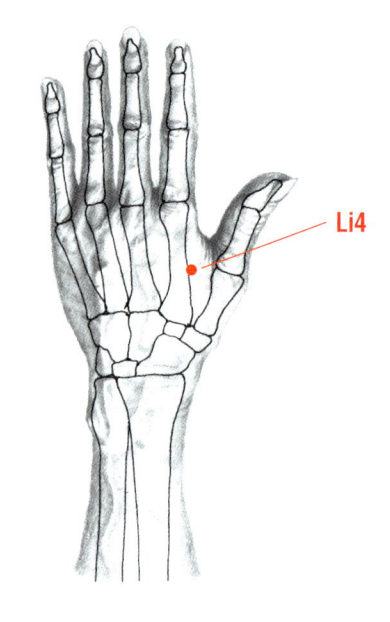

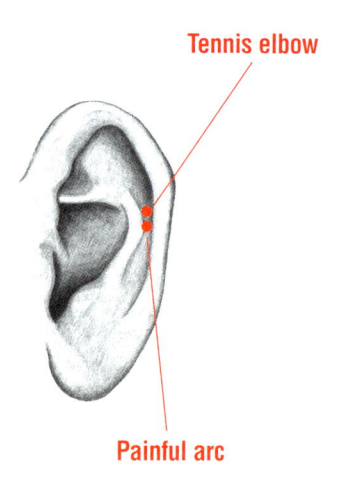

9. SPORTS & INDUSTRIAL INJURIES

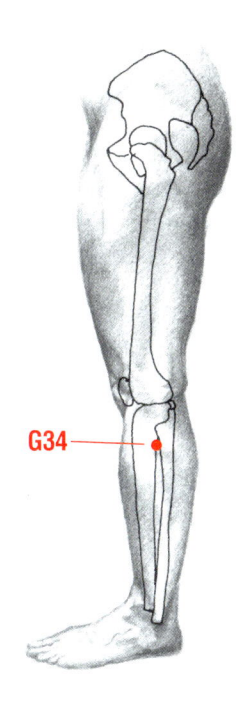

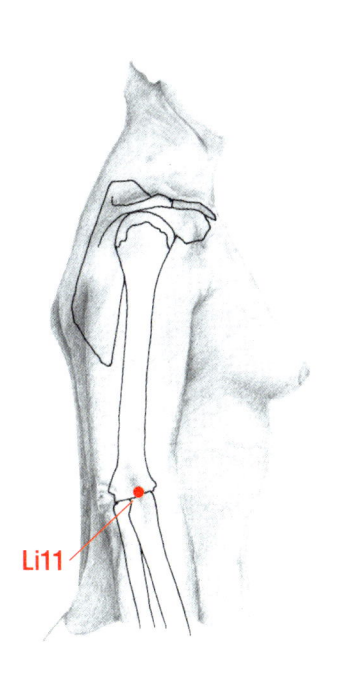

Tennis Elbow

This is usually an over-use injury in which the origin of the extensor muscles situated in the back of the forearm are overstretched and become inflamed. Pain is felt on the outer side of the elbow on gripping, lifting or controlling any heavy object such as a bat or racquet.

POINTS

G34 This is just below and in front of the knobbly head of the fibula, which is the bone just below the outer side of knee. This point is in a slight depression and is sometimes tender when pressed with a finger tip.

Li11 This lies 2cm beyond the end of the outer elbow crease with the arm bent.

Ah Shi Any local tender acupuncture points to be found in the area of pain that give a reaction when stimulated

Ear Ear point

Rehabilitation:

Allow six weeks for recovery.
Rest from the activity causing pain and as the condition improves strengthening exercises may be started.

1. Improve grip by squeezing the following:
   (a) Ball of wool
   (b) Squash ball
   (c) Tennis ball

2. Only when squeezing with (a) is painless, may you progress to (b) and so on.

3. To stretch the muscle insertion:

   a. Stand facing a wall at a distance of 18 inches. Place the back of the hands on the wall at shoulder height. Bend the arms until the forehead touches the hands and then return to the starting position.

   b. When pain free it is advisable to strengthen the area by wrist rolling exercises. Stand with arm in front of you at shoulder height. Hold a towel in the hands. Keeping the arm straight try to roll the towel into a cylinder. When returning to racquet games elbow supports should be used.

9. SPORTS & INDUSTRIAL INJURIES

Golfer's Elbow

This is a similar condition to tennis elbow but occurring on the inner side of the elbow. It affects the origin of the common flexor muscles situated on the inner aspect of the forearm. Pain is caused by bringing the open palm upwards against resistance and also by forming a grip in certain positions.

POINTS

Ah Shi — Any local tender acupuncture points to be found in the area of pain that give a reaction when stimulated

H3 — This is at the end of the inner elbow crease.

Ear — Ear point

Rehabilitation:

Allow six weeks for recovery.

1. To strengthen grip. Improve grip by squeezing the following:

    (a) Ball of wool
    (b) Squash ball
    (c) Tennis ball

    Only when squeezing with (a) is painless, may you progress to (b) and so on.

2. To stretch the area. Stand 18 inches from a wall. Place palms on the wall, fingers inwards. Bend at the elbows until the forehead touches the hands and then return to start position.

3. To strengthen. Sit with the arm resting on the leg, palm facing upwards. Bring the wrist up towards you. To progress try the exercise while holding a can of food.

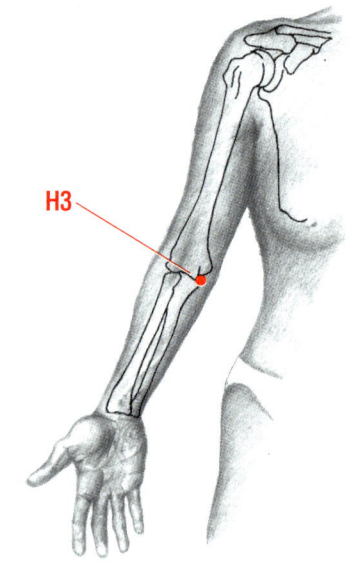

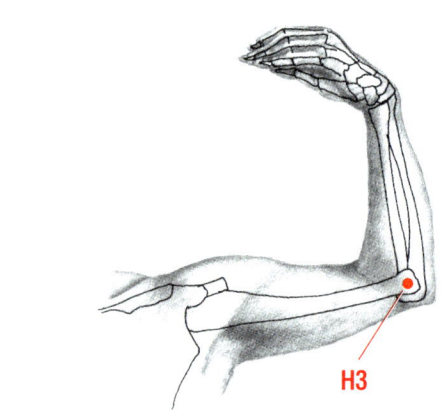

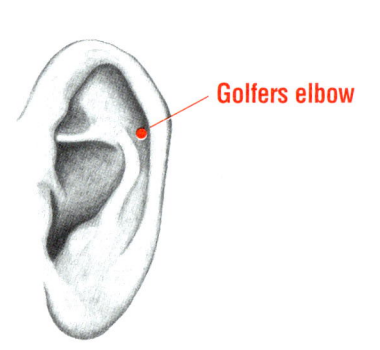

9.6

9. SPORTS & INDUSTRIAL INJURIES

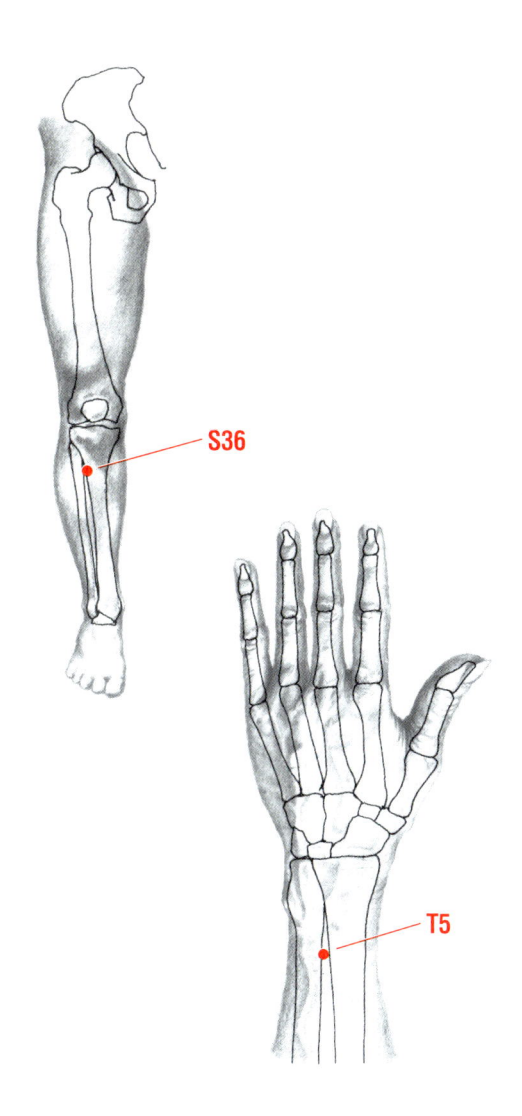

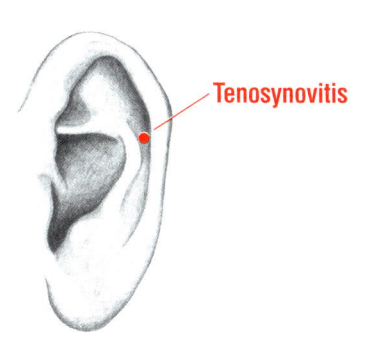

Tenosynovitis (Inflammation of Forearm Tendons)

This is inflammation in the extensor muscles, running down the back of the forearm. It is caused by repetitive movements such as rowing, screwdriving, etc. This tendon often becomes swollen and feels rough (when the wrist is moved). If not treated early enough rest and strapping with a crepe bandage is required. Electro-Acupuncture is therefore an ideal "First Aid"

POINTS

S36 — This lies three thumb's width below the joint under the kneecap lying on the outer side of the knee. One finger's width back from the sharp edge of the shin bone.

T5 — This lies on the back of the wrist, two thumb's width towards the elbow from the wrist crease.

Ah Shi — Any local tender acupuncture points to be found in the area of pain that give a reaction when stimulated

Ear — Ear point

Rehabilitation:

Allow 8-10 weeks for recovery.

When pain and local swelling subside, gradually return to exercise - keep the number of repetitions low.

To strengthen grip.

1. Improve grip by squeezing the following:
   (a) Ball of wool
   (b) Squash ball
   (c) Tennis ball

2. Sit with the arm resting on the thigh palm down. Raise the back of fingers towards the face keeping the elbow still. To progress hold a can of food in the hand.

9. SPORTS & INDUSTRIAL INJURIES

Wrist Injuries

Wrist sprains are common in contact sports. They are often caused by falls. It is very important to eliminate the possibility of a fracture, particularly an undisplaced Colles fracture of the lower end of the radius.

POINTS

Li5   This lies in a depression right at the very base of the thumb, almost at the wrist joint, the depression being much more obvious when the thumb is spread away from the index finger.

Si5   This lies on the edge of the wrist joint crease on the little finger side of the hand.

T4   This lies on the back of the wrist, one finger's width towards the elbow from the wrist crease and next to the small prominent bone.

Ear   Ear point

Rehabilitation:

Allow 4-6 weeks for recovery.

1. To stretch the muscle:
   Stand facing a wall at a distance of 18 inches. Place the back of the hands on the wall at shoulder height. Bend the arms until the forehead touches the hands and then return to the starting position.

2. When pain free it is advisable to strengthen the area by wrist rolling exercises. Stand with arm in front of you at shoulder height. Hold a towel in the hands. Keeping the arms straight try to roll the towel into a cylinder.

   Improve grip by squeezing the following:

   (a) Ball of wool
   (b) Squash ball
   (c) Tennis ball

   Only when squeezing with (a) is painless, may you progress to (b) and so on.

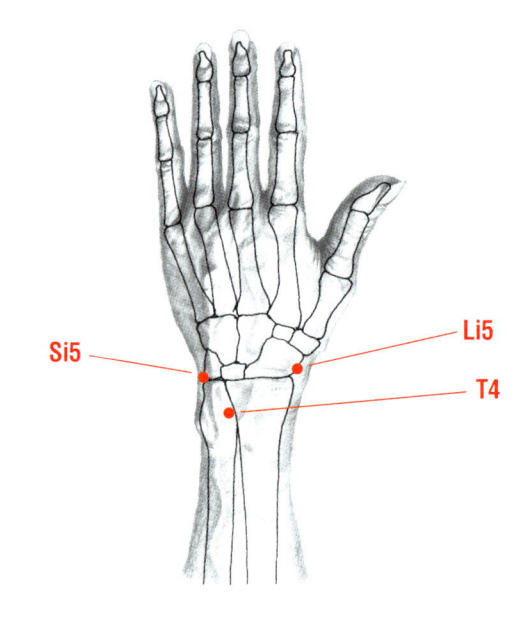

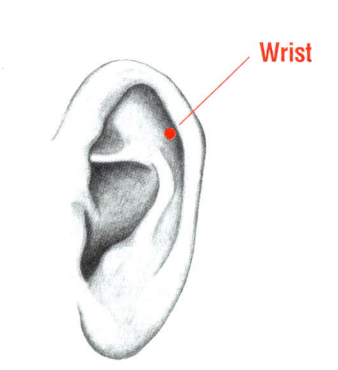

9. SPORTS & INDUSTRIAL INJURIES

Carpal Tunnel Syndrome
(Pain and Tingling in the Fingers and Thumb)

Tight arm bands or heavy hand work can sometimes cause a pressure neuritis and typical pain and tingling (in thumb, index, middle and part of the ring fingers). This is characteristic of carpal tunnel syndrome. The fingers often feel abnormally large. Some patients describe their fingers as feeling like a "bunch of bananas". If there is no improvement after two weeks consult your doctor.

POINTS

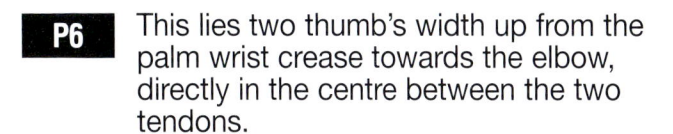

P6 — This lies two thumb's width up from the palm wrist crease towards the elbow, directly in the centre between the two tendons.

P7 — This lies in the centre of the wrist crease palm side of hand.

Ear — Ear point

Rehabilitation:

When the fingers begin to feel better the best form of rehabilitation is to use the hand as normally as possible.

No specific exercises are required.

Take up to 100mg of Vitamin B6 daily.

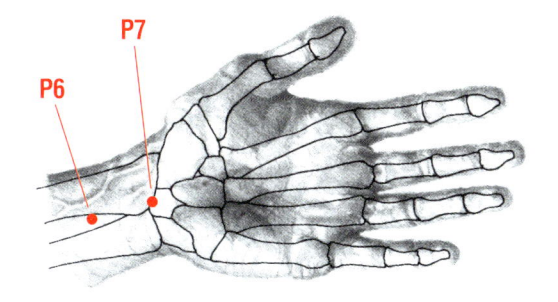

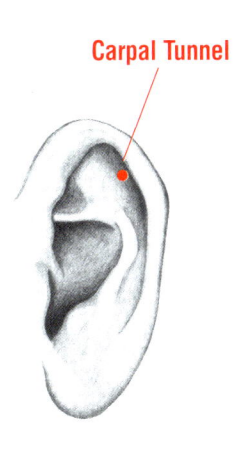

9. SPORTS & INDUSTRIAL INJURIES

Sprained Thumb and Fingers

Sprained thumbs and fingers are common sporting injuries, often caused by the thumb or finger being forced back by contact with another player or during a clumsy sporting action.

POINTS

L9 — This is situated at the end of the radius bone, by the thumb, on the palm side, in the depression just before the wrist crease.

L10 — This is situated on the palm side of the thumb, one finger's width from the thumb knuckle, towards the wrist.

L11 — This is situated on the outer side of the nail bed of the thumb.

Li4 — This lies on the side of the bone which runs from the forefinger knuckle down towards the wrist. See page 8 for a detailed description of this point.

Li5 — This lies in a depression right at the very base of the thumb, almost at the wrist joint, the depression being much more obvious when the thumb is spread away from the index finger.

Ah Shi — Any local tender acupuncture points - particularly on the line of creases as shown.

Ear — Ear point

Rehabilitation:

Allow 2-3 weeks for recovery.

These exercises should be started two days after injury and with the hand in a bowl of hot water.

1. Open and close the fist.
2. Open and close the fingers and thumb.
3. The hand may be immersed in hot water for 15-20 minutes.

   As pain lessens improve the grip by squeezing the following:

   (a) Ball of wool
   (b) Squash ball
   (c) Tennis ball

   Only when squeezing with (a) is painless, may you progress to (b) and so on.

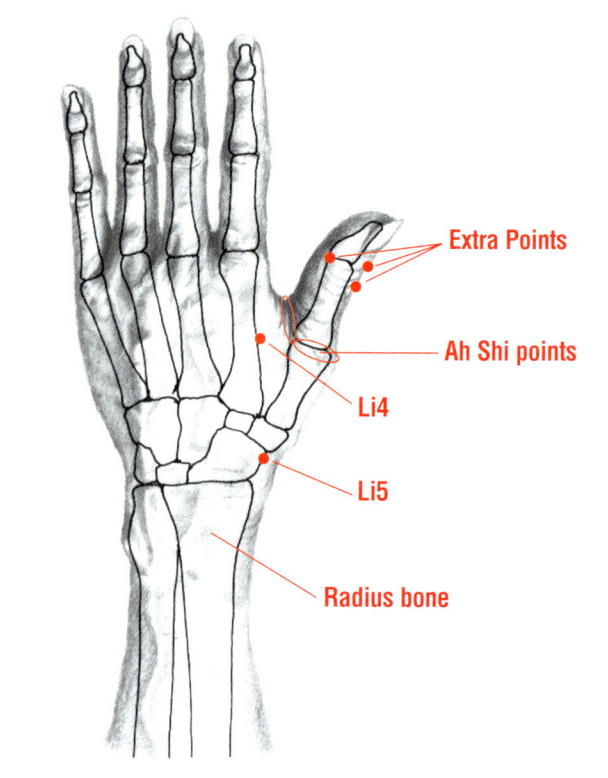

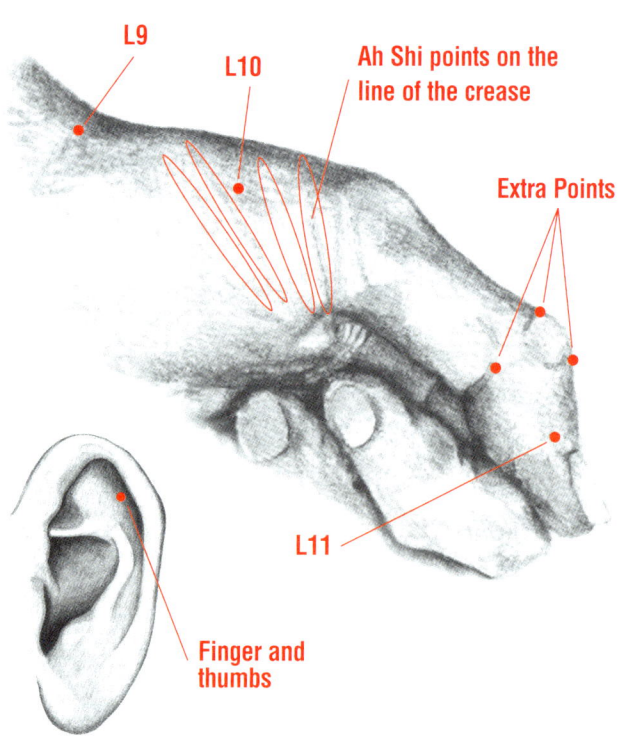

9. SPORTS & INDUSTRIAL INJURIES

SPINAL INJURIES

The spine comprises three areas:

Cervical spine: The neck

Lumbar spine: The lowest quarter of the back

Thoracic spine: The area between the cervical and lumbar spine.

Injuries to the spine fall into two distinct categories:

1. Direct trauma such as a knock or fall. This type of injury, if the patient is in great pain, must be treated by a qualified medical practitioner.

2. Physical Stress Injuries such as those caused by lifting or pushing.

    There may also be damage to muscles, ligaments, or even minor displacement of the vertebrae themselves. Previous back injuries can be the cause as can wear and tear due to repetitive strain injuries (Sports or occupational).

Spinal Injury

Injury to the Spine is less common in sport than injury to the limbs.

"Acute on chronic" situation - straining a chronically bad back is the most common occurrence..

9. SPORTS & INDUSTRIAL INJURIES

Neck Injuries

Neck injury is often caused by forcible extension (a backwards movement) of the head. While Electro-Acupuncture can be useful in treating this, it is wise to seek a qualified medical opinion.

POINTS

G20 — Just below the skull bone and outside the muscle bulge.

G21 — This lies halfway between the knob of bone in the centre at the bottom of the neck and the tip of the shoulder, in the fleshy mass of muscle passing over the shoulder.

Gv14 — This lies just below the most prominent knob of bone at the base of the neck in the midline.

Li4 — This lies on the side of the bone which runs from the forefinger knuckle down towards the wrist. See page 8 for a detailed description of this point.

Si3 — With the fist clenched, this lies at the end of the main crease of the palm at the junction of the red and white skin (It is easier to locate unclenched).

Ah Shi — Any local tender acupuncture points to be found in the area of pain that give a reaction when stimulated

Ear — Ear point

Rehabilitation

Acute neck injuries often require a surgical collar. This removes the weight of the head from the cervical spine. Exercises are used to regain mobility and on no account should there be any forced neck movement.

1. Lie (on your back) on the floor, turn your head from side to side.
2. Seated on a chair: bend your head to the side until your ear touches your shoulder (as near as possible will do), repeat to both sides.
3. Seated on a chair: lower your head until your chin touches your chest. Return to upright position and repeat.

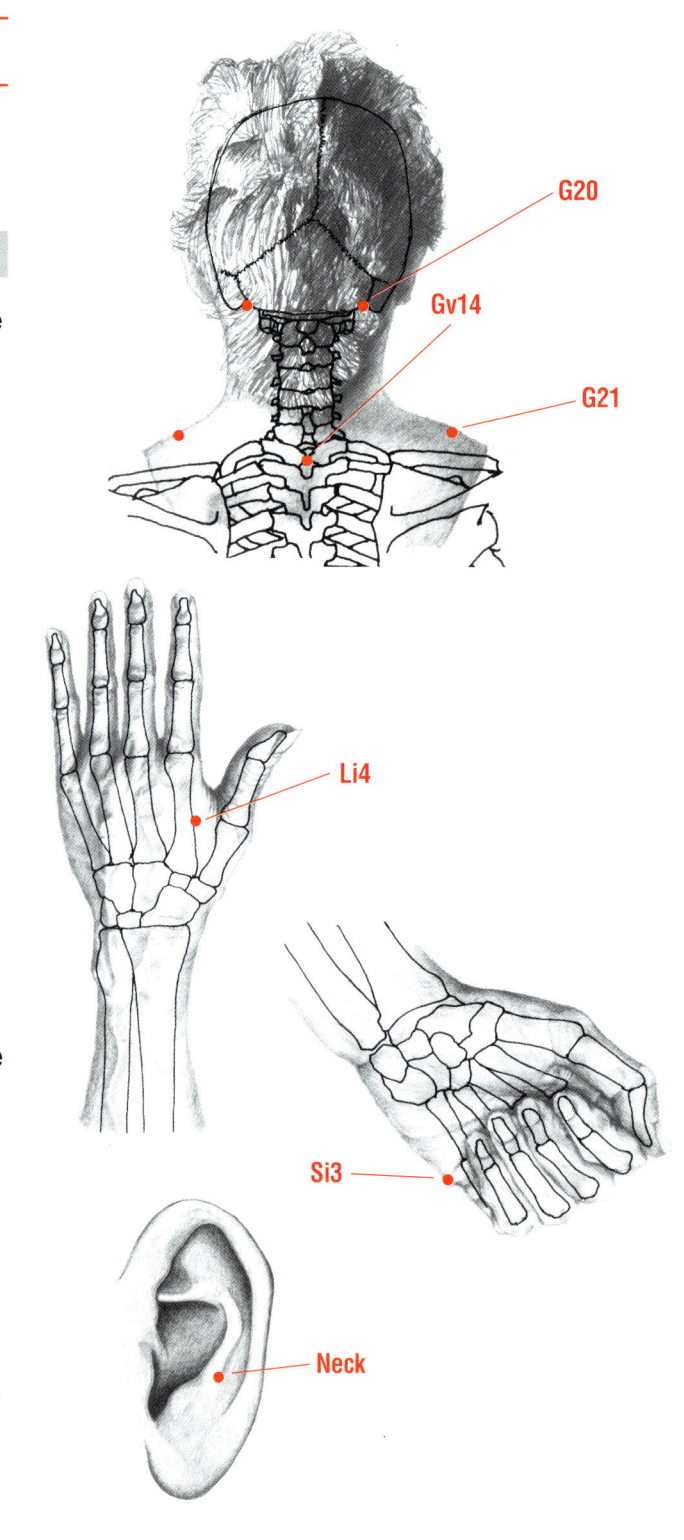

9. SPORTS & INDUSTRIAL INJURIES

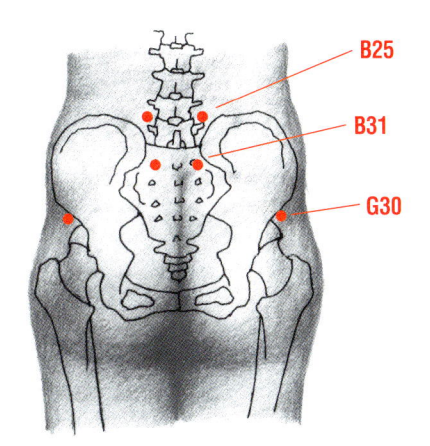

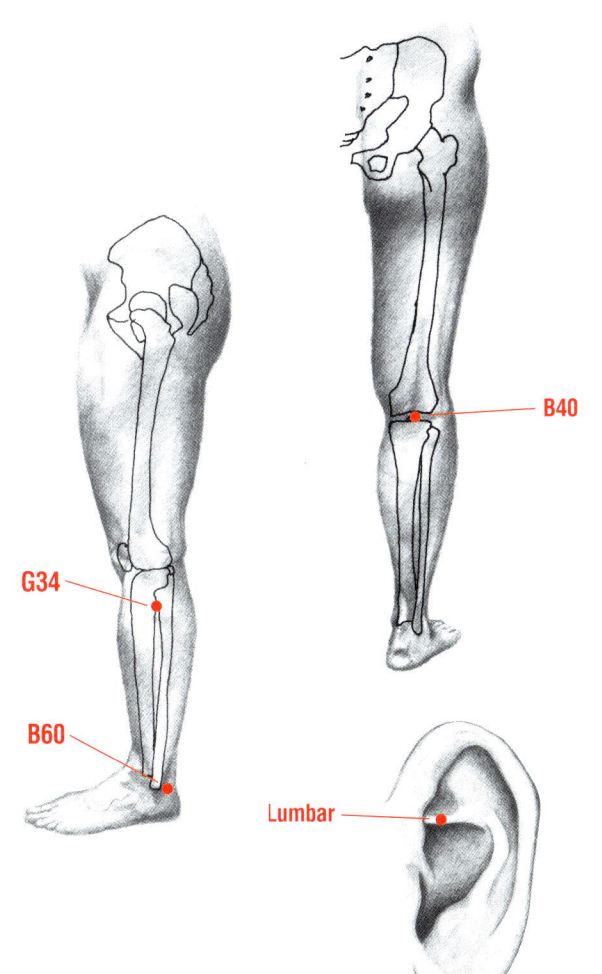

Lumbar Spine

The most common cause is narrow discs in the lower lumbar spine. Discs separate the vertebrae and cushion each from the next. Qualified medical opinion should always be sought but Electro-Acupuncture will usually prove to be the ideal "first aid" and can often be totally successful in the relief of low back pain.

POINTS

B25 — This lies one thumb's width above the sacral bone, one and a half thumb's width away from the mid-line.

B31 — This lies at the top of the sacral bone 1½ thumb's width away from the mid-line.

B40 — This lies directly behind the knee joint in the centre of the crease.

B60 — This lies midway between the tip of the outer ankle bone and the achilles tendon (in the hollow).

G30 — This lies in the upper, outer part of the buttock muscle. It is usually tender on deep finger tip pressure.

G34 — This is just below and in front of the knobbly head of the fibula, which is the bone just below the outer side of knee. The point is in a slight depression and can be tender when pressed with a finger tip.

Ah Shi — Any local tender acupuncture points to be found in the area of pain that give a reaction when stimulated

Ear — Ear point

Rehabilitation: Allow four weeks for recovery.

1. Lie, face downward, with the hands behind the back. Lift the head and shoulders off the floor, lower and repeat.
2. Lie on your back with your feet on the floor and knees bent. Move both legs from side to side.
3. When improvement has begun and the pain gone: stand with your hands clasped behind your back, bend backwards and forwards from the waist, gradually increasing the movements as you are able.

9. SPORTS & INDUSTRIAL INJURIES

Thoracic Spinal Injuries (to the Chest Spine)

Sometimes an injury is sustained to the middle of the spine. Many sportsmen and women suffer with facet joint problems (the small joints at the back of each vertebra). Electro-Acupuncture is an excellent method of treating this problem. *Using your body ruler (page 7) will greatly assist in accurately locating points B12 - B19.*

POINTS

B12 At the level shown on the diagram.

B13 This lies one and a half thumb's width to each side of the centre of the spine at the level of the third thoracic vertebra.

B14 At the level shown on the diagram.

B15 At the level shown on the diagram.

B16 At the level shown on the diagram.

B17 At the level shown on the diagram.

B18 At the level shown on the diagram.

B19 This lies one thumb's width below B18. Again it is situated on both sides of the mid-line.

Ah Shi Any local tender acupuncture points to be found in the area of pain that give a reaction when stimulated

Ear Ear point

Rehabilitation:

1. Lie face down with the hands behind the neck. Raise the head and shoulders as high as possible, lower and repeat.

2. While sitting in a chair, reach sideways towards the floor with each hand in turn.

3. Sit on the edge of a chair, turn to look behind and repeat to the other side.

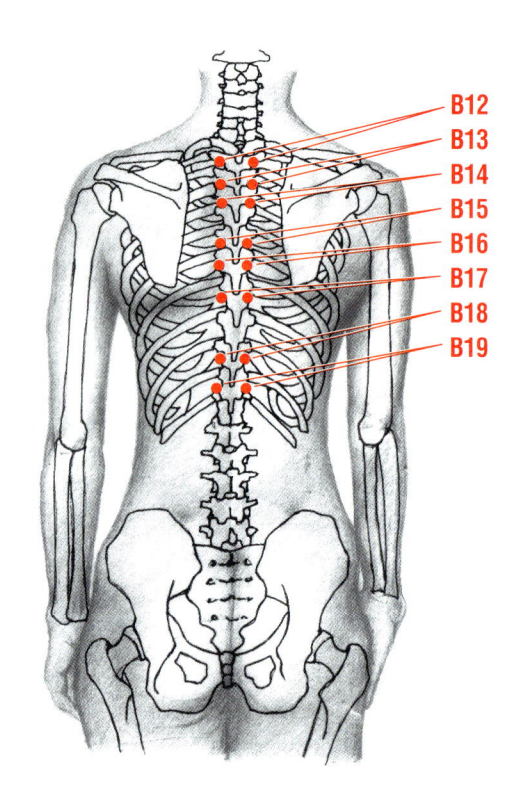

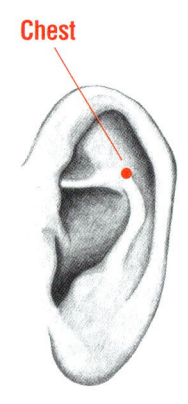

9. SPORTS & INDUSTRIAL INJURIES

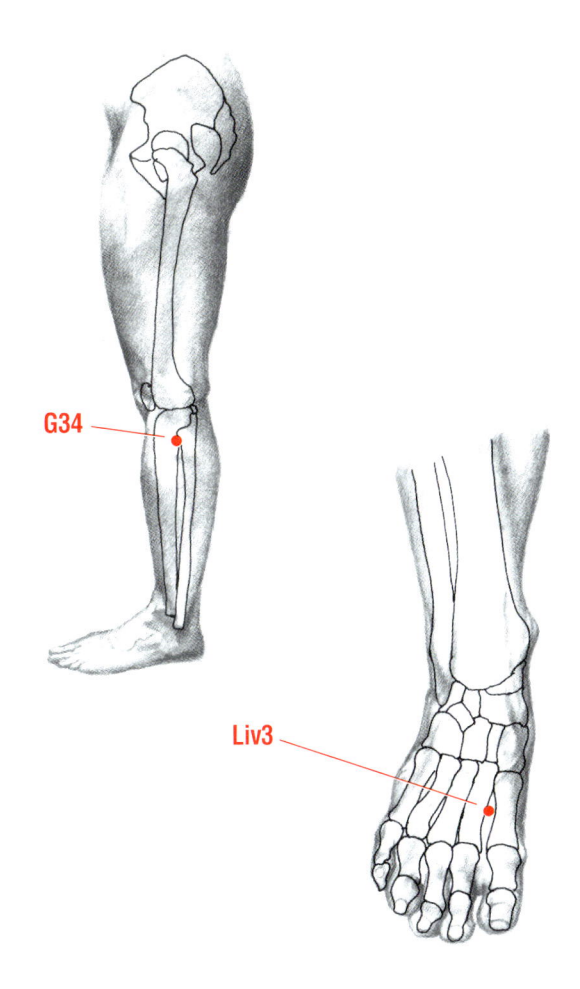

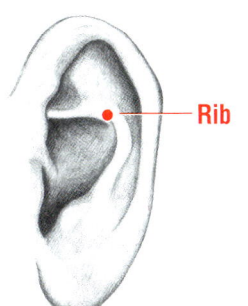

TRUNK INJURIES

Rib Injuries

Bruised, cracked or fractured ribs are common in contact sports and, characteristically, cause pain that is aggravated by deep breathing. Modern treatment does not favour local strapping of the ribs, and therefore some treatment for the pain is essential to facilitate normal breathing. Occasionally rib pain may be caused by the muscles between the ribs being strained. Electro-Acupuncture is ideal in both cases.

POINTS

G34 This is just below and in front of the knobbly head of the fibula, which is the bone just below the outer side of knee. This point is in a slight depression and is sometimes tender when pressed with a finger tip.

Liv3 This lies in between the tendons of the big toe and the first toe, two thumb's width towards the top of the foot from the web.

Ah Shi Any local tender acupuncture points to be found in the area of pain that give a reaction when stimulated

Ear Ear point

Rehabilitation:

Undisplaced Rib Fractures may take 4-6 weeks for recovery. When rib fractures are healed, or as the pain subsides, lie on your back with the arms by the side. Raise the arms above the head. At the same time inhale until the lungs are completely filled or discomfort is felt.

Stand with arms crossed in front, take one arm up and out to the side and continue the movement as far as it will go. Return to the start position and repeat with the other arm.

9. SPORTS & INDUSTRIAL INJURIES

Stitch

This is a cramp-like muscular pain that occurs in the lower part of the abdomen. It occurs during or after exercise. Any lower abdominal pain, which persists after rest, requires a medical opinion. Some people are especially prone to stitch, and in these cases Electro-Acupuncture will be of benefit.

POINTS

Cv6 This lies one and a half thumb's width below the navel.

S36 This lies three thumb's width below the joint under the kneecap lying on the outer side of the knee. One finger's width back from the sharp edge of the shin bone.

Sp6 This lies one hand's width (four fingers) up from the inner ankle joint. It lies just behind the tibia bone at this point.

Ah Shi Any local tender acupuncture points to be found in the area of pain that give a reaction when stimulated

Ear Ear point

Rehabilitation:

Allow 3-4 weeks for recovery and as the pain subsides.

Try the following exercises: Lie on your back on the floor.

Place your feet flat on the floor and bend the knees.

1. Raise only your head from the floor.
2. Raise both head and shoulders.
3. Bend forward to touch the knees with the hands.
4. With arms folded across the chest, sit up and touch the knees with the elbows.

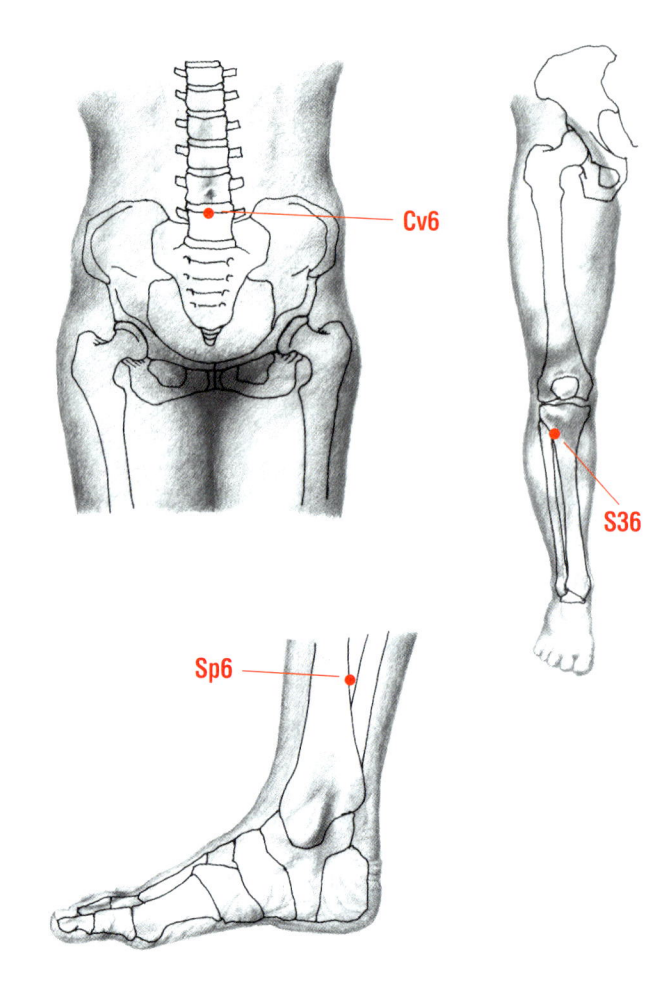

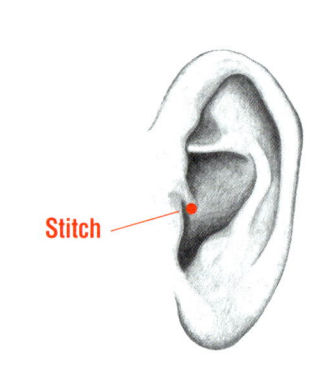

9.16

9. SPORTS & INDUSTRIAL INJURIES

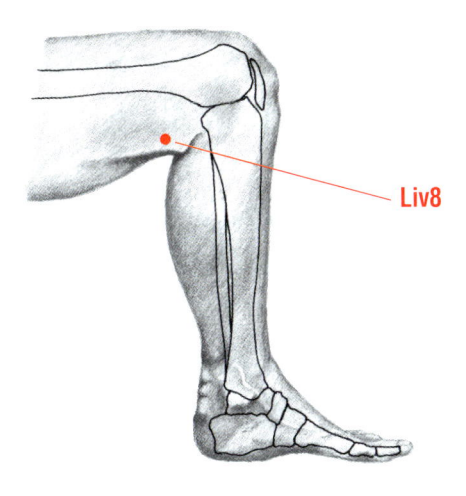

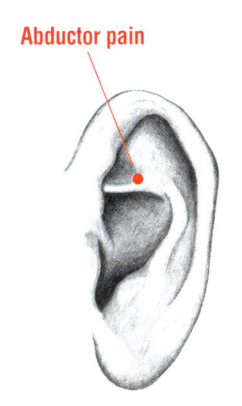

GROIN INJURIES

The groin is situated on the inner aspect of the thigh. Injury occurs when a splits movement goes beyond the body's normal capabilities. Sudden twisting and turning movements can cause the same problem as can kicking, and tackling with the inside of the foot. Pain, higher in the groin (to the ilio-psoas muscle) may also be felt due to repetition of the kicking action. When this movement stops, the injury will usually clear up in 2 or 3 weeks (possibly less with the use of Electro-Acupuncture).

Abductor Pain (Pain on the inside of the Thigh)

If the legs are forced apart during a sports injury, the result can be a strain of the abductor ligament. This is situated at the top of the inside of the thigh. Electro-Acupuncture can also be useful in treating this problem.

POINTS

Liv8 — On the inside of the knee in the hollow between the two tendons when the knee is bent.

Ah Shi — Any local tender acupuncture points to be found in the area of pain that give a reaction when stimulated

Ear — Ear point

Rehabilitation:

Allow 6 weeks for recovery.

It is most important to complete this exercise routine in order to prevent further injury returning to sporting activities.

1. Sit on the floor with legs apart, reach as far forward as possible
2. Stand with legs wide apart, touch the floor as far in front and behind (between the legs) as possible.
3. Stand with the legs wide apart and then attempt to move the feet even further apart.

Strength - improve the muscle power by squeezing:

1. A pillow or football between the knees. Hold the position for ten seconds each time.
2. In the later stages of recovery the leg movements in breaststroke swimming will assist.

9. SPORTS & INDUSTRIAL INJURIES

Abdominal Strain
(Pain in the Rectus Abdominal Muscle)

The rectus abdominis are a pair of muscles lying in the wall of the abdomen passing from the pelvis up to the lower edge of the rib cage. These are often strained by over-use in training or possibly due to a direct blow or by lifting heavy objects. Injury may also occur during a sudden, rough movement as would happen in a judo fall.

POINTS

Cv6 — This lies one and a half thumb's width below the navel.

S36 — This lies three thumb's width below the joint under the kneecap lying on the outer side of the knee. One finger's width back from the sharp edge of the shin bone.

Sp6 — This lies one hand's width (four fingers) up from the inner ankle joint. It lies just behind the tibia bone at this point.

Ah Shi — Any local tender acupuncture points to be found in the area of pain that give a reaction when stimulated

Ear — Ear point

Rehabilitation:

Allow 3-4 weeks for recovery as the pain subsides.

Try the following:

Lie on your back on the floor. Place your feet flat on the floor and bend the knees.

1. Raise only your head from the floor.
2. Raise both head and shoulders.
3. Bend forward to touch the knees with the hands.
4. With arms folded across the chest, sit up and touch the knees with the elbows.

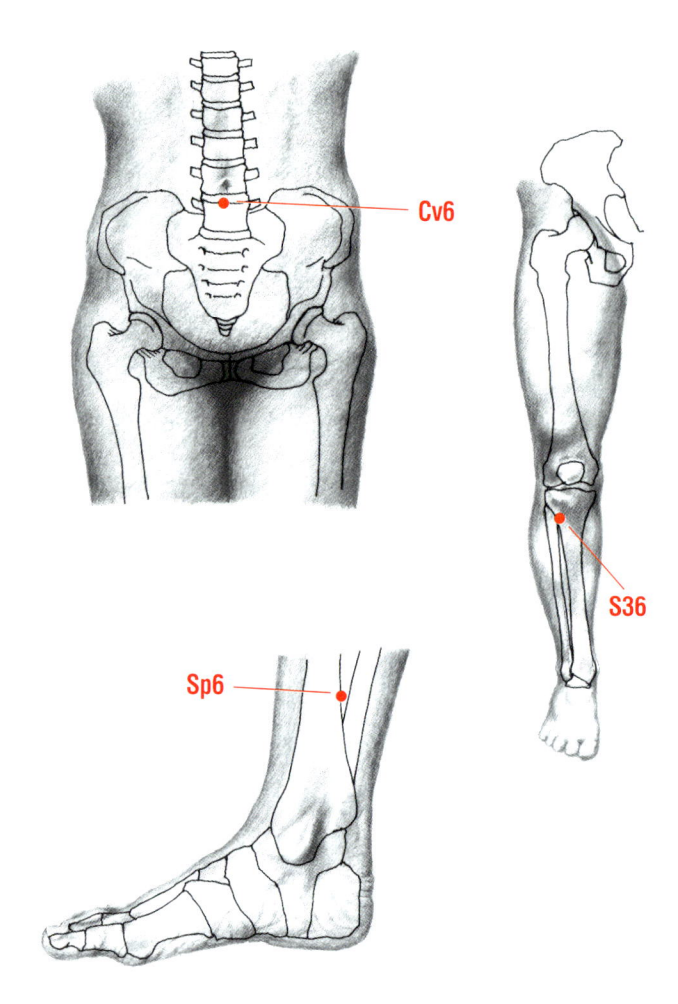

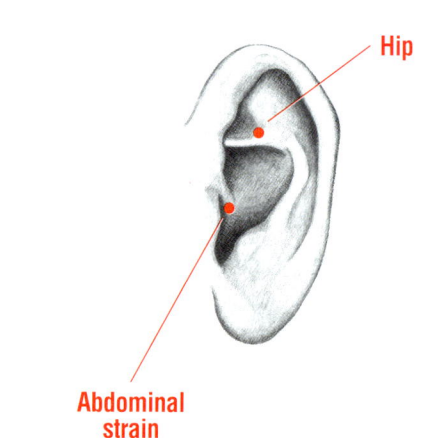

9. SPORTS & INDUSTRIAL INJURIES

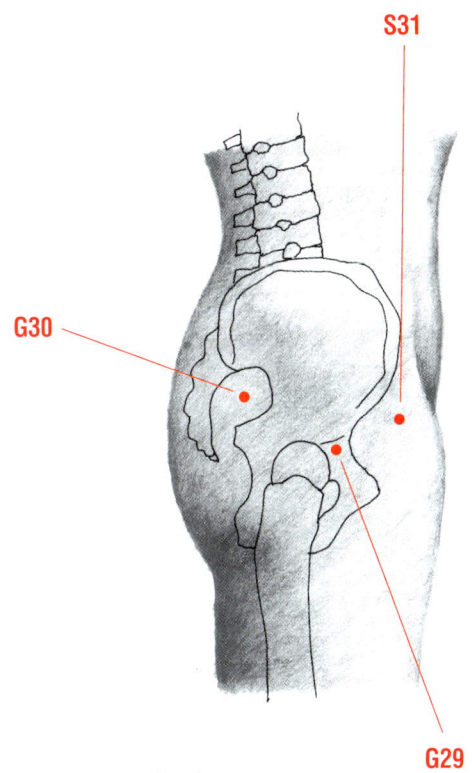

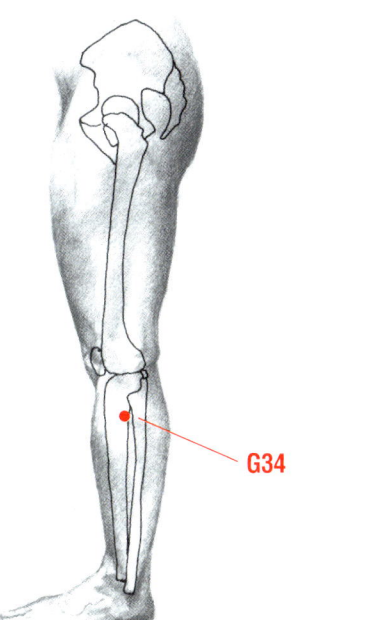

Hip Injuries

The hip is a strong joint and is seldom injured during sport. The outer aspect of the thigh, at the level of the hip, can sometimes be injured by direct contact with the ground or other unyielding surface. Recovery from bruising may take 2 weeks.

POINTS

Ah Shi — Any local tender acupuncture points to be found in the area of pain that give a reaction when stimulated

G29 — This lies halfway between the bony knob found at the top and front of the rim of the pelvis and the bony mass formed by the top of the hip bone, which is situated at the top of the thigh.

G30 — This lies in the upper, outer part of the buttock muscle. It is usually tender on deep finger tip pressure.

G34 — This is just below and in front of the knobbly head of the fibula, which is the bone just below the outer side of knee. This point is in a slight depression and is sometimes tender when pressed with a finger tip.

S31 — This lies on the level of the pubic bone just below the bony knob found at the top and front of the pelvis.

S36 — This lies three thumb's width below the joint under the kneecap lying on the outer side of the knee. One finger's width back from the sharp edge of the shin bone.

Ear — Ear point

Rehabilitation:

Maintaining the range of movement in the hips is vital.

1. Lie face down, raise one leg, keeping it straight. Repeat with the other leg.
2. Lie on your "good" side, keep the injured leg straight, and lift it as high as possible.
3. Lie on your back, bring one knee up to the chest (repeat with the other leg).
4. Sit on the floor, keep the legs straight, and turn the feet inwards and outward.
5. Swimming is recommended when pain begins to subside.

9. SPORTS & INDUSTRIAL INJURIES

THIGH INJURIES

Dead Leg - Thigh Pain

Any muscle may receive a direct blow thereby causing temporary stiffness with pain. The term dead leg is reserved for the muscles on the front and side of the thigh. The direct blow will cause internal bleeding with resultant swelling, pain and the loss of function.

POINTS

Ah Shi — Any local tender acupuncture points to be found in the area of pain that give a reaction when stimulated

G34 — This is just below and in front of the knobbly head of the fibula, which is the bone just below the outer side of knee. This point is in a slight depression and is sometimes tender when pressed with a finger tip.

Ear — Ear point

Rehabilitation:

1-2 weeks may be required for full recovery.

The quadriceps muscle in front of the thigh will soon become weak and therefore the exercises given for knee injuries (see page 9.24) should be followed.

Following the successful completion of these exercises cycling and swimming is recommended.

Return to sport is dependent upon a full pain free movement at the knee and hip joints.

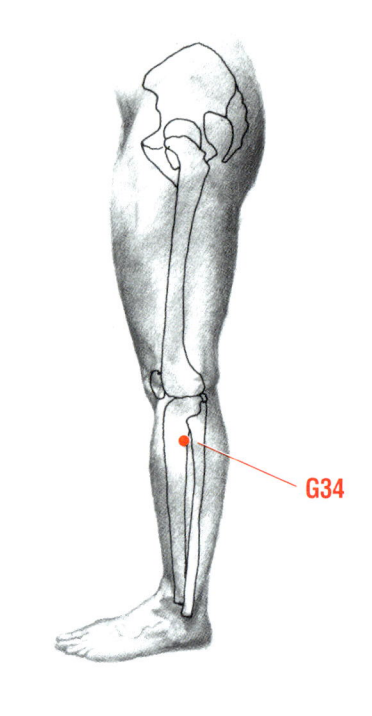

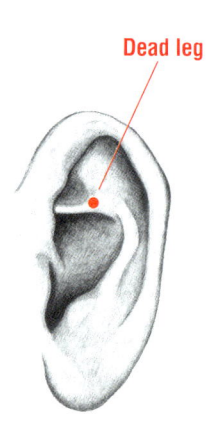

9. SPORTS & INDUSTRIAL INJURIES

Rectus Femoris

This muscle lies on the front of the thigh running from hip to knee. It is injured, in the main, by sprinting and kicking movements.

POINTS

Ah Shi — Any local tender acupuncture points to be found in the area of pain that give a reaction when stimulated

G34 — This is just below and in front of the knobbly head of the fibula, which is the bone just below the outer side of knee. This point is in a slight depression and is sometimes tender when pressed with a finger tip.

Ear — Ear point

Rectus

Rehabilitation:

Allow 4-6 weeks for recovery.

Static Exercise

1. In the sitting position, keep the leg straight and tighten the muscles of the thigh. When correctly performed the heel will lift just off the floor (compare with the other leg). Hold the position for ten seconds.

2. In the sitting position, place a pillow or rolled towel behind the knee. Tighten the thigh muscle and so raise the heel from the floor.

3. Sit on a table, raise the foot to straighten the leg. Lower and repeat
4. Stand leaning on a table, slightly bend both knees and increase the bend as confidence returns.

Stretching

The eventual aim is to bring the back of the head as near as possible to the floor while in a kneeling position. Begin, in the early stages, by kneeling on the floor with the trunk upright; as the pain diminishes, gradually lean backwards using the hands to support the body weight.

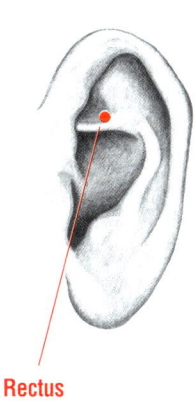

9. SPORTS & INDUSTRIAL INJURIES

Hamstrings

These muscles lie on the back of the thigh. They affect the movement of both hip and knee joints. They are frequently injured in sports, during fast movements, such as sprinting, overstretching, and kicking a ball. Fatigue and lack of warm-up are other factors as are uncoordinated movements and direct violence such as a kick or blow from behind.

POINTS

Ah Shi Any local tender acupuncture points to be found in the area of pain that give a reaction when stimulated

B40 This lies directly behind the knee joint in the centre of the crease.

Ear Ear point

Rehabilitation:

It is very important to maintain or even improve the amount of stretch in the hamstrings following injury:

1. Sit on the floor with both legs straight, raise the injured leg until discomfort is felt. Easier movement will be felt each day.

2. Sit on the floor with the injured leg straight and the other leg bent. Reach forward with the hands to touch the toes of the injured leg. If this is achieved easily, reach beyond the toes.

3. Stand, keeping the legs straight, try to reach the floor and aim to improve each day.

4. Stand on the uninjured leg with the injured leg resting on an object parallel with the floor (such as a table). Reach towards the foot of the injured leg.

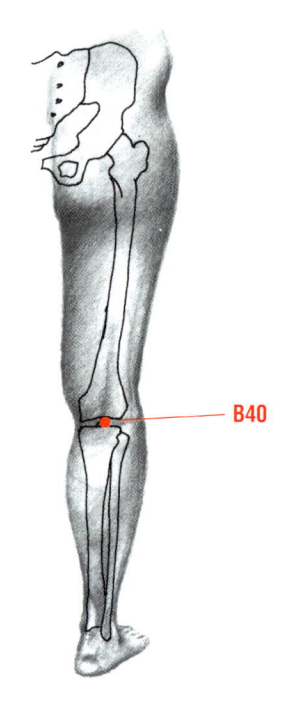

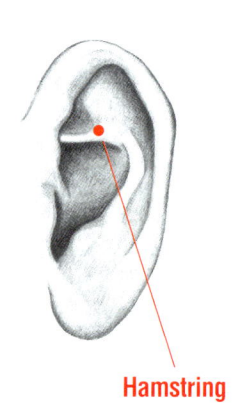

Hamstring

9. SPORTS & INDUSTRIAL INJURIES

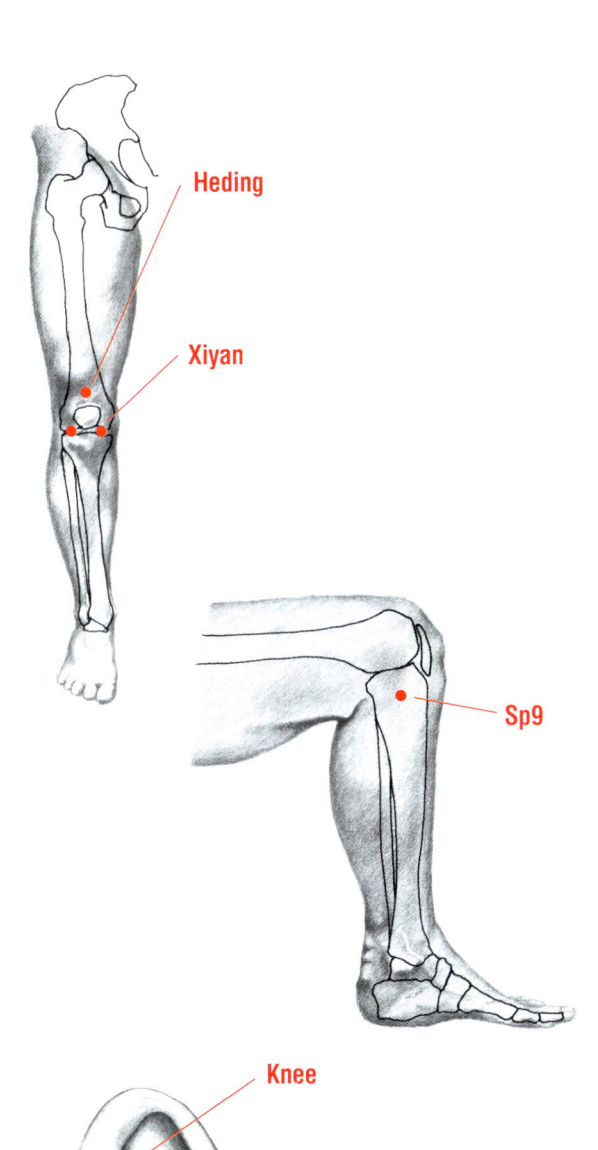

KNEE INJURIES

Cartilages

These are usually damaged due to violent movement of the knee while the foot is stationary, such as twisting. Pain and swelling will result and the knee joint may lock and give way. One or more of these symptoms may be present. While qualified medical help should always be sought treatment with Electro-Acupuncture should help curb the pain and swelling.

Ligaments

These are situated on the inner (medial ligament) and outer (lateral ligament) aspects of the joint. These prevent excessive sideways movement. Inside the joint are the cruciate ligaments which prevent excessive forward and backwards movement. Ligaments are injured when the joint is forced into unnatural positions. At the front of the knee is the ligamentum Patellae which attaches the knee cap to the front of the Tibia.

POINTS

B40 — This lies directly behind the knee joint in the centre of the crease.

Sp9 — This lies just below the inside of the kneecap and below the top of the tibia. This point is usually tender when pressed with a finger tip.

Xiyan — These points lie in the depressions formed on either side of the ligament just beneath the knee-cap. These depressions become obvious when the knee is slightly bent.

Heding — Lies two finger's width above the kneecap in the centre line.

Ah Shi — Any local tender acupuncture points to be found in the area of pain that give a reaction when stimulated

Ear — Ear point

Treatment continued ▶

9.23

9. SPORTS & INDUSTRIAL INJURIES

Ligaments - *continued*

Rehabilitation:

Ligament strains may take 6 weeks for recovery.

It is vital to maintain the size and strength of the quadriceps muscles (those on the front of the thigh, from hip to knee). These exercises should be performed in sequence moving on to the next exercise only when the pain has subsided.

Static Exercises

1. In the sitting position, keep the leg straight and tighten the muscles of the thigh. When correctly performed the heel will lift just above of the floor (compare with the other leg). Hold the position for ten seconds.

2. In the sitting position, place a pillow or rolled towel behind the knee. Tighten the thigh muscle and so raise the heel from the floor.

3. Sit on a table, raise the foot to straighten the leg, lower and repeat.

4. Stand leaning on a table, slightly bend both knees and increase the bend as confidence returns.

5. Stand in front of a chair, bend the knees until buttocks touch the seat (do not sit) then return to start position.

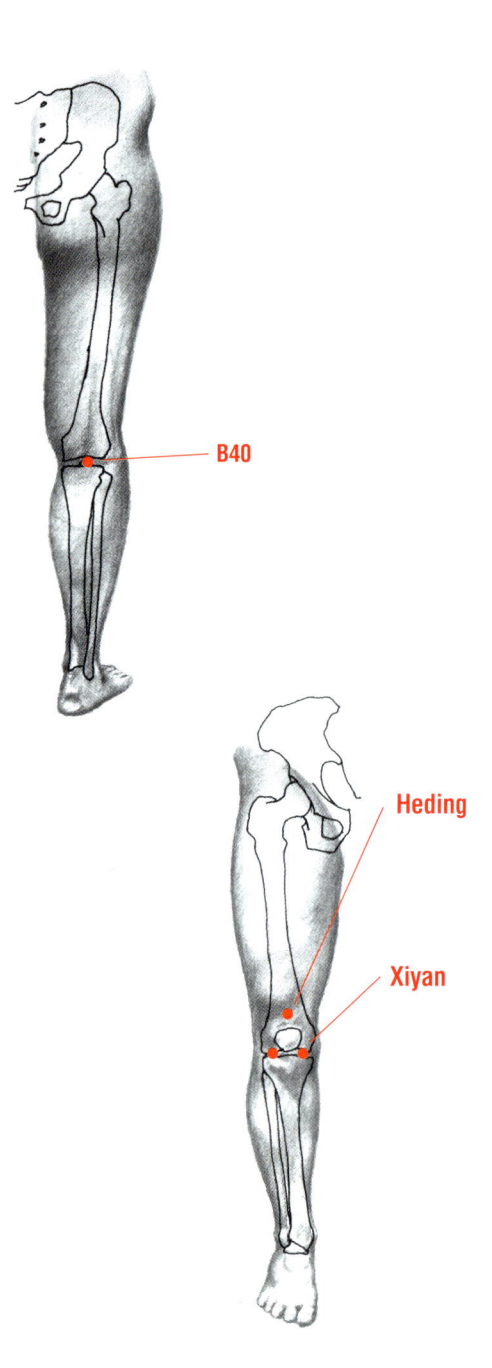

B40

Heding

Xiyan

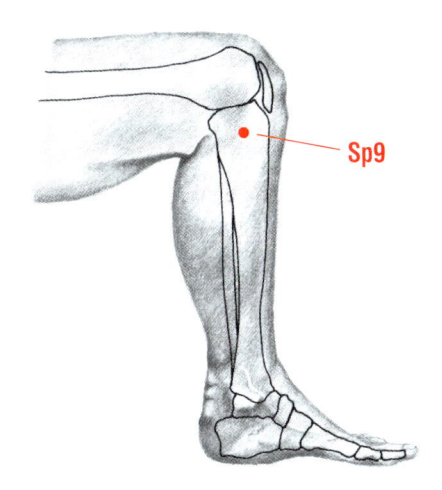

9. SPORTS & INDUSTRIAL INJURIES

Lateral Ligament Strain

(Pain on the Outer Side of the Knee Joint)

Injury occurs when strain is put onto the outside of the joint as in a tackle or from a bad landing such as in basketball when the player lands on the outer side of the foot.

POINTS

Ah Shi — Any local tender acupuncture points to be found in the area of pain that give a reaction when stimulated

Ear — Ear point

PLUS - Treatment Points and Rehabilitation as for Ligaments

Sp9

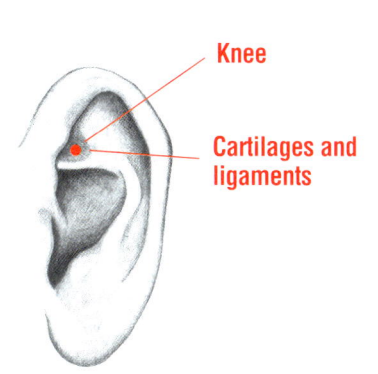

Medial Ligament Strain

(Sprain of the Ligament on the Inner Side of the Knee Joint)

Injury occurs when strain is put onto the inside of the joint as in a tackle or from a bad landing such as in basketball when the player lands on the inner side of the foot.

POINTS

Ah Shi — Any local tender acupuncture points to be found in the area of pain that give a reaction when stimulated

Ear — Ear point

PLUS - Treatment Points and Rehabilitation as for Ligaments

Knee
Cartilages and ligaments

9. SPORTS & INDUSTRIAL INJURIES

LOWER LEG INJURIES

These injuries are the classic sports related injuries. They are common to long distance runners, aerobics teachers and athletes who change, too often, the surface on which they train and compete. Qualified medical help should be sought to remove the possibility of stress fractures and Anterior Tibial Syndrome. Electro-Acupuncture should help in many cases and help control the pain in more severe situations.

Shin Soreness

Sometimes known as shin splints, this is common in runners. It produces pain on or next to the tibia (the major bone in the lower leg) when standing, walking or running.

POINTS

Ah Shi — Any local tender acupuncture points to be found in the area of pain that give a reaction when stimulated

S36 — This lies three thumb's width below the joint under the kneecap lying on the outer side of the knee. One finger's width back from the sharp edge of the shin bone.

S41 — This lies directly over the middle point of the front of the foot joint.

Sp9 — This lies just below the inside of the kneecap and below the top of the tibia. This point is usually tender when pressed with a finger tip.

Ear — Ear point

Rehabilitation

Allow 6-8 weeks for recovery.

Rest from the offending exercise.

The use of shock absorbing inner soles is recommended.

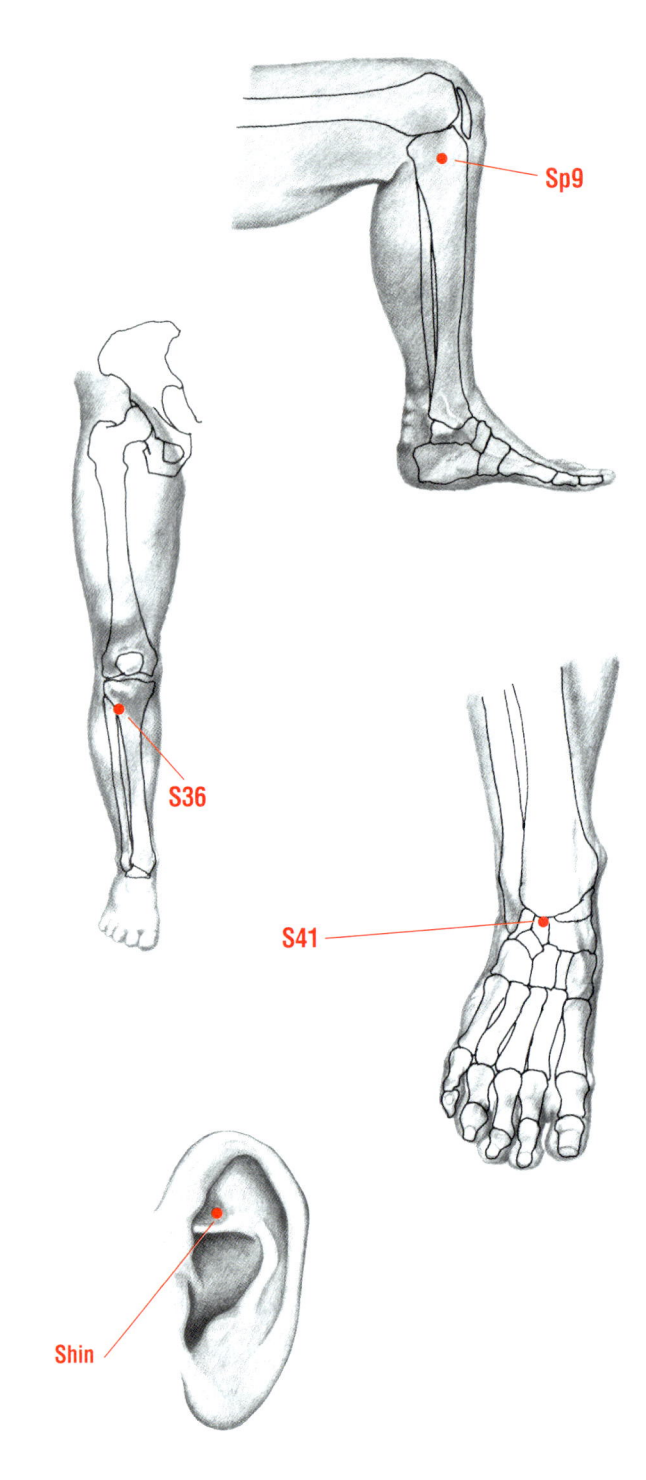

9. SPORTS & INDUSTRIAL INJURIES

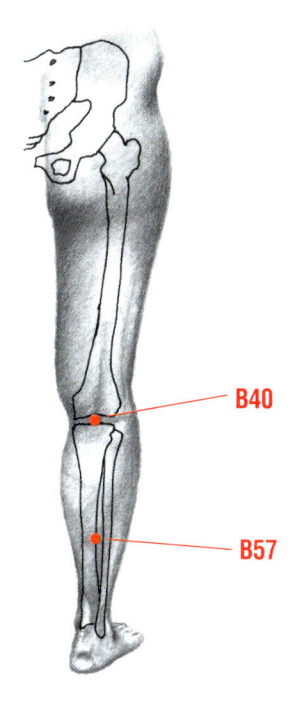

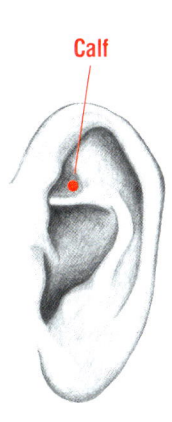

Calf Strain

Calf muscles lie in the back of the lower leg. There are two main muscles, the gastronemius and soleus muscles. They both insert into the Achilles tendon which attaches to the heel bone. These muscles are injured through insufficient warm-up, sudden changes of direction, (such as in tennis and squash) fatigue during the closing minutes of a game, or direct violence, such as a kick.

POINTS

B40 — This lies directly behind the knee joint in the centre of the crease.

B57 — This lies in the centre of the back of the calf, just where the fleshy mass of muscle narrows down into tendon.

Ah Shi — Any local tender acupuncture points to be found in the area of pain that give a reaction when stimulated

Ear — Ear point

Rehabilitation:

1. These should be done in the following sequence as pain subsides.

2. Lie on a sofa or on the floor with the legs elevated. (Feet above the hips.) Stretch the toes away from you and return.

3. Sit in a chair with the feet flat on the floor, raise and lower the heels.

4. Lean on a table, raise and lower yourself on your toes, while taking your weight on your arms.

5. Stand, raising up and down on your toes.

6. Repeat 4 on one leg at a time.

Stretching Exercise

Stand facing a wall with both hands against the wall, gradually walk backwards, away from the wall. Keep the hands in position on the wall and try to keep the heels on the floor.

9. SPORTS & INDUSTRIAL INJURIES

Achilles Tendonitis
(Inflammation of the Achilles Tendon)

In this condition pain is felt in the Achilles tendon just above the heel. The tendon is often painful to touch. Rupture of the Achilles tendon is uncommon. However, should the tendon be partially or completely ruptured competent orthopaedic treatment must be sought. Electro-Acupuncture is then a useful assistant to recovery.

POINTS

B60 — This lies midway between the tip of the outer ankle bone and the achilles tendon (in the hollow).

G40 — This lies just in front of the knob of bone on the outside ankle bone.

K3 — This lies midway between the tip of the inner ankle bone and the achilles tendon (in the hollow)

Ah Shi — Any local tender acupuncture points to be found in the area of pain that give a reaction when stimulated

Ear — Ear point

Rehabilitation:

These should be done in the following sequence as pain subsides.

1. Lie on a sofa or on the floor with the legs elevated. (Feet above the hips.) Stretch the toes away from you and return.
2. Sit in a chair with the feet flat on the floor, raise and lower the heels.
3. Lean on a table, raise and lower yourself on your toes, while taking your weight on your arms.
4. Stand, raising up and down on your toes.
5. Repeat 4 on one leg at a time.

Stretching Exercises

Stand facing a wall with both hands against the wall, gradually walk backwards, away from the wall. Keep the hands in position on the wall and try to keep the heels on the floor.

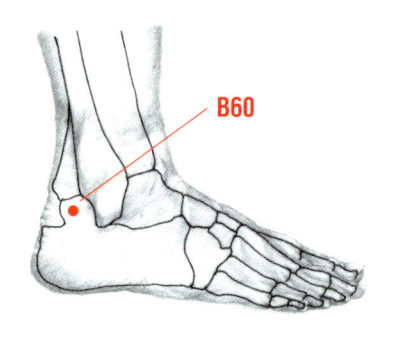

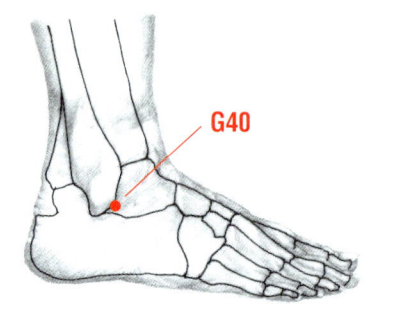

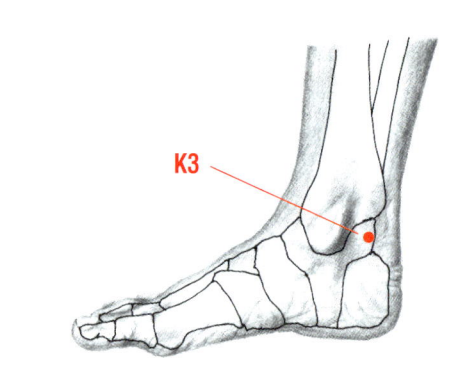

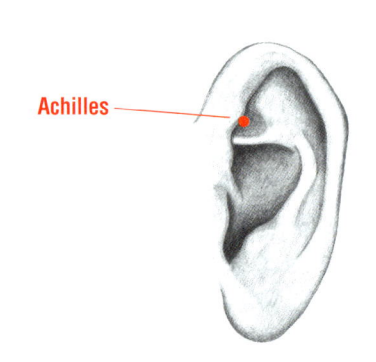

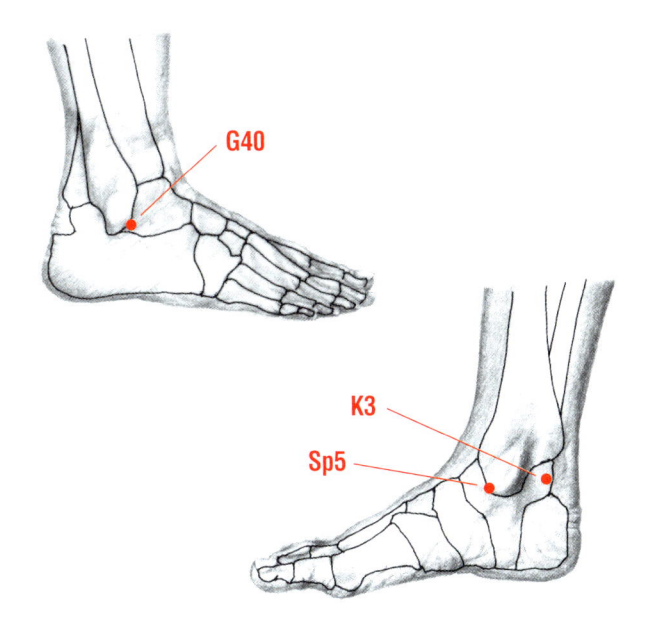

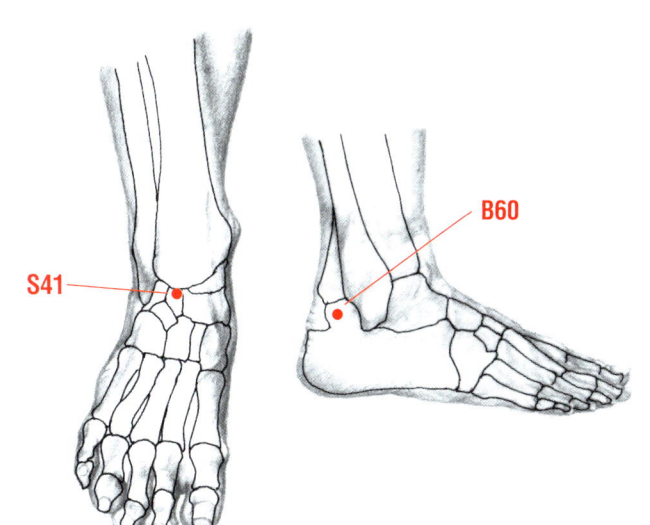

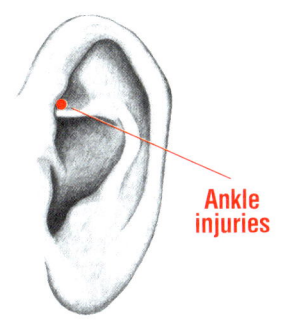

9. SPORTS & INDUSTRIAL INJURIES

Ankle Injuries

Ankle sprains are often caused by a forced sideways movement to either the inside or the outside of the ankle. The ligaments on each side of the joint capsule may be stretched or torn and may bleed internally or externally.

POINTS

B60 — This lies midway between the tip of the outer ankle bone and the achilles tendon (in the hollow).

G40 — This lies just in front of the knob of bone on the outside ankle bone.

K3 — This lies midway between the tip of the inner ankle bone and the achilles tendon (in the hollow)

S41 — This lies directly over the middle point of the front of the foot joint.

Sp5 — This lies just in front of the knob of bone on the inside ankle bone.

Ah Shi — Any local tender acupuncture points to be found in the area of pain that give a reaction when stimulated

Ear — Ear point

Rehabilitation:

The following exercises should be done in sequence as pain diminishes:

1. Sitting with the leg elevated
   (a) Stretch toes away from you and pull them towards you.
   (b) Turn the foot inwards and outward.
   (c) Describe circles with the foot.

2. Sit on a chair, feet flat on the floor, raise and lower the heels.

3. Stand, leaning on a table, raise and lower the heels.

4. Stand, raise and lower the heels

Balance

Ankle injuries cause a temporary loss of balance and therefore reorientation is required.

1. Stand on the injured leg only and try to remain in this position for one minute. Having achieved this repeat the exercise with eyes closed.

2. Try to stand on the tiptoes of the injured leg for 30 seconds.

9. SPORTS & INDUSTRIAL INJURIES

FOOT INJURIES

Metatarsalgia (Pain on the Ball of the Foot)

This is pain under the ball of the foot where the supporting ligaments of the metatarsal heads become strained in the line of the toe joints. This is common in people whose work involves a lot of standing. It can also be caused by running or jumping on hard surfaces, or running in hard soled shoes. Appropriate footwear and metatarsal support is essential in these cases.

POINTS

G34 — This is just below and in front of the knobbly head of the fibula, which is the bone just below the outer side of knee. This point is in a slight depression and is sometimes tender when pressed with a finger tip.

Liv3 — This lies in between the tendons of the big toe and the first toe, two thumb's width towards the top of the foot from the web.

Extra foot points — These lie at the web point between each toe.

Ah Shi — Any local tender acupuncture points to be found in the area of pain that give a reaction when stimulated.

Ear — Ear point

Rehabilitation:

Refrain from the sports or exercise which caused the problem.

The use of shock absorbing inner soles is recommended. A metatarsal bar of foam rubber or felt may also assist in relieving the pain. This can be purchased from a chemist or chiropodist.

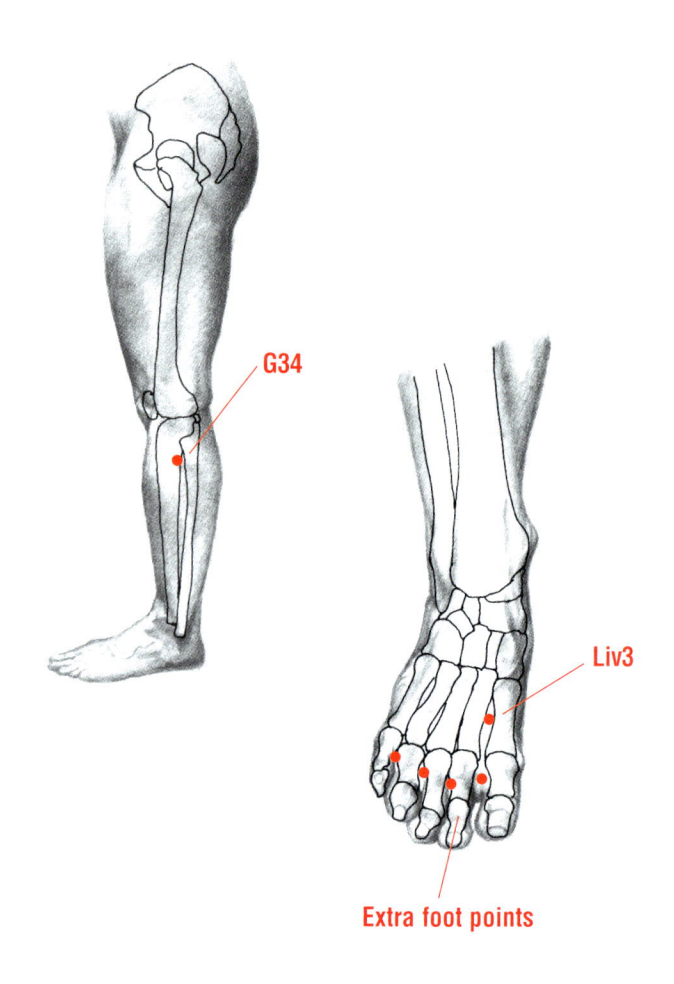

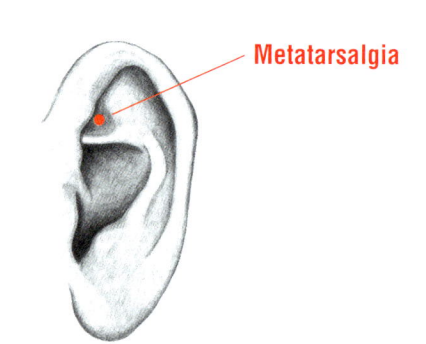

9. SPORTS & INDUSTRIAL INJURIES

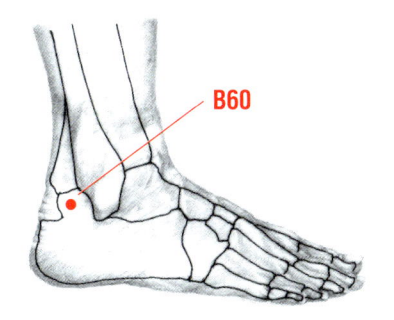

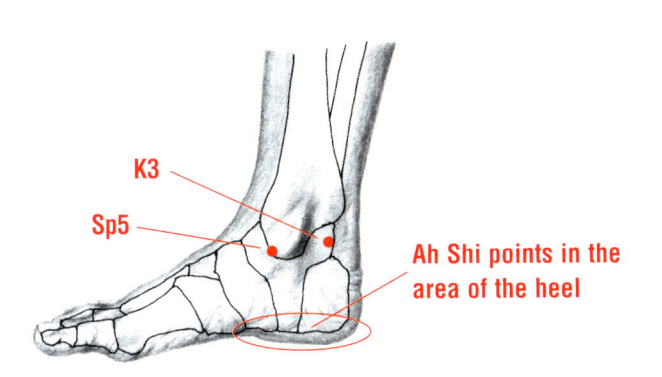

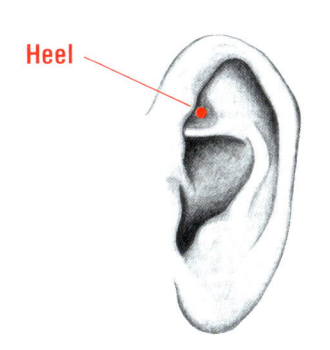

Bruised Heel - Heel Spur

In these injuries pain is felt beneath the heel, which is often due to simple bruising. This can occur when landing during jumping or hurdling.

POINTS

B60 — This lies midway between the tip of the outer ankle bone and the achilles tendon (in the hollow).

K3 — This lies midway between the tip of the inner ankle bone and the achilles tendon (in the hollow)

Ah Shi — Any local tender acupuncture points to be found in the area of pain that give a reaction when stimulated.

Ear — Ear point

Rehabilitation:

Refrain from the sport or exercise which caused the problem.

The use of shock absorbing inner soles is recommended. Use foam rubber to build up additional support for the arch of the foot.

9. SPORTS & INDUSTRIAL INJURIES

Bunion pain (Hallux Valgus)

This is pain in the big toe joint and is common in older sportsmen. Excessive use of tight footware combine over the years to cause bunions, which are swellings of the joint at the base of the big toe. This is often followed by diversion of the joint from its original straight line, towards the outer side of the foot, the characteristic deformity of hallux valgus.

POINTS

Liv3 — This lies in between the tendons of the big toe and the first toe, two thumb's width towards the top of the foot from the web.

Sp1 — This is situated on the outer side of the nail bed of the big toe.

Sp2 — This is situated on the outside edge of the big toe, in a depression, level with the web of the toe.

Sp3 — This is situated on the inside edge of the foot, two thumbs width towards the ankle from Sp1, in a depression, up against the large knob of bone.

Sp5 — This lies just in front of the knob of bone on the inside ankle bone.

Ah Shi — Any local tender acupuncture points to be found in the area of pain that give a reaction when stimulated

Ear — Ear point

Rehabilitation:

The use of shock absorbing inner soles is recommended in all footware.

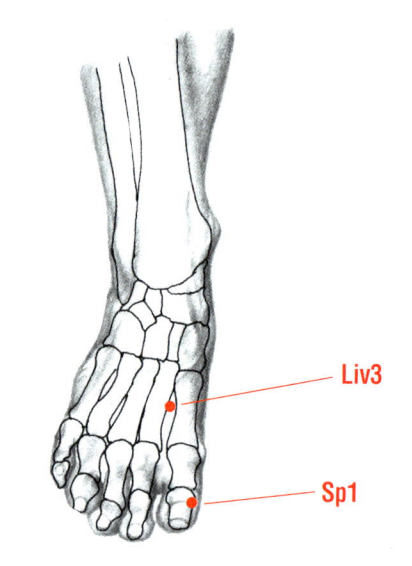

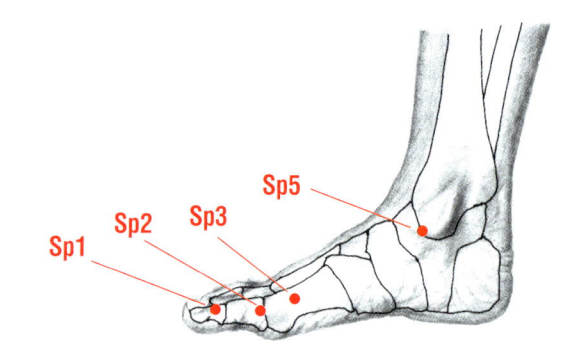

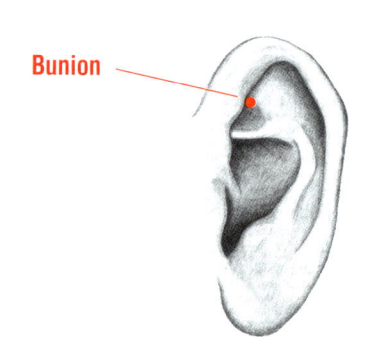

9. SPORTS & INDUSTRIAL INJURIES

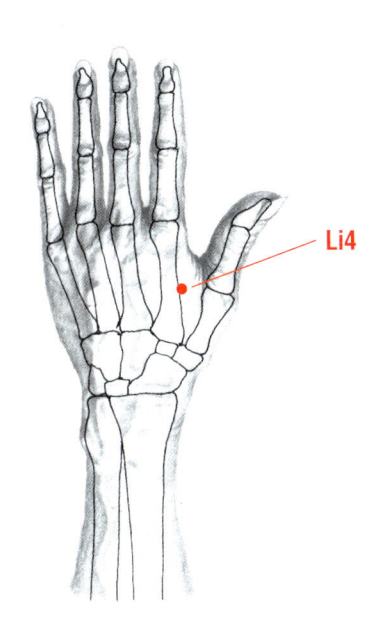

IMPROVEMENT OF PHYSICAL PERFORMANCE USING ELECTRO-ACUPUNCTURE

A recent study was carried out in Norway that tested the exercise response to electrical stimulation. An electrode was applied to Large Intestine 4 (Li4) and the treatment was continued for thirty minutes on each hand.

An improvement in running, swimming and ergo meter cycling was regularly observed following this stimulation.

Apply Electro-Acupuncture over large intestine 4 (LI4) for approximately 10 minutes on each hand. This can be carried out during the rest period prior to sporting activity and need be carried out once daily only.

This improvement in physical performance is almost certainly due to the release of natural chemicals in the body. The most important of these is endorphin.

EAR TREATMENT POINTS

	Page	Point
Abdominal Pain - Upper	4.7	31
Acne	5.2	37, 44
Angina	3.1	29
Ankle Pain	1.18	13
Anxiety	8.18	18, 59
Asthma	6.2	41
Back Pain - Lower	1.15, 9.13	21
Bedwetting	7.1	6, 18
Bells Palsy (Facial Paralysis)	2.1	66
Bladder - Irritable	7.2	25
Bronchitis	6.3	41
Carpal Tunnel Syndrome	9.9	3
Chest pain	3.1	29
Chilblains	3.1	10
Conjunctivitis	8.21	63
Constipation	4.3	40, 22
Coccyx	1.28	17
Cramp	1.25	14, 16, 23
Depression	8.15	16, 34
Diarrhoea	4.5	31
Dupuytrens Contracture	1.12	7
Earache	1.8	61
Eczema	5.3	34
Elbows	9.5, 9.6, 1.11	28, 30
Eye Pain	8.20	62
Facial Neuralgia	1.7	65
Facial Paralysis	2.1	66
Fainting Attacks	8.9	29, 53
Fever	8.9	5
Foot Pain	1.18	8
Gout	1.27	8
Haemorrhoids	4.4	22
Hand - Finger Pain	1.12	3
Hangover	8.17	39
Hay Fever	8.3	53
Headache	1.2 - 1.5	49, 51, 60
Heartburn	4.3	36
Hiccoughs (Hiccups)	8.13	35
High Blood Pressure	3.5	45, 46
Hip Pain	1.16, 9.19	15, 18
Hot Flushes	8.11	1, 22, 55
Impotence	8.17	20, 22, 58
Incontinence	7.3	5
Insomnia	8.8	18
Intercostal Neuralgia	1.19	27
Irritable Bladder	7.2	25
Itchy Skin - Pruritis	8.13	54
Jaw Pain	1.6	57
Knee Problems	1.17, 9.23/5	14
Lactation	8.16	19, 33
Laryngitis	2.3	48
Liver Problems	4.6	46
Libido - Increase	8.3	20, 25, 42
M.E.	8.14	18, 21, 47
Menopause - Hot Flushes	8.11	1, 22, 55
Menstruation - Painful or Cramps	1.24	21, 25, 50
Migraine	1.2, - 1.5	49, 51, 60
Morning Sickness	8.15	36
Mouth Ulcers	2.3	36

	Page	Point
Neck Problems	1.9, 9.12	47
Nosebleed Epistaxis	2.7	45
Palpitations	3.5	18, 35
Periods - Painful	1.24	21, 25, 50
Perspiration - Excessive	8.11	45
Premenstrual Tension PMS	1.24	21, 25, 50
Prostate Problems	7.2	25
Pruritis (Itching)	8.13	54
Radio Ulna Joint Strain	1.14	12
Relaxation and Stress Treatment	8.18	18, 59
Renal Colic Kidney	1.23	4
Sciatica	1.20	16, 17
Shoulder Problems	1.10	42, 47
Sinusitis	2.2	56
Smoking	8.19	45
Stress and Anxiety	8.18	18, 59
Stroke Recovery	8.2	8, 9, 13, 21, 32
Sweating - Excessive	8.11	45
Tennis Elbow	1.11, 9.5	30
Tinnitus	2.4	38, 43
Toothache	1.6, 1.7	61, 63
Tonsillitis	2.7	24
Urinary Incontinence	7.3	6
Urinary Retention	7.4	11
Wrist Problems	1.14, 9.8	9

Sport and Industrial Injuries

	Page	Point
Abdominal Strain	9.18	36
Abductor Pain	9.17	16
Achilles Tendonitis	9.28	8
Ankle Injuries	9.29	13
Bicep Tendonitis	9.3	7
Calf Strain	9.27	13
Carpal Tunnel Syndrome	9.9	3
Cartilages	9.23	14
Dead Leg	9.20	18
Fingers and Thumbs	1.12, 9.10	2
Golfers Elbow	9.6	28
Hallux Vulgus - Bunion Pain	9.32	8
Ham Strings	9.22	18
Heel	9.31	8
Hip Injuries	9.19	15, 18
Lateral Ligament Strain	9.25	14
Ligaments	9.23	14
Lumbar	9.13	21
Medial Ligament Strain	9.25	14
Metatarsalgia	9.30	8
Neck	9.12	47
Painful Arc	9.4	32
Rectus Femoris	9.21	16
Rib Injuries	9.15	26
Shin Soreness	9.26	13, 14
Shoulder	9.2	42, 47
Spinal Injuries	9.11	7
Sterno - Clavicular Pain	9.3	26
Stitch	9.16	36
Tennis Elbow	9.5	30
Tenosynovitis	9.7	30
Wrist Injuries	9.8	9

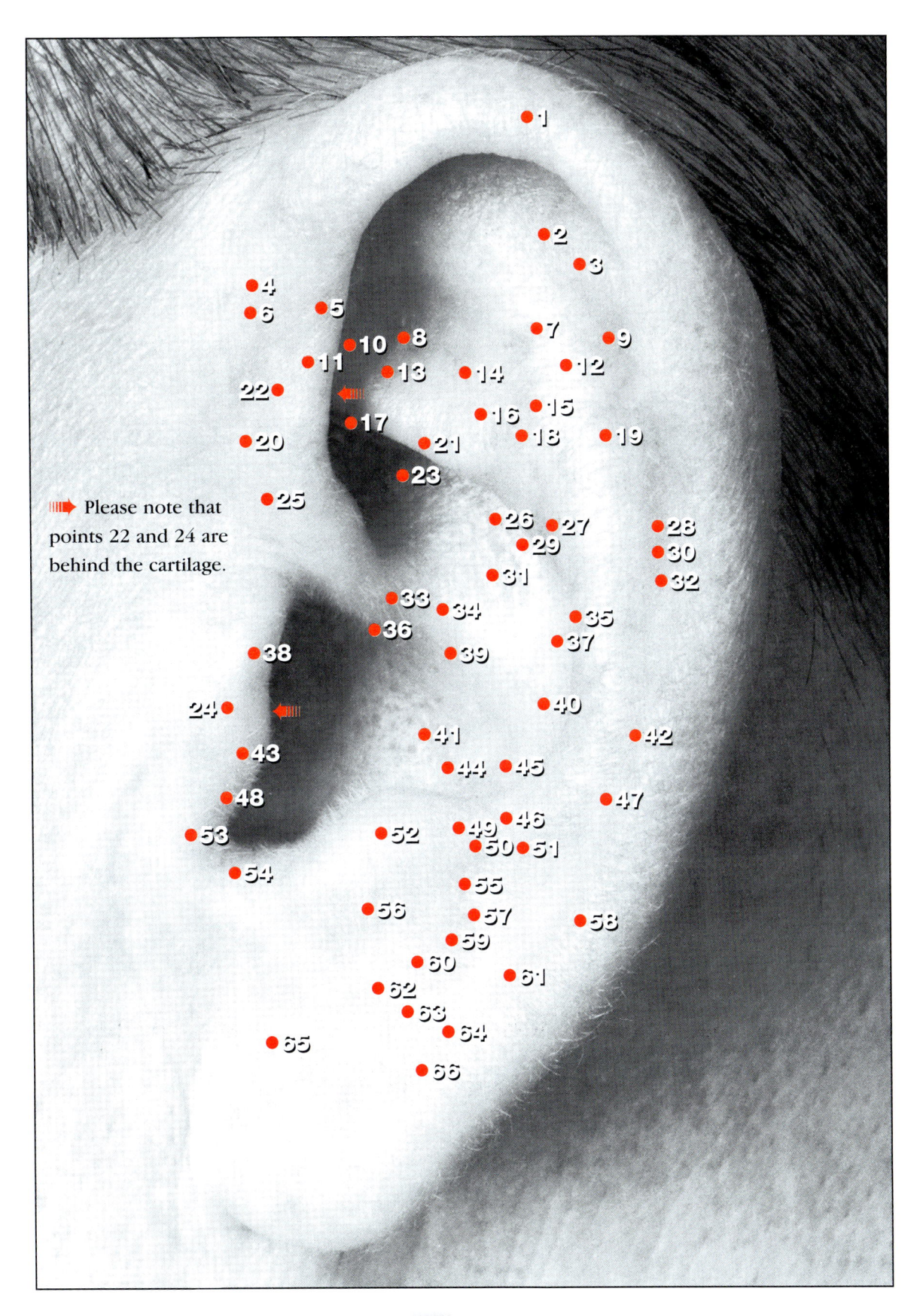

Please note that points 22 and 24 are behind the cartilage.

10.2

INDEX

Painful Disorders:

Ankle Pain	1.18
Arthritis - Refer to the relevant painful joint in this index and treat the points shown	
Back Pain - General	1.15
Back Pain - Lower - Lumbar	9.13
Back Pain - Middle - Thoracic	9.14
Back Pain - Upper - Neck	1.9
Big Toe Pain - Gout	1.27
Coccyx - Painful - Coccydynia	1.28
Cramp	1.25
Curvature of the Spine - Scoliosis	1.26
Ear Pain	1.8
Elbow Pain - Arthritis	1.11
Facial Neuralgia (Tic Doloreux)	1.7
Foot Pain	1.18
Frozen Shoulder	1.10
General Pain	1.1
Gout - Pain in Big Toe	1.27
Groin Injury	1.22
Hand, Finger Pain	1.12
Headache (Migraine) - Frontal	1.2
Headache (Migraine) - Occipital	1.3
Headache (Migraine) - Temporal	1.4
Headache (Migraine) - Vertex	1.5
Hip Pain	1.16
Intercostal Neuralgia	1.19
Jaw Pain	1.6
Knee Pain	1.17
Neck Pain	1.9
Period Pain (Dysmenorrhoea) P.M.S.	1.24
P.M.S.	1.24
Renal (Kidney) Colic	1.23
Repetitive Strain Injuries (R.S.I.)	1.19
Sciatica	1.20
Scoliosis - Curvature of the Spine	1.26
Shingles	1.23
Shoulder Pain	1.10
Tennis Elbow	1.11
Thumb Pain	1.13
Toothache (lower jaw)	1.6
Toothache (upper jaw)	1.7
Varicose Veins	1.21
Wrist Pain	1.14

Ear, Nose and Throat Problems (ENT):

Bell's Palsy	2.1
Deafness - Nerve	2.6
Facial Paralysis	2.1
Laryngitis - 'Sore Throat'	2.3
Menieres, Vertigo	2.4
Mouth Ulcers	2.3
Mumps	2.8
Nose Bleeds	2.7
Sinusitis	2.2
Sore Throat	2.3
Tinnitus	2.4
Tonsillitis	2.7

Heart & Circulatory Disorders

Angina	3.1
Chilblains	3.1
Circulation Improvement (Reynaud's)	3.2
High Blood Pressure (Hypertension)	3.5
Low Blood Pressure (Hypotension)	3.4
Palpitations	3.5
Raynaud's Syndrome	3.2

Abdominal Problems

Abdominal Distension	4.1
Biliary Colic	4.9
Colitis	4.2
Constipation	4.3
Crohn's Disease	4.15
Diarrhoea	4.5
Diverticulitis	4.16
Duodenal Ulcer	4.14
Flatulence	4.1
Gallbladder Colic	4.9
Gallbladder Disease	4.8
Haemorrhoids	4.4
Heartburn	4.3
Hepatitis	4.12
Hiatus Hernia	4.10
Irritable Bowel Syndrome	4.11
Liver Trouble	4.6
Nausea	4.6
Sea Sickness	4.6
Stomach Ache	4.7
Upper Abdominal Pain	4.7

Skin Disorders:

Acne	5.2
Eczema	5.3
General Allergies	5.1
Psoriasis	5.4
Verrucas	5.3
Warts	5.3

INDEX

Chest Diseases:
Asthma	6.2
Bronchitis	6.3
Cough	6.1
Croup - Laryngeal Tracheitis	6.4

Genito-Urinary Problems:
Bed-Wetting (Enuresis)	7.1
Cystitis	7.5
Irritable Bladder	7.2
Prostate Problems	7.2
Urinary Incontinence	7.3
Urinary Retention	7.4

Miscellaneous Disorders:
Anxiety & Stress	8.18
Appetite Reduction	8.1
Attention Deficiency Syndrome (ADS)	8.12
Conjunctivitis	8.2
Chronic Fatigue Syndrome	8.14
Depression	8.28
Diabetes	8.26
Eye Problems - Macular Degeneration	8.21
Eye Problems - Cataract	8.21
Eye Problems - Conjunctivitis	8.21
Eye Problems - Glaucoma	8.21
Eye Problems - Multiple Sclerosis	8.23
Eye Problems - Squint	8.21
Fainting Attacks	8.9
Fever	8.9
Fluid Retention	8.10
Heel Spur	9.31
Hangover	8.17
Hay Fever	8.3
Hiccoughs (Hiccups)	8.13
Hot Flushes	8.11
Hyperactivity (ADS)	8.12
Impotence	8.17
Insomnia	8.8
Itching (Pruritis)	8.13
Jet Lag	8.19
Lactation	8.16
Libido - Decreased	8.3
Mastitis	8.16
M.E.	8.14
Menopause Problems	8.11
Morning Sickness	8.28
M.S. (Multiple Sclerosis)	8.22
M.S. (Multiple Sclerosis) - Eye Problems	8.23
Parkinson's Disease	8.24
Perspiration - Excessive	8.11
Post-Viral Syndrome (M.E.)	8.14
Pruritis (Itching)	8.13
Restless Legs	8.7
Sleep Apnoea	8.8
Smoking	8.19
Snoring	8.8
Stress & Anxiety	8.18
Stroke Recovery	8.4
Thyroid - Balancing	8.27

Sports and Industrial Injuries:
Abdominal Strain	9.18
Abductor pain	9.17
Achilles Tendonitis	9.28
Ankle Injuries	9.29
Biceps Tendonitis	9.3
Bunion Pain	9.32
Carpal Tunnel Syndrome	9.9
Calf strain	9.27
Dead Leg	9.20
Elbow - Golfer's	9.6
Elbow - Tennis	9.5
Hamstrings	9.22
Heel - Bruised	9.31
Hip Injuries	9.19
Knee - Cartilages	9.23
Knee - Lateral Ligament Strain	9.25
Knee - Ligaments	9.23
Knee - Medial Ligament Strain	9.25
Lumbar Spine Injuries	9.13
Metatarsalgia (Pain in Ball of Foot)	9.30
Neck Injuries	9.12
Painful Arc (Shoulder Pain)	9.4
Physical Performance Improvement	9.33
Rectus Femoris	9.21
Rib Injuries	9.15
Shin Soreness	9.26
Shoulder Joint	9.2
Spinal Injuries	9.11
Spinal Injuries - Lumbar	9.13
Spinal Injuries - Neck	9.12
Spinal Injuries - Thoracic	9.14
Sprained Thumb & Fingers	9.10
Sterno Clavicular Pain	9.3
Stitch	9.16
Tenosynovitis (Forearm Tendons)	9.7
Thoracic Spine Injuries	9.14
Wrist Injuries	9.8